Free Your
Magnificent
MIND

Free Your Magnificent MIND

Insights on Success from José Silva

José Silva

with José Silva Jr. and Ed Bernd Jr.

MEDIA

Published 2023 by Gildan Media LLC
aka G&D Media
www.GandDmedia.com

Front Cover design by David Rheinhardt of Pyrographx

Interior design by Meghan Day Healey of Story Horse, LLC

Library of Congress Cataloging-in-Publication Data is available upon request

ISBN: 978-1-7225-0625-4

10   9   8   7   6   5   4   3   2   1

CONTENTS

PART 2
SOME BASIC TECHNIQUES FOR YOU TO USE

Contents

PART 3
SOME PERSONAL REFLECTIONS

Contents

PART 4
IDEAS CAME FROM MANY SOURCES

FOREWORD

by Ed Bernd Jr.

Working for José Silva as editor of his company newsletter the last seventeen years of his life was the best job I ever had. I also got to help him edit books he was writing, and was coauthor of his last four books, helping him to "arrange the words," as he put it.

I could ask him anything about his research, the results, his interpretation of the results, and how people could benefit from them, and he would tell me. He didn't hold anything back . . . and neither did I.

He said that I must have asked him "at least a million questions." He might be right.

Since his passing twenty-five years ago, it has been an honor, privilege, and pleasure to work with my best friend, José Silva Jr., to help him continue his father's mission.

Joe observed and documented his father's research. His observations and recollections have given me many new insights.

His father demonstrated his confidence in Joe when he named him President of Silva International in 1994, when he put Joe in charge of a new company to manage his ultimate course: the Silva

UltraMind ESP Systems in 1998. He also named Joe executor of his Will, and Trustee of the José Silva Trust.

In this book, you get to enjoy the best of both:

José Silva's breakthrough insights that have helped millions of people worldwide over the last fifty-five years.

Joe's "inside look" at what his father was really like.

Thank you for joining us on this journey of discovery.

INTRODUCTION

From Poverty to Prosperity

José Silva's life is more than a great American success story. It has transcended time and space to become one of the world's all time great success stories. It reveals the determination, the greatest, and the divinity of humanity itself.

Orphaned at age four, he never attended school a day in his life as a student; yet the reading and research that he undertook to help his own children, unlocked secrets of the mind and human potential that had remained hidden for thousands of years.

José Silva's twenty-two years of dogged determination to dig out these secrets has literally changed the world.

He actually found the secret of success.

José Silva Was a Unique Individual

As a youth, he was a successful businessman, earning more money than most adults in Laredo.

As a young man, he displayed athletic skills as a competent boxer.

As an adult, he learned to sing, and was so good that he was offered a scholarship to study voice in Italy for a year.

Though he never attended school a day in his life as a student, this self-educated man established an electronics training facility at Laredo Junior College that was named the best in the state of Texas by the Veterans Administration. He has lectured at many major colleges and universities about his trail blazing discoveries.

The achievements for which he will be remembered the longest, of course, concern his mind training systems.

As a thinker and philosopher, millions of people seek his guidance through his writings and lectures.

As an inventor, he holds several patents, including the first patent ever issued stating that "Human concentration turns on an education program."

As a scientist, he has won the respect of many other scientists, despite the fact that he holds no degrees.

Leading by Example

Here is a man who truly symbolizes what he teaches.

He first started working with his own children in 1944 to help them get higher test scores and better grades.

Then in the 1950s and 1960s helped his neighbors learn how to actually use the untapped power of their minds to get whatever they wanted. While he never asked them to pay him, he was rewarded greatly with more knowledge on this subject than anyone else on the planet.

From 1966 to 1998 his Silva Mind Control Method helped millions of people worldwide, and since 1998 his Silva UltraMind ESP System is leading the way into what he called "the beginning of the second phase of human evolution on the planet."

This man with no formal schooling wrote the book on mind development—in fact, he's had more than a dozen books published by major publishers, in two dozen languages.

Prior to his passing in 1999 he developed a new course—actually more than a course, he calls it a system: The Silva UltraMind ESP System.

In addition to helping people develop and use their own God-given intuition, the UltraMind ESP System includes a new scientifically-based technique to communicate with higher intelligence regularly and reliably to obtain help and guidance in carrying out your mission in life.

While José Silva may have moved on to new assignments, his work is still going strong, both in live seminars and in convenient home study courses.

There are many courses that are "based on" his work, but the only courses still being taught that he authored himself, based on his twenty-two years of scientific research, are the Silva UltraMind ESP System, and his Holistic Faith Healing System.

The José Silva Story

Even though he was born to poor parents in Laredo, Texas, on the Mexican border, José Silva was always successful. His story is a true American success story. In fact, his story transcends time and space: It is one of the world's great success stories.

As a six year old boy he began to support his family, after watching his father die as the result of a terrorist act during the Mexican revolution.

José learned to read and write on his own—in both English and Spanish.

Instead of going to school, he earned money for his family by selling newspapers on the streets of Laredo, shining shoes, and doing odd jobs.

By the time he was a teenager, he was an employer and hired other youngsters to work with him, going door to door to sell merchandise he purchased in San Antonio. The youngsters were earning as much money after school as their parents earned working full time. And young José was earning as much every day as the typical adult in Laredo earned in a week.

One day José came across an electronics course, borrowed it, studied it, and went into the radio repair business. Eventually he built the largest electronics repair business in south Texas.

This was pretty impressive for a youngster who had educated himself, had supported his family since age six, and had earned the respect of people in the community.

But there was one area where José's hard work and street smarts weren't paying off.

Why Weren't His Children Like Him?

Even though José had experienced success in many areas, his children were not following in his footsteps. Some bad report cards convinced him that he had to find the answer.

The answer seemed to be in the way that super successful people—like himself—used their minds.

He made good decisions, but his children sometimes failed to do the correct thing.

He could concentrate on a task and complete it. His children didn't seem to have that same ability.

José was usually in the right place at the right time, and this had led to much of his success. But his children, like so many other people who never see their dreams come true, sometimes seemed to wind up at the worst possible place at the worst possible time.

He was never ill, but his children got the usual childhood diseases.

This raised several questions in his mind:

Why could some people learn more easily than others? José learned without ever attending school, while his children were bringing home some F's on their report cards.

Why were some people so much better at earning a living than others?

He felt that the answer was in the mind. But how could he explore the mind?

Studying the Mind

José began to study psychology—the study of human behavior. One of the things he learned is that the brain operates on a small amount of electrical energy, and that this electric current vibrates or pulsates at different rates.

Sometimes the brain's electrical energy vibrates rapidly, twenty times every second, referred to as twenty cycles per second, abbreviated twenty cps. Sometimes it vibrated slower, at ten cps, or five cps.

He wondered why this was so.

Then he drew on his experience in radio repair, and realized that some radios sound better than others.

What makes the difference in a good electrical circuit, and a bad one, he wondered? He already knew the answer:

In electronics, you seek the circuit with the least impedance, because that is the circuit that provides you with the greatest power.

Since the brain operates on a small amount of electrical energy, the same principle should hold true: Find the operating mode where it has the least impedance and the most power, and you've found the best mode for mental activity.

The mind did not reveal its secrets to José Silva easily. He persisted, investing his own time and money, continuing even though critics scorned him. Today he is recognized as the leading researcher in the world in the field of the mind and human potential.

And José Silva's UltraMind ESP System is leading humanity into the second phase of human evolution on the planet: Learning how to use your ESP to obtain guidance and support from higher intelligence so that you can fulfill your mission in life.

Why This Book is Valuable to You

In 1979, after more than a dozen years of teaching his Method to the general public, José Silva estimated that more than 3 million people had learned his System for using more of their mind the way that ultra-successful people do.

With help from his brother Juan—and Juan's business contacts throughout the world—they had trained thousands of Silva Lecturers in the United States and in fifty other countries around the world to teach his Method, with courses being taught in a dozen different languages.

Many "knock off" copycat courses had sprung up too. But they often made grossly exaggerated claims about what to expect from the course.

José Silva knew that the *real* benefits would change people's lives for the better—physically, emotionally, and spiritually—so he decided to write about them in the company newsletter.

This book has ninety-nine of those *From the Founder* columns and articles with about success.

The *From the Founder* columns quickly became the most popular feature in the *Silva Method Newsletter*. It ran in every issue for the last twenty years of his life.

They cover a wide range of subjects dealing with success in life, written by a self-educated, self-made millionaire who is known to millions of people around the world.

Some of the columns deal with his science, like how he used hypnosis to fool the body's healing mechanism and cause it to send healing even when none was needed.

Other columns are based on his observations and life experience, like the common denominators he observed in the most successful Silva Instructors, and another column with his thoughts about why we should act our age. Like many ultra successful people, he was great at giving simple explanations for complex subjects.

A Feast to Nourish Your Soul

These brief articles are easy to read whenever you have a few minutes for some inspiration and motivation.

Joe Jr.'s commentary at the beginning of each section of the book provides insights into the man and his research that have only been known to his family and a few close friends . . . until now.

To help you take full advantage of José Silva's wisdom and advice, the book includes an appendix with three ways to learn to enter the alpha brainwave level, and many of the problem-solving techniques to help you change your life for the better.

Joe Jr. made sure that the coursework presented in this book is exactly the way his father researched it.

The benefits you will receive by acting on José Silva's insights are far greater than the false promises made by the knock-off copy-cat courses.

Pick José Silva's Magnificent Mind

If you have taken any of the Silva training, then you already know how to use more of your mind. If not, you can take the training for free in this book.

Then as you read José Silva's reflections and analysis of how he and others have used their mind to achieve exceptional success, you can do the same with your own Magnificent Mind.

Newsletter Helped a Subscriber Change from Negative to Positive

(This note was sent to the Silva Method Newsletter *in 1990 by Frieda Cahn of Flushing, NY)*

"The *Mind Control Newsletter* articles and lectures changed my life from a negative thinking person to a happy person, young at heart.

"Seventeen years ago I developed cancer, and was very ill.

"I joined Silva Mind Control. The articles and tapes and lectures made a healthy and happy person out of me.

"I just celebrated my seventy-seventh, birthday, and there is no more medicine I have to take, and I am still working, to take care of newborn babies.

"Write more success stories of people who have been helped."

Meet José Silva Jr.

Known as Joe Jr. to his friends, José Silva Jr. is one of the last links to his father's pioneering research.

Here is what Mr. Silva had to say about Joe when he named him President of Silva International Inc., in 1994:

"Joe has been involved with the Silva Method since we first started conducting research," Silva said. "He functioned as a research subject, an assistant, and even as historian—Joe has tape recordings of many of the sessions that we conducted, including the age regression sessions when the young subject was describing scenes in Paris and giving us French recipes.

"Joe worked with me in the electronics business," Silva continued. "When we started Silva International in 1967, he became our first financial officer, and he has held that position ever since."

A couple of years later Mr. Silva named Joe to be the Executor of his Will and Trustee of the Trust established to manage his Estate after his passing.

Joe's knowledge has been invaluable in helping to carry on his father's mission. You will hear from Joe from time to time as you read this book.

Now let's get started and hear directly from José Silva himself.

PART 1
ACTION LEADS TO PROSPERITY AND FULFILLMENT

1 Belief Breeds Confidence and Success
(1983)

People who are successful, who achieve a great deal, have a certain attitude, a unique feeling of confidence, that is easily identified by other people, particularly other successful people.

Every time you have a success, you get a special feeling that you can obtain only by having success. These feelings of success help build an inner confidence within you that creates a special power to bring you even more success.

When you have that confidence, when you have that unique feeling of success deep within you, you feel differently, you think differently, you act differently than a person who lacks that confidence.

When you have that feeling of confidence and success, you speak out boldly, you offer suggestions without apprehension about the results—either to yourself or to others. The words you need come to you, yet your words are only a part of the communication you have with others. Your presence, your bearing, your enthusiasm, your expressions and posture all communicate your confidence, your leadership.

Much of this can be faked, of course; you can learn the language of successful people; you can take acting lessons and learn to play the part of a confident person. This will fool a lot of people, but not people who actually have these qualities.

People who have this inner feeling of confidence, people who know their true value, instinctively recognize others who have it. And they are attracted to each other. The "lucky break" comes to the person who has the inner qualities to take advantage of the opportunity.

How can you develop this inner confidence if you do not have it, and enhance it if you do? How can you become part of this network of successful people who reinforce and help each other?

You can do it by using your inner conscious levels, your alpha brain wave levels, your alpha level of mind. If you haven't taken any of our Courses, you can learn right now with any of the Free Training options in appendix A.

Whenever you have a success, even a small success, you will get that unique feeling of success that comes only when you succeed.

Reinforce this success.

Reinforce this success many times. At your alpha level, recall it to mind, review this success, live it over and over again, recalling the feelings associated with it, and visualizing it over and over.

By doing this at your alpha brain wave level, and using visualization and imagination, you are developing your right-brain hemisphere. And this is the one big success "secret" of the most successful people: they use the right-brain hemisphere creatively, clairvoyantly, and effectively.

To develop effective use of the right-brain hemisphere, practice visualization and imagination at your alpha level.

Some people report having difficulty visualizing and using their imagination. Remember that visualization is recalling what something looks like. Imagination is thinking what something would look like when you have never seen it before.

Various people receive information in different ways. Some people easily recall conversations and sounds; they are auditory in the way they perceive information. Other people get a sense about things, they experience the feelings. And still others are visual, are strong "imagers" and project strong mental pictures.

When you function in this manner at level, practicing and reviewing successes, you are programming yourself for success.

When you do this, you do not need to build up so many successes in the physical dimension. You will speed your progress toward fulfilling your potential and becoming a better problem solving agent on this planet when you function in this manner.

2 People Who Achieve the Most Overcome the Most Challenges *(1981)*

Some people look on challenges as something bad, something to hinder progress and achievement.

At Silva Mind Control, we view challenges as opportunities.

Adversity is something that helps us grow, helps us learn new ways to do things, helps us become more versatile and creative.

We spend our entire lives overcoming challenges. And the result of our overcoming these challenges is to get still greater challenges.

Why do we do this? Why solve one problem, just to face a still greater problem?

When we are born, we are confronted with vast problems. We have to learn to communicate effectively.

We learn to take care of ourselves. We learn such things as how to walk and how to persuade people to help us.

A good parent has so much compassion, so much desire to help, that the parent will let the child face challenges and overcome them.

We could carry a child everywhere. But if we did that, the child would never learn to walk. And if the child never learns to walk, then the child will never learn to run and play games, will never learn to dance, will never learn to ski.

Do you see the pattern that emerges? When we solve a problem, we are given a still greater problem to solve. But at the same time, we are given a greater sense of satisfaction when we solve the problem.

There is a special sense of satisfaction that comes from solving problems. There is no other way to get that sense of satisfaction except by solving problems.

The bigger the problem you solve, the greater the sense of satisfaction.

The people who overcome the most challenges are the people who get the greatest sense of satisfaction.

We presented more than fifty awards to Silva Mind Control lecturers at this year's International Convention. The lecturers who got the greatest sense of satisfaction surely were those who have overcome the most challenges.

Rosa Argentina Rivas of Mexico, recipient of this year's World Cup as the top lecturer in the world, faced many challenges as she went to Central America alone to introduce Silva Mind Control to people there many years ago.

Paul Grivas of New York City, who received the President's Cup this year as most outstanding lecturer in the United States, has faced countless challenges working in the biggest, most sophisticated city in the country.

Dr. Marcelino Alcala of Puerto Rico, who received the President's Cup for other countries, also faced many challenges, including legislation designed to make it impossible to present the Silva Mind Control Method in Venezuela.

Thanks to the creativity that comes from many years of successful problem-solving, Silva Mind Control is stronger than ever in Venezuela.

We have all faced many problems in the past.

The Silva Mind Control Method does not exempt us from having problems; it gives us more alternatives for coping with them.

And as we successfully deal with those problems, we get our rewards:

That special sense of satisfaction that comes with achievement; and a bigger problem to solve.

To achieve more than you already have, you must solve more problems.

The first step in solving more problems is to review your most recent successes, and use these as points of reference.

If you know how to crawl, review that point of reference before you try to walk.

If you can walk, review that special feeling of success you got with that accomplishment before you try running.

Whatever challenges you face in life, review your most recent successes and then apply your techniques so you can achieve even more.

The people who overcome the most challenges are the people who achieve the most.

Note: If you have not taken any of our courses, you can learn to enter the alpha level with any of the free training options in the appendix of this book.

You can learn how to obtain guidance and help from higher intelligence with the MentalVideo Technique in appendix D.

3 Energy, Commitment and Silva Mind Control *(1979)*

As has been the case in the past, 1979 has been a tremendous year for Silva Mind Control, and this was evidenced in the enthusiastic people who attended the 1979 Silva Mind Control International Convention in Laredo, Texas.

But ours is a life-long mission, one that is made pleasant and satisfying by the realization that our work is not only treading on uncharted courses but is helping out humanity in the process.

As a matter of fact, it is because our work is so attached to the betterment of humanity that it has become a world-wide movement.

However, The Silva Mind Control Method demands continuing practice and commitment, and what I offer here are chiefly some observations which other persons have found useful in becoming successful lecturers of the Silva Mind Control classes.

The key to success, of course, is to be thoroughly familiar with the method itself.

Also, the personal appearance and personal life of the lecturers ought to reflect the ideals of Silva Mind Control.

The overriding ideal is that only by serving humanity can such a program find success. One cannot detach the Silva Mind Control

Method from the continuous striving of humanity to perfect itself and find peace and harmony.

The Silva Mind Control method is a tool for humanity achieving these goals, and we ought to be humble—and proud—that we are but a means by which this process is carried out.

This is the reason why the successful Silva Mind Control practitioner shares the enthusiasm that is life's, savors the spontaneity that sparks imagination, imitates the best qualities possessed by successful human beings, and continues studying and reading to attain an even greater professionalism.

Being involved in Silva Mind Control is not an easy task. It is a commitment not only to ourselves but to our fellow humans on this planet. If practiced right it is a tremendously satisfying task.

I wish everybody could have seen the eagerness, the commitment and the energy that poured forth from every Silva lecturer who attended the Laredo international convention.

That was the spirit of the whole movement—communicating, studying, practicing, meditating, reading, and enjoying.

All of this within the framework of comradeship that is the Silva Mind Control family.

More than anything, I witnessed success at the convention.

It was a personally gratifying experience I shall always carry with me, and it is such experiences that provide the strength to continue.

We owe it to ourselves to be successful Silva Mind Control practitioners.

Humanity can expect no less of us.

Note: If you have not taken any of our courses, you can learn to enter the alpha level with any of the free training options in the appendix of this book.

4 Here's How You Can Know What to Do with Your Life *(1993)*

I believe that we were placed on this planet for a purpose.

Whoever put us here must have had some reason.

Whoever put us here, I refer to as higher intelligence.

They must have more intelligence than I have, because I didn't have any choice about whether I came here or not, or if I did have a choice, I don't remember it now. I found myself here.

So what am I supposed to do while I am here? There must be some reason I am here. What should I be doing?

It makes sense that if somebody sent me here, it would probably be to help correct problems.

Help Correct Problems

It seems like we haven't finished the evolutionary process yet. We are still inventing things to make life better, and there seems to be more that needs to be done.

So perhaps I'm here to correct problems. That does make sense doesn't it? If you are employed by somebody, they employ you to do a good job. If you do a good job they pay you for it. If you don't do a good job, they'll quit paying you for it, won't they?

If you do an outstanding job, they'll promote you. They will give you more responsibilities—and more pay. You will enjoy life that much more, you will get more satisfaction.

The more problems you solve, the more rewards you are going to get. It sure seems to work like that, in life as well as in business.

Cause and Effect

What happens if we are creating problems?

If I am out there creating problems, why should higher intelligence even want me around.

Maybe that's why people who create problems end up having so many problems. Maybe not at first, but sooner or later that law of cause-and-effect seems to balance out.

This approach has worked for me for my entire life. And for more than a quarter of a century it has worked for Silva graduates who apply it.

When you program to correct problems, and keep in mind what your needs are—plus a little bit more—then you will get everything you need to continue to be successful and happy.

Finding Your Purpose

If you want to know what your purpose in life is, then enter your level and ask. You will get answers.

It is important to ask at deep levels. Practice the Silva Centering Exercise—relaxing parts of your body, then relaxing your mind, until you are very deeply relaxed both physically and mentally.

From this deep level, you will get in touch with your "higher self" as some people call it. I call it the other side. On the other side—in the spiritual dimension—I believe that there are beings who have been assigned to help us.

These beings are not limited by time and space the way that we are. They have access to more information than we do. They can formulate better plans than we can.

So enter your level. Deepen that level by using any of the deepening exercises as you learned in the Basic courses (relaxation, countdowns, etc.) and ask what you should be doing here.

Find something to do that is of a constructive and creative nature, then do it, and all things will be added unto you.

Note: If you have not taken any of our courses, you can learn to enter the alpha level with any of the free training options in the appendix of this book.

5 How to Identify Your Purpose in Life
(1995)

Because of my experiences, I believe that we were sent here to planet earth to correct problems and to help complete the job that the Creator started.

But not everybody agrees with me.

So why am I convinced that my belief is correct?

It is because of my experiences.

For some reason, I have always been interested in solving problems. Whenever I see that something needs to be done, I want to do it.

That is how our research on the mind began.

I started studying psychology, and applying what I learned.

Before long, I was seeing results.

That's when my neighbors started asking me to work with their children. Eventually they began to ask me to also teach my techniques to them.

Of course, I helped them. I helped everyone who asked for my help.

And I never charged for my help. I never even let them reimburse me for my expenses.

Can you imagine someone working for a year, two years, five years, ten years, or more, without getting anything out of it? Who would do something like that?

Why would I do something like that?

I asked myself those same questions. My research was helping a lot of people, but it was taking me away from my family and my business. It was costing me money, and depriving my children of a full time father.

So why should I keep doing the research?

Actually, I didn't just decide to keep on doing it.

I quit.

In fact, I quit two times.

Each time, within two hours, something happened to get me to continue.

The first time I quit it was two o'clock in the morning. Shortly after going to bed, I had a dream. There was bright light, and two sets of numbers: 2-3-2 and 2-7-2. Eventually, late in the day, a friend who was helping me found a lottery ticket with one of those numbers. Of course we purchased it. It paid $10,000. That was about two years salary for the average person back in 1949.

I felt like this was a message from the other side, from high intelligence, telling me to keep working.

I kept working.

The next time I quit was on a rainy Saturday morning. As I sat there pondering my decision to quit, my son ran in with some rolled up papers in his hand. I noticed something strange about them immediately:

Even though it was raining outside, the papers were dry.

I unrolled the papers. On the top was a picture of the face of Christ.

I felt like He was scolding me for stopping. After all, hadn't I been given $10,000 a few years before, to encourage me to continue my work?

That "personal visit" was the last incentive I ever needed. I kept working, and am still working today, to show people how to actually use more of their minds to help themselves and their loved ones.

So, based on my own personal experience, and of my observations of thousands of other people, I believe that when we are centered, then we are guided by high intelligence on the other side.

They tell us what to do.

They don't speak to us of course; they are spiritual beings, not physical.

They send us ideas, when we are at level, as you learn in our Courses and with any of the Free Training options in appendix A.

Results Confirm Validity

Our job is to recognize the ideas that come from the other side. We must find a way to distinguish those ideas from our own ideas.

A sure way to tell is by noticing the results that you get.

When you are working on a project, you will probably encounter obstacles.

The first time you encounter an obstacle, notice how long it takes you to deal with it.

Then the next obstacle you encounter, how long does it take to deal with it? If it takes twice as long, this might be a sign from the other side that you are going in the wrong direction.

If it takes half as long to solve the problem, then this could be a sign that you are moving in the right direction.

Keep going. When you encounter another obstacle, does it take more time or less time to deal with it?

If the obstacles continue to become more and more difficult, and take longer to remove, then you are probably going in the wrong direction. If you take two steps backward for every one step forward, you are losing ground.

Enter your level. Analyze the project. Figure out what you must do so that you take two steps forward for every one step backward. That is the way most projects go: you encounter a problem, take a step back and then go forward again.

Then do something different.

When you are on the right track, your efforts will be rewarded. When you are going the wrong way, you will encounter more obstacles.

Take the path of least resistance.

Trust the Process

During our research, I did not always know why I was doing certain things, or where it would lead. I just continued to meditate, to work hard, and to take the path of least resistance.

I always like "lucky coincidences." What that means to me is that God is helping without showing His hand. Now, however, we can see it all. We know how to get help from high intelligence, and know that we are getting it. You can learn our MentalVideo technique in appendix D.

When good things happened during my research, I did more of what I had been doing. When things did not go well, I tried a different path. It paid off then, and that approach still pays off for me today.

That is not to say that you should be quick to quit. Not at all. We have to prove that we are willing to put forth the effort, that we will accept the responsibility that is given to us.

But we don't batter down doors. After you have made a good effort, over a period of time, to open a new door in your life, and the door still won't open, then back up, take a deep breath, enter your level, and look around to see if there is another door.

When you take that one step backwards, you may find a way to take even more than two steps forward before you encounter another problem that you must solve.

Eventually, when you continue to follow the guidance from the other side, you will find that you do not encounter any more obstacles but go straight to your goal.

It does not take a great deal of wisdom to be successful when you follow this procedure. All that you really have to do is to do what you are guided to do.

There was an old joke many years ago. A man went to his doctor with a complaint. The man raised his arm above his head and told the doctor, "Doctor, it hurts when I do that."

The doctor's solution was very simple: "Then don't do that."

If you are having problems in your life, then "don't do that." Enter your level and figure out what you can change. Then make the change, and evaluate the results. When you find something that makes your life better, then do it.

We all want to be happy.

My experience has taught me that happiness comes from solving problems. That's what we were sent here to do. When we do it, we will be well rewarded.

So, enter your level, figure out what you should be doing. Then go do it, and notice the results. If you encounter too many obstacles, and they keep getting bigger and more difficult, then enter your level again and figure out something else to try.

When things are going well, and you are receiving rewards and incentives, and you are happy, then you know that you are doing what you were sent here to do, and that is to make this planet a better place to live.

Take it from me: In my eighty years on this planet, I have found that the people who watch out only for themselves might accumulate a lot of things; but the people who work to solve problems feel a lot better about themselves, and are much happier.

Note: If you have not taken any of our courses, you can learn to enter the alpha level with any of the free training options in the appendix of this book.

6 Ancient Formula Contains Modern Success Strategy *(1991)*

In life, the race is not always won by the one who runs the fastest. The game is not always won by the one who is the best game player.

Take me for example.

When I conducted my research into the mind and human potential in the 1940s, '50s and '60s, I did not have all of the elaborate and expensive equipment that researchers at the universities had.

Yet my research produced more beneficial results than the universities.

I never wrote papers for academic journals, yet millions of people around the world have benefited from my findings.

It didn't happen overnight.

I invested twenty-two years in intensive research to develop a system that can help everybody.

Then I tried to get somebody else to take over. Nobody would.

So at the age of fifty-two I closed my electronics repair business and moved into a new career.

Now, twenty-five years later, the Silva Method of Mind Development and Stress Control is being offered in eighty-eight countries and twenty languages We recently presented it for the first time in the Soviet Union.

Keys to Success

Why was I so successful when so many others achieved so little—especially considering that they had more money, more education, more equipment, more people to assist them, and were able to devote full time to the task?

Some would say that persistence is a big part of it. Anyone who knows me knows that I am persistent, yet I stopped my research . . . twice. There was some other factor involved in getting me to continue on.

How about education? I never went to school a day in my life as a student, so that doesn't explain it.

Some would say that clear thinking leads to good decisions and a better understanding of things. But why me? I never had the opportunity to attend school to study the ideas of the great thinkers who came before us.

There was some other factor involved in my ability to make correct choices.

I have always worked longer hours than most people—I did at six and I still do at seventy-six—but what gives me the energy to do that?

It must come from somewhere.

Many people emphasize the importance of goals. It was never a goal of mine to create a mind development program, yet I always had a sense of purpose in my life, a sense of direction. How did I know what choices to make, which pathways to pursue?

There are cynics who say that you need the right parents, the right contacts, to be successful.

My father died when I was four, and as the oldest son I became both brother and father to my brothers and sisters. I did not have connections to any powerful people, but I had a contact that was more important than all the powerful people in the world.

The Right Stuff

The key to my success—to anyone's success—can be found in my research, and in the Silva Courses.

First, learn to think at the alpha level, where you can use both the logical left brain hemisphere, and the creative, intuitive right brain hemisphere simultaneously.

Doing this gives you a connection with the "other side," where higher intelligence resides.

There is a lot of help available to you there, but you have to have a clear connection in order to receive it.

Second, you must function correctly in that dimension.

What do I mean by "function correctly"?

I mean more than learning the mechanics, more than learning how to use the tools and techniques.

That's important, of course, but there is more.

That dimension is a creative dimension, where you can create.

It is not a dimension to destroy.

What do I mean by create? I mean that you should work to correct all problems that cause human suffering, without creating any new problems.

I think that both factors are necessary for success.

The average person has, at best, a very weak connection with the other side:

An occasional dream. A flash of insight now and then. Once in a while a prayer answered.

Those who establish a stronger connection can accomplish more of the things they set out to do.

To achieve outstanding success, to live an abundant and fulfilled life, you need the second ingredient: To function correctly, by helping to solve problems.

Researchers who had their subjects try to guess the number of spots on ESP cards had only limited success.

In my research, I had subjects enter their level and mentally detect health problems; then I had them mentally correct the problems.

I had far greater success than the university researchers who used only hypothetical cases.

I am not the first to suggest this strategy for success. Here's how it was said 2,000 years ago:

"First enter the kingdom of heaven, and function within God's righteousness; then all else shall be added unto you."

There really isn't any secret to success. All religions say the same thing in their own way. So do the ultra successful people.

Now you have a method to put it into practice in your life: The Silva Method.

Practice. Develop your skills. Use your skills and talents to correct problems, your own problems and other people's problems.

Do this and abundance and fulfillment will be yours.

Note: If you have not taken any of our courses, you can learn to enter the alpha level with any of the free training options in the appendix of this book.

7 What Do We Mean When We Talk About "Mind"? *(1983)*

We have a definition for "mind" that is different from the definition that many people use.

We found it necessary to use the term a particular way so we could better understand and explain what we are doing.

Some people refer to "mind" as your intelligence, what you have learned. Some people refer to the intelligence that human beings have as "human intelligence."

My definitions are different.

We find that there is a dimension where biological intelligence resides, and another dimension where human intelligence resides and functions.

When we refer to human intelligence, we mean the same thing that religious people mean when they talk of the soul or spirit; we mean the same thing as metaphysical people mean when they speak of consciousness.

Instead of saying the soul, or the spirit, we say human intelligence.

Instead of saying the mind, we say human intelligence.

The mind, or the psyche, is a faculty of human intelligence.

To function with it is like the focusing faculty of eyesight to see near and far, and using the faculty of hearing to attune to noises near and far. Human intelligence has a faculty called the mind, to tune to the brain, to become attuned to the brain.

There are two different dimensions, so we distinguish one from the other by speaking of them as the physical dimension where biological intelligence resides, and the spiritual dimension where human intelligence resides.

So human intelligence functions and resides in a spiritual dimension, and brain and body reside in the biological, physical, dimension.

They work together, these two different worlds; we need to first think about things before we act on them. So the world of the mind is always ahead of the world of physics. It has to be thought of first, before it can be acted on and materialized.

The psyche, mind and human intelligence, work together.

When we talk about mind, we talk about human intelligence along with its faculty the mind.

When we talk about mind, we are dealing with human intelligence. You can not separate them; like you can not separate the focusing of the eye from the eye itself; or the attuning of the hearing from the ear; it's part of the ear.

So human intelligence has a system to become attuned to the brain, and we call that system the mind.

Locating Human Intelligence

When human intelligence becomes attuned to the brain, we know where that is, and when that takes place, by measuring brain waves.

We connect the electroencephalograph to an individual, and then we know whether they have become attuned to the beta world, or to the alpha world, or to the theta world, or delta world.

We can know where human intelligence is projecting its consciousness because of its attunement, because when it does this, the brain develops a rhythm that can be measured; otherwise it is discharging erratically, ever so often, but not with a rhythm that can be measured.

We look for the rhythm, and when we find the rhythm, we know where human intelligence is projecting its mind to.

So psyche-orientation means orienting the mind to find a different brain level, and learn to function from that different brain level.

We call it psyche orientation, like psychic education, or mental training . . . that's what it is. That's why we call it thought control, or mind control.

Everything comes through thought control; you need to think about it first, before you can materialize it.

Using Human Intelligence

When you function at the alpha dimension, you are able to function with both the spiritual and the physical dimensions. You are able to use both the left (physical) brain hemisphere and the right (subjective) brain hemisphere.

That is why we developed a method to help people learn to find and stay at the alpha dimension, the center of the brain frequency spectrum.

When you are centered, you have total control.

No other system that we studied takes you to the alpha dimension and shows you how to stay there. Our method is the one that helps a person stay centered.

Practice at the alpha dimension every day and you will benefit from both worlds, the spiritual and the physical. You will be able to influence the physical from the spiritual, and the spiritual from the physical, and your life will continue to become better, better, and better.

Note: To learn how to put this into practice starting today, choose any of the free training options in the appendix.

8 Research Proves Us Ahead of the Times
(1980)

One of the more disheartening facets of our work—and one I am sure is shared by many Silva Mind Control graduates—is the lack of the recognition that our work deserves.

It took us years of painstaking research to prove that the Silva Mind Control method works and that it was, and continues to be, in the vanguard of scientific thought in this area.

Yet, while our method is generally accepted by millions of people throughout the world as the most effective method of achieving personal growth through Mind Control, or mind development, there are those who still refuse to give credit where credit is due.

An example of this is the present research being done in the area of mental training to develop athletic abilities as well as the survival of severe personal crisis, such as being stricken by cancer.

This research, presently being conducted in universities in the United States, is fashioned after the Russian model of training athletes through a systematic method of mental training.

The Soviets, who are getting credit for this breakthrough, in effect have their athletes visualize "optimal" performances, so that later on they can achieve in reality what they had been doing mentally.

"The dramatic approaches used by the Russians are little known in the West," a scientist experimenting in this field is quoted as having said.

But is this really so? Or is it that much of the scientific community in the United States has not been listening to us?

For example, almost every graduate of Silva Mind Control is familiar with a phrase that I put forth to my students, and this is that we should learn from our successes.

Many of us have been trained since childhood to "learn from our successes." In many seminars, I have advocate this concept with the following explanation:

"There is a special feeling you get when you succeed. You should reinforce this feeling every time you begin a project, then you will attune to that same wavelength again and be just as successful as before."

The theory behind this method of mental attitude is that everything people put into their memory bank influences their actions in one way or another. The key, then, is to put successes into it instead of failures.

We literally become that which we think we are, and what we think about ourselves depends upon what we put into our mental bank.

This concept, which we at Silva Mind Control have advocated for decades especially through the Mirror of the Mind technique, is basically the very same thing the Russians are doing with their athletes, and the very same thing United States scientists are "learning" from the Russians.

The Russians believe that the physical follow-through of an intention is the mere after-the-fact duplication of an event. The unconscious mind cannot really decipher reality from imagery.

In effect, this is the same premise we have been advocating for years with our theory of reinforcing our successes.

What we have been advocating for years is that it is okay to look at any temporary defeat; glean anything of benefit from it, and then cancel it out consciously. Once you have dealt with it, there is no reason why you should keep it in your consciousness.

And once that defeat is erased, concentrate on successes, which is another word for what the Russians call "optimal" experiences.

This is not the only area in which many researchers throughout the world are following our path and "discovering" that which we have been advocating for years.

In a way, this should give all of us in Silva Mind Control a deep sense of satisfaction, for these researchers are only proving us correct.

What is a little sad is that our work has not received the recognition that I feel it deserves, although our success is unquestionable.

We have, throughout the years, proven that our work was not only first, but that is getting "better and better."

9 What Gives People the Strength to Carry On When Discouraged? *(1997)*

Life is often hard, and presents many challenges. Yet we must persist and do what we are supposed to do.

I've certainly had many challenges in my life:

My father died when I was four years old, as the result of a terrorist act during the Mexican revolution.

My mother remarried and moved away, while I stayed with my grandmother.

I never went to school, because I was working to bring in money for the family.

I grew up in a border town in the Southwest, where bullies like to pick on kids as small and as light as I was.

I've been through economic depressions—the Great Depression that affected the entire United States, and numerous local depressions that result from such things as bad weather, fluctuating oil prices, peso devaluations, and air base closings.

When I began researching ways to help my children develop more of the natural mental abilities—the research that lead to the development of the Silva Method—many of my friends shunned me and my family, they ridiculed us, and they even called the law on us.

My church—which is supposed to offer spiritual support during hard times—threatened to excommunicate me for trying to help people in ways that they didn't understand.

When I completed my research and tried to show the world what I had done, I was rejected by scientists, by the government, and by the educational and religious establishments.

When I set up a business, many of the people I had taught to teach the Silva Method turned on me, took the course that I had spent twenty-two years and half a million dollars to develop, and began teaching it as their own.

When I told an author that he could write a book that included my copyrighted material and we would split the profits, he walked away and wrote his book with one of the people who had taken my material and was teaching it without my permission. His book was a big seller at the time, but now it is out of print and our books are still being sold worldwide.

Today, I have many loyal people who have stuck with me for two decades or more. Yet I'm still disappointed sometimes when someone I thought was loyal says that I don't know what I'm doing, and goes out to teach on his or her own.

It doesn't make sense sometimes. All I've tried to do my entire life is to correct problems and help people, and to earn enough money by doing so to take care of my own family, so that we don't have to depend on anyone else.

I'm not looking for sympathy. I know that there are people who have had a more difficult life than I have. Everyone has challenges to face.

I was asked what gives me the courage to persist in the face of so many obstacles; how do I know I am doing the right thing; how do I know what I should be doing with my life.

Purpose of Life

My first purpose, when I was six years old, was to take care of myself and my family. Somebody had to earn money, and being the oldest male, I decided I should do it.

This is not difficult to figure out. Even animals take care of their own families. There is really nothing special about it.

I have never been able to understand people who don't try to take care of their own families, or divorced fathers who fail to even support their own children. People like that are not acting like human beings; they are not even acting in as ethical a manner as most animals.

Giving Service

In my efforts to support myself and my family, I learned very quickly that people were not willing to give you money simply because you needed it, but would gladly pay you if you gave them something of value, something that solved a problem for them or helped them to enjoy their life more.

I solved the problem of dirty shoes by shining their shoes. I sold them newspapers, cleaned their offices, took them shopping, cooked in their restaurants, helped them build buildings.

I found that I could earn even more money by helping more than one person at a time. For instance, when I sold household items like needles and thread door-to-door, people appreciated my service. When I recruited several more young people to help me take my merchandise door to door, I helped even more home-owners, and helped these young people earn some money for their families also. As a result, I earned much more money than before.

The more people you help, the more valuable your services are, and the more money you make.

Did I enjoy doing all that work?

Not particularly.

Was it satisfying?

It is always satisfying to fulfill your obligation to take care of your family. And It made me feel good to know that I was helping people.

Some people always pick jobs that they enjoy. They seem to be compensated by the enjoyment; but if they are not correcting a lot of problems, if they are not helping a lot people, they will probably not receive a great deal of money.

Some people choose jobs that are very satisfying, because they help people in need. Again, they may receive the bulk of their compensation in feelings of satisfaction rather than cash.

Different people have different needs.

My needs were to take care of myself and my family.

And I found that the best way to do that was to help as many people, as much as possible.

Eventually, in the 1960s I was employing crews of workers to install television antennas so that Laredo residents could get good television reception, even from the San Antonio stations 150 miles away.

This was hard work, but I was helping the workers that I employed, as well as helping the people who watched the television after we installed the antennas.

Then I found something that helped a lot more people, and helped them a lot more than any television set ever could: I began teaching people how to use more of their minds to be healthier, luckier, and more successful in life.

Helping Millions

The Silva Method has helped millions of people, in every way you can imagine.

Our files here at the office are bulging with testimonials and thank you letters from people who have overcome terminal illnesses, who have learned how to earn all the money they need to support their families, who have overcome challenges and gotten the education that they need, and so much more.

It is interesting that during the twenty-two years when I was conducting my research, I always had plenty of money for my family and also enough left over to invest in research.

I was actually earning more money than other people in similar businesses, even though they were helping as many people with their business as I was with mine.

Why was this?

I attribute it to the fact that I was committed to helping people with research.

I don't mean involved; I mean committed. Do you know the difference?

The difference in being involved and being committed is like ham and eggs. The chicken is involved; the pig is committed.

I was doing much more than helping my own children.

When other parents saw that my children had started getting better grades, they asked me to help their children. I did so.

When people learned that I could help them with holistic faith healing techniques, they came to me looking for help. I attempted to help all who came. In fact, my brother Juan and I used to go out looking for people to help.

When other adults in Laredo saw what the children could do, they asked me to teach them my techniques also.

Eventually I was teaching my method to groups of people. I did not do it for money, but to help them. Eventually I began to accept a small amount from those who came to the meetings to help pay the cost of the room and refreshments.

Help from Higher Intelligence

I believe that Higher Intelligence, on the "other side" as we like to say, guided me in the correct direction because I demonstrated my commitment to use what I learned to help people, and to use it to correct problems.

Many people get involved and promise a lot of things. I was committed, and I was producing. From the very beginning, I shared everything I was learning with anyone who wanted to know.

How did I know that I was doing the correct thing?

I didn't always know.

Did I ever have doubts?

You bet I did.

Calling It Quits

One time I got so discouraged while reading psychology books late one night, after everyone else had gone to bed, that I threw the book across the room and it slid under the sofa. That was it, I hadn't found the help I needed for my children, I was frustrated and ready to quit.

Why should I continue to take the abuse and criticism from people in the community?

Why should I, who had learned to read and write with the help of my sister and brother because I never attended school, try to understand books that college students found difficult?

Why should I continue to put my money into something for other people's benefit?

That's how I felt.

So what caused me to change my mind, to realize that part of my purpose in life was to continue my study and research?

A dream.

I had a very strange dream that same night, a dream that contained numbers, and I spent all of the next day trying to figure out what the dream and the numbers meant.

That evening, somebody suggested we look for a lottery ticket with those numbers. In Nuevo Laredo, Mexico, we found the ticket, and it won me $10,000.

Well, I found out what the numbers meant, but what did the dream itself signify?

I sat down by myself and thought about everything that had happened, both before and after the dream.

The one thing that stood out, that was different from my normal routine, was by the violent episode when I threw the psychology book across the room and vowed to end my research.

Could there be a connection? Could it be that that book slamming into the wall woke up somebody else besides by wife? Could it have gotten the attention of somebody on the other side, who realized that they needed to send me an sign to let me know I should keep going?

Was that the way of compensating me for the work I was doing?

That was the conclusion that I drew from the episode.

So I went back to work, studying, testing, trying out many different things to see what would work.

A few years later I got discouraged again.

That was when Christ—the symbol of my religion—came to me.

It was actually a picture of Christ that my son Ricardo put into my lap one morning shortly after I had packed all of my books away in the attic. At least this time I wasn't throwing them around.

Ricardo came running in from the rain and tossed the rolled up papers to me.

When I picked them up, they were dry. How could that be?

When I unrolled them, the life-sized face of Christ was looking me straight in the eye.

It hit me as hard as any fist has ever hit me. I felt as if he was asking me, "Didn't I tell you to continue your research? Why are you not obeying me?"

I went into the bathroom and locked the door. I didn't want my family to see me cry.

Knowing What's Right

Here are some of the conclusions that I draw from my life experiences:

We have been sent here to help correct problems, in order to make this world a better place to live.

Correcting problems means that we should be doing constructive and creative things. We should not destroy or do anything to make life more difficult for anyone, but should make life better whenever we can.

The more problems we correct, and the more people we help, the more compensation we will receive.

Our helpers on the "other side," the helpers that I refer to as Higher Intelligence, offer us guidance. It is up to us to listen and to heed the guidance.

When you are centered, when you function at the alpha level, you will receive the guidance from the other side. It is not just ideas that count—they might be coming from your own imagination. Notice what happens in the physical world. When things are going well, you are on the right track. If you have too many problems in your life, you may be going in the wrong direction.

I believe that I was one of the fortunate ten percent of humanity that naturally functions at the 10 cycles alpha brain wave frequency. I was centered. I used those levels naturally, without even realizing it. I was at the correct level, and had the correct attitude—helping people—so I got the messages.

Now you can do the same. Enter level with the 3 to 1 method that you learned in the Silva Method Basic Lecture Series. Ask for guidance. If you are sincere, and if you are demonstrating your sincerity by taking action—if you show that you are really committed—then you will be guided to know what is right.

And when that happens, it is easy to press on, to persist, to have faith, to trust, and to do what you know in your heart is right to do.

As it says in the Bible, "If God is with you, then who can be against you."

Note: To learn how to put this into practice starting today, you can choose any of the free training options in the appendix.

You can learn how to obtain guidance from higher intelligence with the MentalVideo Technique in appendix D.

10 Eliminate Enemies of Your Immune Mechanism *(1983)*

Your immune mechanism is what heals all health problems. If that immune mechanism weakens, then you are in for serious problems, so we need to keep that immune mechanism strong. Doctors and medicines assist the immune mechanism in healing the body.

What is the greatest enemy of the immune mechanism?

Guilt is the worst enemy of the immune mechanism, and starts weakening the system.

Whoever deals in wrong dealings, wrong dealings in business, in family relations, in everything, develops a guilt complex, and starts wearing down the immune mechanism, confusing it.

If that immune mechanism starts weakening on you, it is called stress . . . negative stress, something we don't like.

There are other enemies of the immune mechanism: stress, tension, worry, and so on, but guilt is the worst.

When the immune mechanism starts weakening, the person starts getting problems like insomnia, then migraine headaches, then peptic ulcers, then high blood pressure. If the problem is not corrected, it starts getting worse.

Now come the chronic diseases: diabetes, arthritis, glaucoma.

This is the second warning; if these second level health problems are not corrected, then come leukemia, cancer, heart attacks, strokes . . . and death.

How to Be Strong and Healthy

The way to strengthen the immune mechanism is the simplest thing ever: we can do it by going to our alpha level, the center of the brain frequency spectrum, and staying there fifteen minutes a day.

Why is this so? Many reasons.

It has been found that if we stay at our level fifteen minutes a day, analyzing our problems, our past experiences, making adjustments, noticing what we did that was wrong that we didn't want to do any more, getting rid of all guilt complexes, planning for the future taking inventory, and making our readjustments to go forward, we will stay healthy.

But you must be sure you are at ten cycles. If you haven't already learned how to do this, you can learn quickly with any of the Free Training options in appendix A.

We have found that a person at ten cycles, a person who stays at ten cycles consciously aware for fifteen minutes, will be there enough time to do away with—dissolve—the stress enzyme, a substance that accumulates in the blood stream as a result of tension and worry and weakens the immune mechanism.

Perhaps we find it so beneficial because we attune ourselves to a ten cycle per second pulsing that scientists have discovered between planet earth and the ionosphere.

Scientists don't know the origin of this pulsing, they don't know where the generator is, but they suspect it to be the depths of the universe; God's creation.

When we function at the alpha level, we attune to this pulsing of the universe, to charge our immune mechanism, charge our bodies up, strengthen our immune mechanism, to continue to be healthy, so no health problems will bother us.

Can you imagine, if everybody would get to their level, and stay fifteen minutes a day, we would not have a health problem left.

Can We Live Forever?

People come and ask, "If we go to our level fifteen minutes a day, we will never get sick?"

I answer, "That is right."

They say, "Do you mean to say, we are never going to die?"

"We don't mean that," we say; "we will die in perfect health."

We are conditioned to accept that disease will kill us.

Disease should not kill people.

People should die of natural means, healthy.

Once a way has been found to keep diseases from killing people, then people are going to die in perfect health.

We call it transition.

Make it a point to set aside fifteen minutes a day for yourself, and spend this time at your level, recharging your immune mechanism, getting rid of the guilt complex.

Then you will maintain perfect health.

Any disease is a sign you are doing something wrong.

Take the time to do this when it is convenient for you. That is much better than getting sick and being forced to find the time to get well.

Note: To learn how to enter the alpha level and relieve tension and stress, you can choose any of the free training options in appendix A.

11 Good Things Happen When You Do What You Were Sent to Do *(1988)*

Life goes through cycles. It is much like the tide: sometimes you are riding high, but when the tide goes out, you ride much lower.

During the high tides, abundance comes easily. We feel good, we prosper, and the world looks good.

During the low tides, times are leaner, there is less to choose from, and we must work harder.

It is important that we also work hard during the high tides so that we have a little something extra to help us out during the times when the tide is low, when the tide goes out.

Entering your level every day, and centering yourself will help you have a smoother life. The cycles will still be there, but you can manage them better when you are centered.

When you stay in touch with your source, you receive sound guidance, you make good decisions, and you get positive results.

When you stay centered, you will know instinctively when you can splurge and when you should save.

These cycles go beyond our ability to completely control them. Many other people are involved.

You may be correcting problems and helping the creator, but others around you may not be. If that is the case, you can be swept along as the tide goes out.

Of course, when the tide is rising, it will lift you up too, perhaps higher than the others.

When you are centered, when you are doing the work you were sent here to do, and when others are also fulfilling their mission, and the tide is high, that's when unexpected good things can happen to you.

We had a good example of that recently when we won a new $24,000 Cadillac in a charity raffle.

How did I program to win the car?

I didn't.

I did not program to win it.

I have been purchasing tickets every year for many years from the Laredo chapter of the Alhambra organization because the proceeds are used to provide help for the local mental health and retardation programs.

I never program to win. I just continue to program to fulfill my mission on this planet.

When Arturo Barrera of Alhambra handed me the keys to the car, I considered that to be a sign that I am doing what I should be doing. It lets me know that those around me are also doing what they should be doing.

I interpret this to mean that we are on the right track with the Silva Method, that we are moving in the direction we are supposed to go.

This movement is more than just me. It involves all of us.

You are an important part of the movement. It is due largely to you that we have grown so much.

We now offer the Silva Method throughout the United States and in seventy-four countries and territories around the world, in sixteen different languages.

Millions of people have benefited.

And there is a simple formula to continue bringing the benefits of the Silva Method to the population of the planet:

One plus two equals five billion.

That's right:

If each Silva graduate will just bring two more people to the Silva training, then by the end of this century we will have reached all five billion souls on our planet.

Enter your level and find out the names of the people you know who can benefit from the Silva Method, and who are ready for it now.

And as always, enter your level every day, and from time to time, check to make sure that you are fulfilling your mission.

When you fulfill your mission, and the people around you are centered and work to fulfill their missions, then you will have more high tides in your life.

And that's a lot more effective than programming to win a lottery.

Note: If you have not taken any of our courses, you can learn to enter the alpha level with any of the free training options in the appendix of this book.

You can learn how to obtain guidance from higher intelligence with the MentalVideo Technique in appendix D.

12 Here's How You Can Tell if You Are Living Right *(1990)*

There are many ways of looking at troublesome situations, not all of them dark, gloomy and negative.

For example, I was talking with one of our graduates recently. He noted that he did not have much money or a new car or a big house, but he added, "I have everything I need, and most of what I want, so I'm doing all right."

That is certainly true. I know many people who have big cars, big houses, big mortgages, mountains of bills, and migraine head-aches. They have a lot of things, but they are not happy.

I have a lot of things. But it is not the things that make me happy. Things come and things go. If you are attached to the things, you will find it difficult to be happy, because you will always be worried about losing the things, or getting the latest and newest things before everybody else gets them.

Happiness
What makes me happy is knowing that I am doing what I was sent here to do.

How do I know what I was sent here to do? I have a very simple formula that I use: If my life continues to get better and better, then I know that I am doing what I was sent here to do. If things get worse, then I know that somebody is telling me I am on the wrong track.

How does that manifest in my life? Here's what I have found.

When I am helping to correct problems, I find that I am given everything that I need, and even more.

On the other hand, I have observed that people who are not correcting problems, usually do not get very many of the things that they want, or if they do get the things, the things don't make them very happy.

I have observed that when people feel good about themselves and their lives, they are usually healthy.

But when people are doing something that is wrong, and they know it is wrong, their immune system tends to break down and they get sick.

During my research, many people asked me to heal them, to use the holistic faith healing techniques I was studying to help them get well.

Before I would help anyone, I would ask them a question:

Why do you want to get well?

If they said that they wanted to enjoy their family, to travel, to enjoy some of the things they had never had a chance to do before—if they answered like that, I knew I had my work cut out for me. I would explain to them that they were put here to help correct problems. If they are not helping to correct problems, then it would be difficult to heal them.

But if they would change their attitude and agree to help correct problems, then they would qualify for help. Not help from me, but help from higher intelligence.

When we are doing what we were sent here to do—which is to correct problems—then we will receive everything we need so that we can continue to help perfect the creation and convert our planet into a paradise.

Is that the way life really works? My research indicates that it is.

Observe Your Results

To put it in very simple terms, if your life is not as good as you would like it to be, then enter your level and think about whether you are fulfilling your obligations.

You get a lot of feedback in life. If you are encountering more and more problems, more and more obstacles, this is feedback that you are moving in the wrong direction.

If your life is continuing to get better and better, and if you can solve each new problem more quickly and easily, then you are moving in the right direction.

The more problems you are able to correct, the more people you help, the better your life will be, and the happier you will be.

13 Build Prosperity On Spiritual Foundations *(1983)*

All programming for prosperity should be built on spiritual foundations.

The first step is to enter the subjective (world of the mind) dimension, the alpha level, and determine what your purpose in life is. Find out what you are here for, what you are supposed to do with your life.

Then you take steps to meet your obligations.

If you don't already know how to do enter the subjective dimension, you can learn with any of the Free Training options in appendix A.

When programming for money or other material things, the first thing to think about is what you are going to do when you get it.

You don't want to just go away on a vacation and forget everything else.

Your obligations continue while you are still alive and still have breath of life. Even if you have to drag yourself across the ground, you still have the same obligation to try and do your best to correct the problems on the planet. When you are not here any more, then you cease to be obligated.

If you do the right job, then money will come to you. Because people who need you will request, will ask for you, will attract you, and will be willing to pay you for your services. If you are a good worker, then everybody wants you, and will be willing to pay a fair amount. But if you're not, they don't want you.

This was why whenever I went to look for a job, when I was in the service and needed to supplement my income, everywhere I'd go they'd ask what I wanted to earn, and I answered, "Whatever you think I'm worth. Try me out, and pay me accordingly."

Spiritual Foundation

In the subjective dimension, you determine what your purpose in life is. Then you plan how to go about doing it. Then you transfer it to the physical dimension.

That is the concept of the man who said, "Whatever the mind conceives in the subjective dimension, and believes enough to transfer to the physical dimension, you will achieve." So the achievement was the transference of that particular thing that was created in the subjective world of the mind, into the material, physical world.

It is just like the materialization of thoughts. You have to first create them subjectively, and then you use them in the physical world, to make sense with them, to serve a purpose with them. It is no good to just test them in one dimension. You have to go from one to another and have them make sense in both dimensions.

The subjective has to be first; we have to think about it before we act on it.

And remember, when programming, you do not program just because you *want* something, but because you *need* it. You may not always get what you want, but you can get what you need. And that depends on what you are going to need it for. If it is to correct problems, you will probably get it.

I program to attract whatever we need.

I do not program to receive more than what we need, but I sure put emphasis on receiving *no less* than what we need.

Of course, you need to know in your own mind just what it is that you need. You don't have to ask for it, but keep it in mind and everything will be automatic from there on.

You don't need to ask specifically for $50,000 if that's what you need; just keep your goal in mind, and program for all bills to be paid, or to have the things you need.

Program to see your projects completed, and keep in mind what it takes to do it, as though somebody were looking in and wanting to know what you need so they can send it your way, whatever your needs are.

If you don't keep it in your mind, there is no way for whoever is trying to help you to know.

It is always best to program in increments. For instance, suppose a person wants a lot of money and decides to program to start earning a lot of money.

It is better done in small steps. For example, some people lose their wits; they get spoiled when they get too much of what they are not used to having.

Some people are destroyed by their first failure, while others are destroyed by their first major success. So let's have successes in small amounts, leading up to being able to be successful.

Sometimes when people are too successful too rapidly, they go off in all directions, and don't know how to cope with it. We say do not be spoiled by your first failure, or by your first success.

As long as you keep yourself centered, and are fulfilling the purpose you were sent here for, you will succeed and be prosperous in all areas of life.

Note: To learn how to put this into practice starting today, you can choose any of the free training options in appendix A.

In appendix C you can learn how to use the Mirror of the Mind and the 3-Scenes Technique to solve problems.

You can learn how to obtain guidance from higher intelligence with the MentalVideo Technique in appendix D.

14 The Truth About Prosperity
(1987)

Prosperity is a topic of continuing interest to people, and we are frequently asked how to program for more prosperity.

I tell people that it is easy to get a million dollars if you need it: Just give ten million dollars worth of service to humanity and you will qualify for your million dollars.

We also talk about how faith plays a big part in programming for prosperity—or for anything else for that matter.

Yet is seems that most people continue to program improperly: They program for more money, or they program for more of the things that money will buy. They program themselves to like money. They program themselves to believe that they deserve money.

My research and my personal experience indicates that this is not the best way to program for prosperity—for money.

How to Program

For many years writers have written about the law of compensation. You find it in all the religions: As ye sow, so shall ye reap. In the East it is called "karma," which means simply that you get what you deserve.

Please notice that first you must sow. First you must pay.

Or as I said above: You must qualify for your million dollars, and you do so by giving ten million dollars worth of service to humanity.

Perfect Programming

Let me give an example of a graduate who fulfilled the laws of programming perfectly and received what she most wanted: Good health.

Marge Wolcott, of Port Isabel, Texas, attended the Silva Basic Lecture Series in January of 1970. She had multiple sclerosis, was wearing a full body brace, a neck brace, had to be carried into the classroom and placed in a special chair that she used.

Doctors had given up hope for her. In fact, she had almost died a couple of times.

How did Marge Wolcott program herself to get well? Did she spend all day trying to heal her body? Not at all.

Marge Wolcott is a very religious person. For many years, she has prayed for people who need help.

After she completed the Silva training, when people would ask her to pray for someone, she would use the Silva case working technique.

She was doing this three times a day.

At the end of her programming session, she would visualize herself in perfect health also. "I had little hope," she said. "I was not concerned about it. If I got better, that would be great. If not, I could accept that."

She recovered, and outlived the doctors who pronounced the death sentence on her.

She recovered so well that specialists in MS cannot even tell she ever had the disease.

Why It Worked

Why did her programming work so effectively?

Because she followed some very important universal laws.

When you follow those same laws, your programming will work as well, whether it is for healing, prosperity, relationships of whatever.

First, she qualified for help because she was helping others. For many years she had helped others. And she was applying her Silva techniques first to help others.

By working cases on people who needed help, and by really desiring to help them, she got herself into a perfect frame of mind for programming. Then when she programmed for herself, that programming had tremendous power.

If you have a job and receive a salary for that job, you probably have to do the work first, and then you get paid. If you do get paid before you work, it is probably because you have a long history of doing a good job.

When you serve humanity, you qualify for help from High Intelligence. If you have a long history of serving humanity, then perhaps you already qualify for help. If not, then get to work:

At level, ask what you can do to help humanity, and then do it.

Have Faith

As you recall, faith is made up of three elements: Desire, Belief and Expectancy, also known as Hope.

Marge Wolcott had a lot of desire.

Desire is not something artificial that you can call up on demand. You cannot force desire.

Desire is the result of need.

Marge Wolcott had a great need—she was badly crippled and her life was threatened. Therefore, she had great desire.

To increase your desire, repeat mentally or verbally what you desire, and think of all the reasons you have for accomplishing your goal.

When you find a product or service you can offer that will help humanity, then enter your level and think of all the ways it will help humanity.

How many people will benefit? How about their families?

The more reasons you can think of, that your product or service will help humanity, the more desire you will have. And that means you will have more faith.

Marge Wolcott obviously believed the Silva techniques would work. She believes in God.

She believes in helping people, and that her prayers could make a difference.

And by the time she had worked health cases on several people, she was at the, ideal level—the ideal state of mind—for correctly visualizing her desired end result.

At that deep alpha state of mind, she expected to get better.

She did not push and expend effort and "try" to force her body to get well.

Instead, she visualized and "expected" her body to heal. She had a little bit of hope. Not much, but some.

"The Bible says that whatever you do for others, comes back to you ten-fold," Marge Wolcott said. "Apparently when I programmed for other people, I was helping myself, too."

Prosperity Is Yours

By following the examples of people like Marge Wolcott, you can have all the prosperity you desire.

First: Help humanity. By doing this, you will qualify to obtain more for yourself.

Build your faith.

Increase your desire by programming to help as many people, in as many ways, as possible.

Build your belief by practicing all of the Silva techniques and developing more confidence in them and in your ability to use them successfully. Successful experiences builds confidence and a strong belief that you will succeed again.

And program yourself at a deep alpha level, the kind of deep level you reach when you have been programming to help other people.

Program to help humanity, and keep in mind what you need . . . plus a little bit extra.

There is no need for force prosperity. It will come to you when you use the correct ingredients, in the correct manner, as we have outlined here.

Keep in mind always to "Do unto others what you like others to do unto you."

If you haven't taken our ESP training and want to learn to use the Alpha level and the same techniques that Marge Wolcott used, please see appendices A, B, and C.

15 We Must Evolve, and Keep Our Sense of Values In Perspective *(1982)*

Throughout our lives, we are constantly evolving. Growth is the natural way to function for a human being.

But some people get stuck along the way.

When children are very young, they like to play with dolls and cap pistols. They push little toy cars and trucks around the floor. They make houses in their sandboxes.

It would look foolish for a grownup to spend a lot of time playing with dolls or cap pistols or playing in sandboxes.

Later, as children get older, their interests change. They become interested in girlfriends and boyfriends and cars and football and baseball and dancing and having fun and many more things.

This is a natural state of affairs, and you expect to see it at a certain point in a person's development.

But some people get stuck along the way. We should go through those phases, learning all we can at that point in our development. But then we should move forward and put our knowledge and experience to use.

As we mature, we have things to do. It seems foolish to see a grown man so obsessed with watching other people play football that it dominates his life.

As children, we start out playing with little tiny toys. Take away the toy and it breaks the child's heart.

We learn to ride tricycles, and motorcycles. At a certain age, that becomes the most important thing in life.

But it looks foolish to see an old man wearing helmet and gloves racing around on a motorcycle, trying to act like a teenager.

As we grow older and mature even more, social life becomes the most important thing to us. Take away his girlfriend, or her boyfriend, and the adolescent feels that he or she might die.

All of these phases are okay. They are all natural. When we come into this world, we begin to establish points of reference in the physical dimension.

We have been programmed with certain survival programming, so it is natural to do many of these things.

The problem is, many people get stuck along the way. They get stuck on some phase or some activity that was important at a certain point in their development.

That is why we see some people for whom watching football or baseball has become a whole way of life.

Then we find people in old age who play these games. Imagine a person in old age, still chasing girls. If he catches one, he doesn't know what to do with her!

Instead of getting stuck, we should continue to grow, to evolve. We should put our knowledge and experience to work solving problems, to help convert this planet into a paradise.

This does not mean that we cannot play and have fun; of course we should enjoy life and live balanced lives with the proper proportions of productive work, relaxation, play, social relationships, growth and discovery.

What we should avoid is getting stuck on a child-like pleasure and letting that dominate life so much that we become useless to ourselves and others.

Repeatedly we see where sports and athletic activities have become such big business that they cease to be fun.

Youngsters used to just have fun when they played games; now it is like they are training for a career.

Let us keep a balanced perspective in things. Let's not be like a scratched record, stuck in one groove, repeating the same notes over and over rather than completing the symphony of our life.

Let's make this a better world to live in by bringing back a correct sense of values; let's start spending more on research to help humanity than we spend on entertainment.

16 Anxiety is the Main Problem Today
(1981)

While most of us think of inflation and the economic insecurity it creates as one of the top national—and international—problems today, there is yet another malady that is perhaps even more damaging, and it is one that has not been given the attention it deserves.

This malady is the increase in anxiety and tension among people who are in a position where their decisions affect the course of humanity, both politically and economically.

Anxiety and tension create not only a problem that affects the health—both mental and physical—of these individuals, but they are directly responsible for the decline in creativity, productivity, intuitiveness, and innovations we are experiencing in the modern world.

Heads of state, business executives, college professors, laboratory researchers, or production line workers whose lives are filled with stress and anxiety are not going to operate at their full potential.

At one point or another, the quality of their work declines, their decision-making becomes less pragmatic and effective, their creativeness wanes and their production becomes boring and less innovative.

All of these factors lead us, as a society, towards the road to mediocrity instead of the road that achieves excellence.

Already there is ample evidence all around that there is indeed a significant increase in anxiety, depression, hypertension, heart disease, sleeplessness and chronic headaches. Unfortunately, many of these key persons, in finding it difficult to cope with these stressful situations, turn to alcohol, drugs and other stimulants and depressants for symptomatic relief.

The result of this is not only a loss of productivity but a strain on their family and personal lives.

In Silva Mind Control, these modern-day ills are given priority, for we have always felt that people can become more wholesome and can more fully integrate their personality only if they can cultivate the ability to relax and to control the tensions imposed by modern living.

How can we go about encouraging ourselves to increase our ability to relax and take life without stress while at the same time becoming better integrated individuals and thus more creative and productive?

The answer has been offered to Silva Mind Control graduates since our course was developed and implemented almost fifteen years ago.

I firmly believe that providing people with this ability has been one of our greatest contributions.

For one, an individual has to have the ability to relax. This, I fully believe, is easier said than done, but at Silva we have developed techniques that effectively help us learn to relax almost at will.

What we need to do is to further cultivate these techniques so that we can become even better practitioners.

Second, we must develop the ability to focus our attention on a particular problem—or problems—so that we can concentrate on their solutions without interference from other non-related and often obstructive problems.

However, this is not the type of concentration that most people think of, such as the hard thinking with the hands on cheeks and deeply furrowed brow.

Far from it, Silva Mind Control helps us to practice the type of concentration that is much more effective, that which comes from a relaxed focus of attention so as to let the inner conscious come through with what often is the correct answer to a particular problem.

Thirdly, our graduates have been given the essential tools to accept subjective phenomena to aid us in relaxing and problem solving.

This is perhaps our greatest tool because learning to be receptive to subjective experiences will allow an individual the full use of the messages, the images, the dreams, the ideas, and the impressions of the inner self, which are truly more valuable in making effective decisions.

In essence, what Silva Mind Control helps us to learn is to use four levels by which we can become more productive and better problem-solvers.

These four levels are the physical, the emotional, the mental and the spiritual.

The tragedy of modern life is that we are much too busy—or at least we act like it—that we do not find time to relax and reflect.

By first providing a person with the ability to relax and look inward, Silva Mind Control has opened the doors to a world in which an individual can become more "fully realized."

Once this happens, humanity will be that much better off, and the whole world will be on the road to becoming "Better and Better."

Note: To learn how to put this into practice starting today, choose any of the free training options in appendix A and follow the simple instructions.

17 Researchers Say Silva Does the "Impossible" (1987)

The "experts" said it couldn't be done, but once again research has demonstrated that the Silva Method is the most powerful program available to help people manage stress and live happier, healthier, more successful lives.

The investigation took place within the framework of the Department of Psychology of Haifa University, Israel, in 1984, under the direction of Dr. Moshe Almagor, who authorized its publication.

I'd like to comment on the results of the research from my own point of view.

Life Changes

People have been telling us for a long time that their life changes when they learn the Silva techniques. This research shows one of the important ways this happens.

This study focuses on two kinds of tension and stress:

Things that happen that threaten us, anger us, worry us—that can cause a stress reaction. This is called state anxiety.

Personality traits and characteristics that causes a person to have a high potential to react with state anxiety when faced with a situation that the person perceives as menacing. This is called trait anxiety.

You have heard it said many times that we cannot always control what happens, but we can control our reaction to it.

The problem is, people develop habits through the years; they develop ways of reacting to situations.

In addition, there are certain personality types that are just more prone to worry.

Until now, the "experts" have said that the only way to change these "traits" is through long, drawn out treatment.

You certainly could not expect a forty hour program, presented over two weekends, to do it, the experts claimed.

Lasting Results

What is so impressive is not just that people were less anxious, and more relaxed after the Silva training, but that they continued to become even more relaxed even after the training.

The most exciting part is that Silva graduates were not only able to act more relaxed (manage state anxiety), but actually were more relaxed (decreased trait anxiety).

"The specific feature of the Silva Method is to teach the subject to think in a state of relaxation, and while they are in this state, to utilize proper programming technique to accomplish fixed goals," the research report observes.

"The Silva Method is not hypnosis, because subjects are conscious and are completely in control of themselves while practicing the techniques; he remains mentally active during the exercise, depending on no external agent.

"As opposed to biofeedback, (the Silva Method) provides techniques for the solution of specific problems, and it requires no apparatus."

In those statements, the researchers summed up the "secret" of the Silva Method's success.

Anything applied from the outside only treats symptoms.

When you do it yourself, you treat the cause.

That is why the Silva Method has worked better than hypnosis, yoga, biofeedback and other procedures.

The Silva Method succeeds where they succeed, and also succeeds where they fail—because you are helping yourself.

Outstanding Results

That is why we can see results like those on this chart:

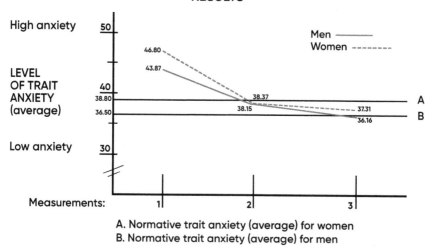

A. Normative trait anxiety (average) for women
B. Normative trait anxiety (average) for men

Naturally, the average level of trait anxiety was "significantly lower" at the end of the training (point 2) than at the beginning (point 1).

In addition, the average level of trait anxiety six months later was "significantly lower" again.

As you might expect, there was greater improvement for those who practiced regularly than those who did not.

"These facts illustrate the importance of daily practice in reducing the level of trait anxiety," the report notes, "although the trait anxiety level of those who did not practice daily, also improved considerably."

In other words, even if all you ever do is take the training and never practice, you still get long term benefits.

If you practice once, twice or three times a day, you get even more benefits.

And everyone will benefit. It made no difference whether the person had high or low trait anxiety levels at the beginning, as far as practicing and improvement were concerned.

The researchers did note that, "participants in the (Silva Method) course, have a higher-than-normative level of trait anxiety; it is therefore possible that this was one of their motives for taking the course. "

Women's Results

Women showed higher stress levels than men, and showed greater improvement.

The researchers observed that this could be the result of women's tendency to be more open to people, more critical, and more sensitive. Also, one study found that women are more suggestible than men.

"It is possible," the researchers said, "that women are more open and perceptive to the course material, and thus the practice during the course, and the irregular practice after finishing the course, sufficed for the women (more than for the men who practiced at the same rate) to reduce the level of trait anxiety."

They added, "It is likely that women have a more positive attitude than men towards the course, but this is only a hypothesis which must be proven."

Six months after the training, "women participants attained a level of trait anxiety significantly lower than normative, while men reached the normative level."

Conclusions

"The results contradict Spielberger's theory, which asserts that relatively short methods will not reduce the level of trait anxiety, but only the level of state anxiety," the report says.

They suggest several possible explanations for this (quoted directly from the report):

1. The course provides a more positive attitude towards life experiences, and emphasizes the importance of positive thinking.

2. The course provides specific programming techniques which can be utilized by the individual as a means for the solution of daily problems.

3. The course is a practical one, and it encompasses practice of all the techniques.

4. The pleasant atmosphere during the course, as well as the positive attitudes, contribute to relaxation and tranquility

And the final comment reads:

"In accordance with the results obtained, the course provides efficient means for reduction of the level of trait anxiety. There are indications that, in spite of the influence of modifying variables, the method exerts significant influence on trait anxiety."

We certainly appreciate this scientific confirmation of what we have been saying for more than a quarter of a century: The Silva Method offers you the tools that you can practice and use to get Better, Better, and Better.

Note: To learn how to put this into practice starting today, you can choose any of the free training options in appendix A.

In appendix C you can learn how to use the Silva problem-solving techniques to deal with problems that are causing the tension and stress.

18 How Does Silva Method Compare with Hypnosis, Yoga, Others? *(1989)*

People often ask about the similarities of the Silva Method with other mental training methods.

They ask if the Silva systems are the same as hypnosis, the same as yoga, or the same as some other mental training methods.

To help explain the differences, let me go back to the time when I first became interested in the study of the human mind.

I began my study of the mind and human potential in 1944 after a conversation with an army psychiatrist while I was being inducted into the army. He explained that he could tell a lot about a person by analyzing how they thought.

This made sense to me, and I felt that I might be able to help my children to be more successful if they used their minds in ways that would help them succeed.

The first goal I had was to find a way to improve my children's IQ factor by devising a way to help them memorize and recall information better.

The first step in research was to find a way of slowing brain activity while maintaining awareness.

Upon investigating methods such as yoga, Zen, Transcendental Meditation and hypnosis, we found that all method require the student to be trained to practice with their eyes closed.

Later our research indicated that the reason for the closure of the eyes was not only to prevent distractions.

We found that when a person attempts to focus their eyes to see something, the brain stays on twenty cycles per second rather than slowing to a lower brain frequency, which was our goal.

At first we thought we could use hypnosis as a major tool to reach our goal, but later research revealed that hypnosis was not giving us the end results we wanted.

We wanted to train a person to function normally at ten cycles brain frequency with as much awareness and consciousness as when a person normally functions at twenty cycles brain frequency.

We found that the brain activity of a person active mentally and physically under hypnosis was twenty cycles per second.

We wanted the person to be active mentally and physically but with the brain at ten cycles.

Another thing we found was that a person under deep hypnosis never asks questions. The hypnotized subject only answers questions.

We also found that a person who is hypnotized has a very strong tendency to forget what transpired while in that state.

These are some of the ways that people functioned abnormally.

What we needed was just the opposite: for people to function normally while the brain was at ten cycles.

We wanted people to be able to ask and answer questions, not just answer. And we wanted them to remember more the deeper they entered, rather than forgetting.

All of the other systems that we investigated also had drawbacks and deficiencies that caused them to fall short of the goals that we had.

We began to realize that we needed a new mental training exercise, similar to existing ones, yet different in ways that would make it possible for us to attain our own objectives.

We realized that all mental training methods led the student in the same direction: into a state of mind-body relaxation.

What became apparent was that all disciplines for training the mind were directed to find an ideal level of mind-brain function that a person could use to attain goals that are difficult to attain.

We also found that the name given to the system, whether yoga, Zen, Transcendental Meditation or hypnosis, was the name given to the step-by-step procedure used to find the ideal level of mind-brain function.

After studying these various disciplines we found that the ideal level of brain-mind functioning is the same for everybody, and that ultimately all disciplines help to find the same ideal mind-brain function level, regardless of the name given to the method used.

The difference in what we developed is that our method allows people to function normally, and to be active both mentally and physically, while maintaining that ideal level of mind-brain function.

With the Silva systems, you can learn to do all the things that are done with hypnosis, and more.

With the Silva systems, you can learn to do all the things that are done by yogis, and more.

With the Silva training, you can learn to do all the things done by Zen meditators, and by Transcendental Meditators, and more.

With the Silva training, you have the choice of functioning in any of those ways, or differently.

It is your choice whether you maintain control, or decide to follow the guidance of another person, or of Higher Intelligence.

When I say Higher Intelligence, I mean God.

Many people have "knocked off" the our work. That is, they have taken parts of it, and specialize in doing only a few of the things that are possible for Silva graduates.

Instead of expanding human ability as they claim to do, they are actually restricting people by teaching only a small portion of what can be done.

To make sure that you get the tools you need to live up to your potential, make sure that you learn the original Silva techniques. Practice the genuine article, not the partial products you find on the market today.

With the freedom of choice that you have with the authentic Silva training, there are no limitations to how far you can go, because there are no known limits to the human mind.

19 The Difference I see Between Silva and Hypnosis by José Silva Jr.

After having observed my dad from his earliest research on through the development of the Silva Mind Control Method, I've seen many, many differences.

Of course, all of the wording is different.

In hypnosis, the hypnotist is always telling you what to do. The hypnotic operator gives you suggestions, commanding you, and telling you what to think and what to do.

For instance, a hypnotist may tell you that you can't open your eyes, and if you accept the suggestions, then sure enough you can't open your eyes.

In very deep hypnosis, the hypnotist will tell you that things are there when they really aren't there, but you will imagine that you see them.

That's called hallucination. You really believe the dog *is* there.

Or the hypnotist can give you the suggestion that something that *is* there, *is not* there, and you will *not* see it. You will believe it is *not* here.

When you are under deep hypnosis, when the hypnotist suggests something, you will do it. When the hypnotist gives a command, you will obey it. Of course, you will not obey the command if it is something that goes against your moral or ethical standards.

Strong Rapport With the Hypnotist

Hypnotized subjects are very intuitive.

Hypnotized subjects will do whatever the hypnotist wants, so long as it doesn't violate their moral code.

So if the hypnotist suggests that the subject do something that would be wrong or might hurt someone, but the hypnotist never intends to let the subject actually carry out the instructions, then the subject—who is functioning clairvoyantly at the time—will play the game and pretend they are trying to carry out the instructions, even though they know the hypnotist will stop them.

And the subject will never admit they knew that the hypnotist would stop them, even under hypnosis, because they know the hypnotist doesn't really want them to.

Limitations of Hypnosis

When you first start hypnotizing people, you can ask them questions and they will answer. But they won't ask questions or try to figure things out for themselves.

But after you have hypnotized them so many times, it is like the body develops a mechanism to defend itself:

The subjects begin asking questions themselves.

And they begin using their intuitive ability.

Taking Back Control

When my dad first started giving health cases to my sisters, he had to ask them everything.

He would ask if there was a problem in the head, for instance. He would have to guide them to the areas involved and ask them questions so they could find the problems.

But as you know, with the Silva ESP training, it is just the opposite:

The orientologist *avoids* giving any guidance.

Silva-trained clairvoyants are very active in seeking out the problems:

Silva-trained psychics do not wait for a body to "appear," but *visualize* (recall) one.

Silva-trained psychics don't wait for something to happen so they can "perceive" what the problem is.

Silva-trained psychics projects right to the problem. They take an active, dynamic role.

Silva-trained psychics visualize a problem and project it onto the image of the body to see if it fits. If not, they try another problem, and keep on it until they find out what the problem is.

Be Sure You're Right and Then Go Ahead

Silva graduates will never be hypnotized, because they are too active, too curious, too interested to ever give up that awareness and involvement.

Things are not done for Silva graduates. Silva Method graduates do things for themselves and for others.

To me, there are a great many differences between hypnosis and the Silva Systems, and the fact that a few superficial aspects appear similar does not mean that the substance of hypnosis and the Silva Systems are anything alike.

It's the difference in meekly doing what somebody else wants, compared with taking charge of your own life, finding out what you need to know to succeed, and then doing it.

A Better, Faster, Superior Method

While my father started with hypnosis, he realized that his subjects were not functioning at normal hypnotic levels.

He thought back to when he was in the army in 1945 and was assigned to a camp near Bowling Green, Kentucky, the birthplace of Edgar Cayce, the famous "Sleep Prophet."

Cayce would enter a state comparable to light sleep, and while at that state he could detect peoples' health problems and advise them of what vitamins and herbs to take to correct their problems.

My father realized that all he needed to do was to guide people to a level comparable to light sleep, so he devised a very simple way to "fool the brain" into thinking that you wanted to go to sleep.

What do you do when you are ready to go to sleep?

Find a comfortable position, make yourself comfortable.

Close your eyes.

Relax physically.

Calm your mind.

Sound familiar? If you have practiced our Centering Exercise you will recognize those as the steps we take to enter the alpha brainwave level.

That is all it takes. No hypnotic techniques, no need for a hypnotist to take control of your mind and tell you what to do.

We don't take control of your mind. We guide you to enter a level—brain-wise—comparable to light sleep.

Rather than using hypnosis, we might be using a system similar to what Edgar Cayce used.

We are not against hypnosis. There are times when it could be the best and fastest way to get results.

My father always advised to do whatever it takes to solve a problem. Isn't it better to have more tools you can use for problem-solving?

20 It is Easy to Learn How to Have Happiness *(1993)*

What makes you happy?

Different people give different answers to that question.

In fact, the search for happiness and fulfillment has been going on for ages.

People have amassed great wealth, only to find that they are still the same person as they were when they didn't have the money, and the money itself doesn't make them happy.

There are many who have achieved fame, but often their own insecurities keep them from enjoying it.

Even having a loving family doesn't insure happiness.

What Brings Happiness?

In my experience, happiness comes from solving problems.

Don't you feel good when you solve a problem successfully? There is a certain feeling that comes from succeeding; you can only get this feeling by achieving a success. It is a happy, satisfying, fulfilling feeling.

The more successes you have, the more times you get this special feeling.

This leads to wisdom. An accumulation of feelings of successes leads to wisdom.

Doing Our Job

Why does it make us feel good to correct problems? Why does this bring us happiness?

Perhaps because we were sent here to correct problems, and when we are doing what we were sent here to do, we are rewarded with feelings of happiness and satisfaction and fulfillment.

Have you ever wondered who sent you here, and why they sent you here?

I have.

I have wondered if I was sent here to enjoy myself with worldly pleasures. But that doesn't seem to be the case. Too much "wine, women, and song" brings about problems for the individual. I've known many people who have died from too much drinking, and from the stress caused by too much self-indulgence.

If something harms your body and brings about an early death, then you shouldn't do it! That certainly seems simple.

What to Do

On the other hand, I've found that when people are engaged in constructive and creative activities, they prosper.

Nobody pays a person for partying; in fact, it usually costs a person a lot of money for the wine, women, and song.

But people do pay, and pay well, for things that you do that are constructive and creative, for things that correct problems and make this a better world to live in.

I think that higher intelligence also compensates us when we are correcting problems.

We're not here to party all the time. We're not here just to eat and sleep and survive.

We're here to solve problems.

How to Proceed

We used to be told to learn from our mistakes. We were told that we could reach success by climbing on a ladder of failures.

Now we know a better way:

Use your successes to lead you to even greater success.

Whenever you succeed at correcting a problem, you get a certain feeling of happiness and satisfaction.

Afterwards, enter your level and review and relive both the success and the feeling that comes with success.

Every time you review the success, and especially that special feeling of success, at your level, it will be almost like having another success.

Success brings on even more success.

Accumulated successes lead to wisdom. So use your successes—even if you only have a few in the beginning—to bring you more success.

Then you will get the added benefit of knowing, deep within, that you are doing what you were sent here to do, that you have aligned yourself with the creator by engaging in constructive and creative activities.

This will boost your self-image and feelings of self-worth, which will give you greater self-confidence and a sense of fulfillment.

There are no affirmations that can do that for you.

Simply changing your attitude without taking the right action is not enough.

When you become a better person by doing what you were sent here to do, then you will feel like a better person, and more importantly, you will actually be a better person.

21 | Block Out the Cries of Critics Because They Are Destructive   *(1987)*

As we near the 21st birthday of the Silva Method, we began thinking about some of the critics we've encountered along the way.

Some people said it couldn't be done.

Some people said we were just fooling ourselves.

Some people said we were just fooling the public.

Some people said we'd never be able to prove it.

Now, some people are singing a different tune.

Results Prove Us Correct

Today we are offering the Silva Method in seventy-three countries.

Today the Silva Method is being presented in sixteen languages. And that doesn't count the fact that English is different in England than it is in the United States, and French is different in France than it is in Canada.

Today the Silva Method is the most imitated program in the world.

To date the Silva Method has helped more than seven million people, directly and indirectly. It has proven effective in all cultures, for people of all religious beliefs—or no religious beliefs, and at all economic and educational levels.

Today the Silva Method is the most valuable and important movement in the world, to help us convert the planet into a paradise.

Serving Humanity

What makes the Silva Method so successful?

We believe it is successful because it helps people correct problems.

There are many things you can do for entertainment and recreation. The Silva Method focuses first on correcting specific problems.

We believe that is what the Creator sent us here to do.

We believe in having fun, in enjoying life.

We believe that enjoyment and fulfillment are the result of doing the job we were sent here to do.

But don't take our word it: try it yourself and see what results you get.

Creative and Constructive

It has been said that nobody ever erected a statue to a critic.

Critics tear down what others create.

Critics inhibit progress.

It is the people who are out there working creatively and constructively who are responsible for progress in our world.

It is the people who are willing to take a risk who achieve great things.

It is the people who believe in their dreams so much that they can continue to move forward despite the critics who achieve greatness.

It is the people who have a soul to dream, and the energy to do, who are recognized as leaders.

We've been criticized by some of the biggest people and organizations around. Church officials have criticized us. States investigated us for fraud.

Even a major news magazine scoffed at us.

Now they are all singing a different tune: Priests and ministers teach the course.

State legislatures have honored us. And we have received favorable news stories in virtually every major publication in the United States and many in other countries.

To achieve the success you desire, do what we did:

Dream your dreams at the alpha level.

Dedicate yourself to correcting problems and working in a constructive and creative manner to make this world a better place to live.

Then get to work, and ignore the critics.

Do this, and you will have a productive, happy, satisfying life.

22 Mind Getting More Attention
(1980)

October is a good month to reminisce about the work that Silva Mind Control has been doing for many, many, years.

It is a good time because fall itself, with its chilly weather, ushers in a reflective mood, and because October is the month of our annual Silva Mind Control International Convention.

The convention scheduled for the eighteenth and nineteenth of October, may be in progress or even over when you read this, but it nonetheless is an event all of us at Silva Mind Control await eagerly.

For one, I feel that getting people involved with humanity and each other is the only way that we can operate at our top level.

Nobody, for example, can ever break the intense, frustrating and devastating feeling of failure by hiding in a self-made shell or by remaining aloof and emotionally isolated.

On the contrary, this feeling of failure can be removed only through the warmth and understanding shared by other individuals.

This year, about 500 Silva Mind Control graduates are expected in Laredo for the convention, which is our way of getting involved with each other at least once a year, of saying "Hello" to friends who share a common interest and mutual goals.

But the convention is important to all of us for another reason it is a vivid example of how much we have grown as an organization and how much our Method has found acceptance throughout the world.

In addition to being the pacesetter in the research of the mind, Silva Mind Control has also been the catalyst in the opening of new dimensions of learning that heretofore had been rebuffed by people whose minds were solidly entrenched in the traditional methods of learning.

For example, psychics, who utilize the mind in dimensions often deemed unacceptable, are beginning to gain more recognition as truly legitimate and worthwhile practitioners.

I feel that much of the acceptance of this new dimension of the mind is due to the work we have carried out at Silva Mind Control thus providing credibility and legitimacy to the area.

To cite one example, a recent story by the Associated Press told how psychics are being used to assist Texas police officers in solving crimes. This was something that a decade ago would have been found nonsensical.

Yet, the story, which was released last month, quoted Texas police officers as saying they utilize the services of psychics.

Police cited a case of a woman who had disappeared from a self-service gasoline station where she worked.

Unable to find her, or her body, the police officers from Longview, Texas, sought the help of a psychic, who gave the police clues while holding on to the woman's purse and keys.

The body was found at an isolated spot that resembled the scene described by the psychic.

In another instance, the Dallas Police Department sought the help of another psychic to find a criminal. After telling officers of the man's character and description, police were able to arrest him. He is now serving a sixty-year prison term.

Other cases were cited by the Associated Press story involving police departments from other cities in the state.

Another story also tells of identical twins who were adopted at birth into separate families. Yet, while never seeing each other for years, they grew up with striking similarities.

As schoolboys, both liked math and detested spelling; both entered law enforcement careers; both drove Chevrolets.

Also, both of them married and divorced women named Linda and married for the second time to women named Betty.

Both of the twins had sons named James Allen. Also both had dogs named Troy.

In another story, a pair of twins, separated in infancy, were introduced later as children. Each wore their favorite dress for the occasion. The dresses, you might have guessed, were identical.

Also, two British twins, Bridget and Dorothy, named their sons Richard Andrew and Andrew Richard respectively and their daughters Catherine Louise and Karen Louise.

These are only some stories that are making news in mass publications.

And what is important is the fact that much more is being written about the wonders of the mind, wonders that those of us at Silva Mind Control had been extolling for decades.

Much more is still not known, but we can be certain that as Silva Mind Control graduates we not only are going to be in the vanguard of this knowledge but we also are going to give visibility to our work.

In this regard, the convention offers an excellent opportunity to share what we have on a personal matter and to tell the world, "Hey, we have something very important to tell, and we are willing to share it not only amongst ourselves but with everybody else."

23   You Can Be More Accurate Than the Best Commercial Psychics   *(1997)*

You don't need to pay a commercial psychic to tell you about your past.

You can learn to be your own psychic and make correct decisions for your future.

"Psychic hotlines" have become very popular in the United States, with hundreds of thousands of people every week paying almost $5 *per minute* to talk to the telephone psychics.

For a flat fee, you can probably find a local psychic that you can go see in person.

Psychic Authority

We know both kinds. They call us here at Silva International because they know that we have conducted more research on psychics than anybody else, and more importantly, we understand the process so well that we can train anyone to be a psychic.

We've had telephone psychics admit to us that they often just listen and provide comfort to callers. Many times, the callers want an audience more than they want an answer.

When you sit down in front of any good commercial psychic, they can tune in to you and tell you about many of the things that have happened to you in the past.

The past has already been impressed on physics, so it is relatively easy to detect. In fact, in just one weekend of training, our Silva Method instructors teach large groups of people how to detect existing information.

But what about the future? After a commercial psychic has impressed you by mentioning several things from your past, can they provide you with reliable predictions of the future? Can they give you information that will help you make better decisions? Can you correct more problems after paying to consult with a commercial psychic?

Psychic Accuracy

If just one out of every five recommendations turns out to be helpful, that's just average. Anyone can do that by chance alone.

If they can give you two correct recommendations for the future out of every five, then you know that they have gone beyond mere chance, and are actually using their psychic ability.

Good psychics can do even better than that. They will be correct three out of five times, or even four out of five times. Think about that for a minute: Anybody who can make more correct decisions than incorrect ones is going to be very successful. In fact, you can still be pretty successful if you just reach the first step and are correct two out of five times—twice the average of a non-psychic.

How can this be?

Problem Solving

If you have the ability to determine quickly whether your decision was right or wrong, then you know how to proceed:

You can reinforce the correct decisions and keep going.

When the decision is wrong, you can stop whatever you are doing and try again.

In order to do this, you would have to consult the commercial psychic daily—maybe several times a day—to insure that you get information quickly enough to make the necessary adjustments.

This could get very expensive at $5 *per minute*, or $50 per sit-down session with a local psychic.

So why not do it yourself?

For a modest investment, anyone can take the Silva ESP training and learn how to be a psychic. Guaranteed, or your money back.

You even get to try out your psychic ability during the final portion of the course. You detect health information with your mind about people that you have never met, and verify that you are correct!

Then, all you need to do is to practice in order to develop skill at detecting any kind of information that you need in order to correct problems.

Will this help you win the lottery? Probably not. It seems as though the creator gave us these abilities to use to correct problems and make the world a better place to live.

If winning some money is the best way to correct a specific problem, then you'll probably win some money. But something like this will come naturally—if it comes at all; we don't scheme and program for it to happen.

We program to correct a problem.

How It Is Done

We don't use our psychic ability for everything, of course. When your car is low on gasoline, that's a problem. The solution is to go to a gas station and put in some gasoline. Normally, you don't need anything extra to correct that problem.

But supposed when you get there, the gas station is closed. And the gas gauge is on empty.

Now you have a bigger problem.

You did what you normally do to take care of the situation, and it didn't work. Now you need to call on your psychic ability for extra help:

Which way should I go to find the nearest—open—gas station, so that I don't run out of gas and get stranded?

In situations like this, if you are right more times than you are wrong, you will be much better off.

If you are a parent and you encounter a problem with your child, you counsel them and solve the problem.

If your counseling doesn't solve the problem, then you use your psychic ability to gain more information so that you can do a better job.

Does this guarantee that you will correct the problem?

No, it doesn't. Even the best psychics are sometimes wrong. They may be right four out of five times, but this still leaves some times that they are wrong.

The Most Valuable Psychic

If you are your own psychic, you will discover very quickly that your strategy is not working. Then, armed with this additional information, you will use your psychic ability again and you will probably come up with the correct answer.

If you have to wait until you can contact your commercial psychic, then at the very least, it will take longer to correct the problem. And during that time, the situation may get worse.

It is obvious that you will do better functioning as your own psychic than by going to a commercial psychic, even if the commercial psychic is more experienced than you are, and is correct more often then you are.

Your ability to use your psychic ability at any time you need it, to incorporate new information, and to make changes "on the fly" so to speak, is far more valuable to you and to your loved ones than the "expert" guidance of a commercial psychic.

That still doesn't guarantee that you'll solve that particular problem, of course. Everyone has free will. When you are dealing with other people, you cannot control what they do.

If we could control other people, this could lead to huge problems, with everybody trying to control everybody else. No, that just wouldn't work. We need everybody's efforts, everyone's ideas and input in order to correct the problems that the world faces.

A Simple Solution

If you want to improve your life, to be more in control of your own destiny, to be healthier, happier, and more successful, then there is a simple solution:

Attend the Silva ESP training, or learn from a home study course, or learn for free with the Free Training in appendix A of this book.

Then practice, practice, practice.

Correct problems whenever you become aware of them. Not just your own problems, but any problems that you become aware of.

Use your psychic ability:

First to obtain additional information so that you can make correct decisions, and

Second, to program—project your mind—and correct the problems that you detect.

It is easy. For an investment that is just a fraction of what people are paying commercial psychics for the limited help they can provide, you can attend the Silva ESP training.

Then join other Silva graduates to develop your ability by correcting problems, and make this a better world to live in.

24 Do Astrological Signs Indicate a Person's Destiny In Life? *(1986)*

People sometimes ask if astrology can be valuable in helping guide our lives, in making decisions about what path to take.

And many people are curious about why astrology sometimes seems very accurate, and other times mostly wrong.

The positions of the planets is one of several environmental factors that can influence matter.

But let's take a look at just how influential factors such as that can be.

The sign under which a person was born, as well as biorhythms and other environmental factors, can indicate the path that a person might be inclined to take.

But you do not necessarily have to take that path.

Inanimate matter has no control over environmental conditions.

Planets and animals have very little control. They can be programmed, they can be altered, but they cannot program or alter themselves or anything else. They are the victims of the environmental influences.

Humans, however, have the capability to program themselves, and to program animals, plants and even inanimate matter.

But not all humans have this ability.

In order to be able to program, you must be able to use your right brain hemisphere to think with. And in order to use your right brain hemisphere to think with, you must be able to enter the alpha dimension where there is a connection to the right brain hemisphere.

The person who uses only the left brain hemisphere functions only in the biological world, and the environmental influences will influence that person.

To change that, a person needs to learn to use the right brain hemisphere. An individual who learns to use the right brain hemisphere has dominion over everything.

This means that the person can neutralize and cancel out the effects of the environmental influences, depending on the individual's needs.

In order to do this, you need to be able to think with your right brain hemisphere and know what to do to neutralize the effects of the various environmental influences and chart the course you desire in your life.

If you use only your left brain hemisphere, then the astrologer can predict the preferences you have. But once you have control of your right brain hemisphere, then you have control of your destiny.

When you control your right brain hemisphere, then you can select the astrological sign you most like and program yourself to have those characteristics if you desire.

For a person who uses the right brain hemisphere, there is nothing to be gained by consulting an astrologer. It will be just as easy to select another path as to follow the path indicated by the astrological chart.

Of course, a person who does not know how to use the right brain hemisphere might benefit from consulting an astrologer, since that person cannot program or alter the effects of the environmental influences.

It seems strange that some people go on being victims of their environment when it takes only a few minutes a day to use the Silva Method techniques and create for themselves any kind of life they desire.

Use your Mirror of the Mind and 3-Scenes Techniques and the other techniques you learned in the Silva training and enjoy a productive, fulfilled and happy life for the rest of your life.

Note: To learn how to put this into practice starting today, choose any of the free training options in the appendix and follow the simple instructions.

25 Do You Make Things Happen, or Just Watch and Wonder? *(1990)*

The Silva Method is a dynamic program. To put it another way, the Silva Method is an *action* program.

We get results.

Sometimes people think that we are supposed to think about what we want and then sit around and wait for results.

The Silva Method is just the opposite. This is a program to help you *make* things happen.

They say that there are three kinds of people:
- Those who make things happen.
- Those who watch things happen.
- Those who wonder what happened.

Sometimes people program, and then just watch to see what happens.

Sometimes people come to class and just "go through the motions," and watch to see what happens.

Then many of those people begin to wonder why nothing happened for them.

The Silva Method doesn't do it for you. The Silva Method gives you tools to do for yourself. You need to project yourself into the process, to make it happen.

Let me give some examples.

At the very beginning of the class (the way we taught it in the beginning), we ask that everybody who wants to learn our Method, to raise their hands.

People don't just sit and wait for their hands to go up. They consciously raise their hands.

They make it happen.

When we do the Long Relaxation Exercise, we do not just wait for the body to relax. We use our imagination to make it happen. We imagine what it would feel like to feel a fine vibration, a tingling sensation, a feeling of warmth caused by circulation.

If you want the technique to work, you need to *project your imagination* and make it happen.

With techniques like the Mirror of the Mind and the 3-Scenes Technique, you make it happen. You *create and project what you desire* in the white framed mirror, then go out and work for it. Get into action, and make it happen. You function dynamically at the mental level by creating and projecting what you desire, and also at the physical level by getting involved physically.

This is what makes techniques work.

With Hand Levitation, you use your imagination to make it happen.

You make it happen when you imagine calling on counselors and mentors and experts for help. You do not just wait for an image of somebody to appear on its own. You consciously create the image of the expert.

The form of the expert is something you create and project. The information they bring comes from the subjective dimension.

To get that information, you need to get involved and make it happen. If you just sit and wait for your imaginary expert to talk to you, you may sit for a long time. You project the conversation: Imagine what you would ask the expert, and imagine what they would answer.

The answer that you "imagine" will be information from the subjective dimension, providing that you do this at the alpha level of course.

Case working is the same. Sometimes graduates will say that "Nothing comes to me." What you should do is to *project* it.

That is what I meant when I wrote in the "Directives for Orientologists," to "Allow the possibility of afflictions and malfunctions to enter your mind."

In medicine they use what is called a "test sample." That is, a comparison is made between the patient and a known substance.

In working a case, you can do it this way. To check out your subject's heart, compare it to a heart that you know has problems. Does it fit? Does it match?

If so, your subject may have the same kind of heart problems.

Test other organs the same way.

Imagine a diseased lung, and determine whether this fits your subject's lungs.

This is much more efficient than merely sitting around and waiting and watching for something to happen.

The new MentalVideo Technique is a little different: First, you use the MentalVideo *after* you have taken action to try to solve the problem yourself. Then you allow 3 days for higher intelligence (God) to send you help or indications of how to proceed.

Note: You can start learning our techniques right now with the free lessons in the appendix.

26 Practice The Silva Techniques and Continue Your Personal Growth *(1986)*

We come from another dimension and we return to another dimension. While we are here, we use our physical bodies to function in the physical dimension.

A child has to learn to use its biological senses.

As an infant grows, it learns to use more and more of its brain. It learns to use its body more effectively.

But all too often, as the child grows, something is left behind.

Between the ages of seven and fourteen, a child has the ability to use all of its senses. The child still has the use of the subjective senses, which it brought to this dimension, and also the biological senses, which is acquired in this physical dimension.

How easy it is to train your child, between the ages of seven and fourteen years, to recognize and to continue to use both sets of senses: the mental and the biological.

This is because the child's brain still beats at about ten cycles per second, about half the speed of the fully mature brain.

But all too often, the child will take the path of least resistance. Since we function primarily in the physical world, it is easier to use the physical senses to gather information and make decisions.

All of the "things" of the physical world are new, and the child desires to experience them.

And all too often, the spiritual senses are forgotten.

For those who leave the subjective senses behind as the brain continues to develop, it takes time and practice to once again learn to use these subjective senses.

First you must learn to slow the pulsing of the brain to ten cycles per second. At this frequency, you have a connection with both brain hemispheres.

Then you must learn the language of the right brain hemisphere, which is visualization and imagination.

With practice, you can learn to use the subjective senses as well as a ten-year-old child.

And then you can improve your ability to use these senses.

How much better it is for parents to help their children learn to use both sets of senses while they are growing up.

The Silva training helps people learn to find and lock on to the ten cycles per second brain frequency, where you can learn to use both brain hemispheres to think with.

Then the Silva training offers a series of mental exercises that use Beneficial Statements for the left brain hemisphere, and in the ESP portion of the training uses visualization-imagination exercises for the right brain hemisphere.

The best exercise of all, of course, is case working.

This provides for use of the subjective senses to help correct problems in the physical dimension, with both subjective and objective feedback.

This is total functioning. This is the way that humans are supposed to function.

If you are a parent, help your children learn to use all of their senses.

If you are a child, practice and keep what you have, for it will be very valuable to you.

If you are an adult, practice all of the Silva techniques, especially case working, so that you can use all of your abilities to help make this world a better place to live before you leave this dimension.

27 What Are You Doing to Help Solve Problems? *(1981)*

The holiday season is the time of year when people from many cultures pause to recognize and celebrate a special kind of new growth.

Symbolically, as the days cease getting shorter, and begin once again to grow longer, many people take time to reflect upon the growth taking place within humanity, and within each individual on this planet.

This recognition takes many forms.

For Christians, it is the celebration of the baby Jesus . . . the Christ child. It is a time when people think about how they can become more like "Our Father," the all-loving, all-encompassing Supreme Intelligence.

Whether you call this Intelligence "God" or "Jehovah" or "Allah" or "Brahma" or some other name, the striving to achieve union—oneness—with Highest Intelligence, with one another—is the same for each of us.

How, then, can we best achieve this oneness, this closeness to our Creator?

It does not come from flattering the Creator by repeating what the Creator surely already knows: that the Creator is all-powerful, all-knowing, all-loving.

It does not come from looking outward and telling other people how devoted you are to the Creator.

To be a Christian is not to talk about what Christ did.

To be a Christian is to do the things Christ did.

The saints were not saints because they prayed 24 hours a day. They were saints because they were solving problems 24 hours a day. They were programming. They were helping people, all day long.

The only way to be close to the Creator is to solve problems of the Creator's creation, the Creator's children.

Prayer will not do it. If you want to be close to your Creator, get up off your knees and go solve problems.

Come to your level, come to the Alpha dimension, and ask what you should do with your seventy-five or eighty years on this planet. You'll be surprised what answers you will get. And you will get answers.

Then get up and go do it.

After you graduate from Silva Mind Control, the *least* you should do should be better than the *best* you did before.

Many people think they came to this planet for a vacation. They think they are on a constant coffee break, here to have fun, to travel, to enjoy life.

Ask sick people, "Why do you want to get well?" They talk about how they want to travel, to enjoy life and have fun. Sometimes it seems like nobody wants to help solve problems, to meet our obligations. If this is their attitude, there is no reason for them to stay alive, to be here. They have no right to ask for help, because they are just getting in someone's way.

If you're not solving problems, you should get off the planet and leave us to our job. Make room for people who are solving problems.

If you are solving problems, then you are needed on this planet. You have a right to stay here, a right to demand everything you need.

This is the attitude that Christ had. That we are here to solve problems. To do "Our Father's Work." To solve problems as best and as much as we can, to always do the best we are capable of.

This is the message all of the avatars brought to this planet.

This is the new "birth" that must take place in every human being sooner or later. It is the attitude we must have if we are to solve the problems of our world.

It is the true "Spirit of Christmas."

Resolve now to take time during this holiday season to meditate on the growth taking place on this planet, on the growth taking place within you.

Program that you will be, in your own way, a "saint" who helps solve problems on this planet.

Program that you will help the Creator by creating, at your Alpha level, a better world for us to live in.

And then get off your knees and get to work to help perfect this creation.

When you align your powers at all dimensions—heart, soul and mind—then you will have the power that moves mountains.

Best wishes for the best holiday season of your life.

Note: To learn how to put this into practice starting today, choose any of the Free Training options in the appendix and follow the simple instructions. That is our Holiday Gift to you.

PART 2
SOME BASIC TECHNIQUES FOR YOU TO USE

by José Silva Jr.

My father is a great role model for anyone who wants to be more successful.

Confidence brings success. A belief in what you are doing builds confidence. Belief comes from your experiences, from the actions you take that lead to success.

When he shined people's shoes, he earned money and could help support his family. That confidence guided him for the rest of his life: Give value and people will be happy to pay you.

The scientifically-verified results he got with his mind training techniques gave him the confidence to stand up to PhD's, stand up to a world famous researcher, and even stand up to the Monsignors who were considering excommunicating him from his Church for what they *assumed* he was doing.

Now let's begin with a couple of From the Founder columns that reveal some of my father's advice on achieving success in your endeavors, and show his unshakable belief in the Silva Mind Control Method.

28 Small Things = Big Success
(1980)

My brother Juan and I were giving out the awards to the Silva Method lecturers during the recently completed Silva International Convention and, as is usually the case, all eyes were on us and the winners who came to center-stage for their awards.

In the midst of the applause and cheers that the winners received as their names were called out, I became very reflective.

"Why," I asked myself, "are these people getting an award? What made them special in this particular regard this year?"

Becoming conscious of those thoughts, I began to seek a strand that connected all the winners this year. Was there a link to their performances? Did they share something in common?

We are blessed, I think, in having outstanding individuals associated with us as lecturers and graduates, and this fact is a principal reason why the Silva Method has become one of the most significant planetary forces in existence today. It is these people—all of them— that give life to the Method, and it is their zeal that has carried it to almost every corner of the world.

Yet, for this particular year, there were some who had excelled even further. Why?

As I kept thinking of this, that connecting strand eventually appeared. These graduates, it seemed, had been specially careful to notice *small* details.

All of us focus on the bigger things—and well we should. But oftentimes, the small details do not get the attention they deserve. After all, big things are nothing more than the accumulation of small things. It stands to reason, therefore, that small details make big things happen.

This is not as philosophical as it may sound, for the person who does small things well—regardless of their importance—is going to do big things well. Conversely, the person who does not give importance to small things is not going to make big things happen.

In the Silva Method, we have become fully aware of this, and we attempt to better ourselves through the very powerful tool of habit.

Individuals are creatures of habit, and if we program ourselves to good habits, we shall, indeed, become "Better and Better." But the opposite can also be true. Nourishing bad habits will become disastrous to the individual.

Making it a habit to do small things well—day in and day out regardless of how insignificant they may seem—will eventually program us to do big things well. This programming, I felt, was what the winners had in common. The small things had given them their prize.

One of the most useful tools of the Silva Method, I think, is that it allows individuals to assume responsibility for their total self, and to allow them to analyze their total being through the different parts that make them a unique human being.

Our human system is made up of many parts, each one playing a definite but distinct role. All of them are equal, and the ability to blend all of their functions harmoniously is a main task of the Silva Method.

Through the Silva Method, we are provided an effective way to search for self, but once we do that we must assume total responsibility for ourselves, including each and every part of our being and each and every role that we as humans play.

Our journey as humans on this planet is comprised of many decisions, many alternatives, many opportunities, many disillusions, many joys and many sorrows. All of these situations will shape us as human beings, and they will affect our way of life and our way of being. They are significant events in our lives, yet if we look closely we can notice that all of these situations came about because of small things.

That big opportunity arrived in my own life, but it came about because day by day I paid attention to doing my job well, learning as much as I could, possessing a cheerful personality, coping with the stresses and responsibilities of the job.

Yes, we must indeed have our sights fixed on the big events in our lives; but we must never forget those small things.

It was doing small things well that earned those individuals their awards this year, and, in a bigger framework, it is doing small things well that eventually will make us better and better human beings.

29 Do This and Have a Prosperous 1983
(1983)

What are your goals for the new year?

Many people seek health, happiness, and success.

These are excellent goals, and much to be desired. But there is a specific way to go about attaining them.

First, you must be specific in your requests. You must know just what it is that you want, so you can imagine just what your desired goals look like. Then you can program them at level.

But there is more to it than that.

As an example, let us look at the way I believe we should program for prosperity. My beliefs are based on my personal experience, my years of research, and a great deal of time I have spent at level obtaining guidance.

If you want prosperity for the new year, the first thing you should do is enter your level, use your Silva Method techniques, and determine what your purpose in life is. Find out what you are supposed to do during your seventy or eighty years or so that you have on Planet Earth.

There is a purpose for each of us. That purpose invariably involves helping to improve conditions on this planet. We were not sent here for a coffee break; we are not on vacation. We are here as representatives of our Creator, to serve as sensors for the Creator and to help improve conditions as our planet evolves.

Once you have found out what your purpose is, then you should take steps to fulfill that purpose.

When you are doing what you are supposed to be doing on this planet, then you are helping to solve problems, then you have a right to demand everything you need for your survival.

If a person is not solving problems, if a person is creating problems, then that person needs to beg for permission to stay on the planet. There is some question as to whether that person even has a right to stay.

In my experience, I have not found it necessary to program for money.

You know that you reap in proportion to what you sow. Therefore, if you are providing service, and you know that you will be compensated for this service, and all your needs will be met, then you will prosper.

Imagine yourself in the circumstances you want to be in. Imagine yourself with those things you need to have to do your work on this planet, and to be comfortable while doing it.

Imagine your family's needs being met.

Imagine your bills all paid. This is all part of prosperity.

A truly prosperous person is one who is achieving success in all areas of life. A prosperous person is one who is developing his or her spiritual factor, and is in touch with his or her source.

A prosperous person is one who is healthy, one who is strong physically, mentally, spiritually, and emotionally.

A person who is experiencing prosperity is a person who feels good about himself or herself, and about the quality of life.

Merely accumulating material things does not guarantee prosperity.

For this new year of 1983, make a commitment to be prosperous.

Many people have accumulated "things" been unhealthy, unhappy, and unfulfilled.

You do not need to accumulate a lot of money, or power, or prestige.

What you need to do is go to level at least once a day; twice a day is better; three times a day is excellent. Get in touch with your source. Find out what you are supposed to be doing with your life.

Then fulfill your purpose in life, and reap all of the beautiful rewards that come to those who serve

Note: If you have not taken any of our courses, you can learn to enter the alpha level with any of the free training options in appendix A.

30 How to Become a More Positive Thinking Person *(1985)*

Negative thinking causes problems.

Positive thinking causes solutions.

Negative thinking provides a climate for health problems to develop.

Positive thinking provides a climate for attainment and maintenance of good health.

Positive Thinking Defined

Let me refresh your recognition of what is meant by each.

Negative thinking is: guilt, worry, insecurity, fear, jealousy, suspicion, hatred, antagonism, anger, despair, mourning, self-doubt. Negative thinking is being out of synchronization, out of harmony, the persons and things around you.

Positive thinking is: love, appreciation, optimism, security, courage, cooperation, compassion, generosity, friendliness, patience, helpfulness, ambition.

Positive thinking is being in synchronization, moving in step and in harmony, in attunement, with everything around you.

These are just examples, not the whole picture.

You do not need to have the whole picture. You need only to have the picture of your own thinking, especially of any negative components.

Here Is What Hurts Us

The worst stressor is guilt.

Like any component of negative thinking, guilt is stressful. As guilt, or any other type of negative thinking, is practiced, it becomes a habit. The stress it causes becomes chronic. Chronic stress is a killer.

When you feel you have not done enough, or that you have done the wrong thing, or that you have not tried hard enough, you feel guilty.

Continue to feel this way and you can be causing damage to your immune system. That damage can eventually, and maybe quite soon, do you in.

What happens when prolonged negative attitudes are held is that chemical changes take place in the body. A stress enzyme is released into the blood.

This enzyme inhibits the work of the immune system. It appears to confuse and weaken it. Health problems start to build up.

A Healthy Outlook

Positive feelings about yourself and the work you are doing are, therefore, preferable. A healthy outlook contributes to a healthy body.

It is better for you to be optimistic than pessimistic, better for your health and maybe better for your ultimate survival.

It is also better for you to do what you know is right so that you are not plagued by guilt feelings.

It is as if nature, or God, has provided a reward system. Do right and your health thrives.

Do wrong and your health suffers.

Knowing Right from Wrong

What is right is that which is creative and constructive, that which relieves suffering.

What is wrong is causing destruction and suffering.

Any time you feel pangs of conscience about what you are doing, stop.

Enter your alpha level. Identify what action is giving you the guilt feelings. If you don't know how to enter the alpha level, you can use the Free Training in appendix A to learn right now.

Resolve to undo and not again do the thing that brought on the feeling of guilt.

Even the thought of doing something that is not totally fair, considerate, moral, legal or correct can be stressful.

The temptation to do wrong can make you sick, even without your doing wrong.

Here is what to do about that:

Whenever such a thought enters your mind, stop.

Close your eyes, take a deep breath, turn your eyes slightly upward and mentally say, "Cancel—Cancel."

You have just diffused on the spot that source of stress. This is good to do at the onset of any negative thought.

Remember, live a positive life and you will live a healthier life.

31 You Can Overcome Hidden Barriers and Restore Normal Good Health *(1987)*

When you function mentally at the alpha brainwave level, your mind has great power. It can detect health problems even before they fully manifest in the beta or outer physical dimension.

You can intuitively know that something needs attention.

You can detect a problem with the subjective (psychic) senses of the right brain hemisphere before it is possible to detect it with the objective (physical) senses of your left brain hemisphere.

That is because the right brain hemisphere operates at the cause level, while the left brain hemisphere works at the effect level.

So, you can help your doctor help you by suggesting possible preventive procedures.

Your doctor may not necessarily confirm that these procedures are necessary but you could be alerting the doctor to that eventual possibility and the doctor may adopt a, "Sure, why not" attitude.

Overcoming Hidden Barriers

As you mentally picture yourself in radiant health each time you practice at your level, the programming that may be interfering with your health could still be there. Eventually your new programming will replace it. But you can sometimes hasten this process by identifying that old programming.

Identifying it can help to diffuse it. You understand what is happening that is causing the problem.

You stop this mental cause.

Ask Yourself

While you are relaxed and before you start mentally picturing yourself healthy, ask yourself, "Why do I have this physical problem?"

Let your thoughts wander. You will start to think about someone you know and are involved with in some way, or something you are doing that is wrong and you feel guilty about, or some situation that you find unacceptable.

If you identify a relationship with another person as the cause of the problem, then mentally picture the person, shake hands in your imagination, or embrace.

Feel that you are "making up."

Feel forgiveness—mutual forgiveness.

Making Changes

What you are really doing is overcoming hidden barriers to your normal good health.

These hidden barriers to good health can actually be causative factors behind the bad health.

Dissolve the friction mentally and you dissolve the physical results of that mental friction.

After completing this, mentally picture yourself healthy, affirm to yourself mentally, "I will always maintain a perfectly healthy body and mind."

You will find that your relationship with this person shifts for the better in the "real" world.

You have created a change.

You have removed a silent barrier to health.

Note: If you have not taken any of our courses, you can learn to enter the alpha level with any of the free training options in appendix A.

32 Anxiety Can Help Also
(1980)

Anxiety and stress have become household words, and both have been given a negative concept that all too often is taken for disaster.

Both are normal conditions of the human body, and if they have assumed such deadly reputations it is only because people have not been able to deal with them effectively. If one were to do so, anxiety and stress would not be automatically linked with high blood pressure, coronaries, diabetes and other ailments plaguing modern man.

As a matter of fact, anxiety and stress are not necessarily bad. Some people have learned to utilize anxiety and turn it into a catalyst for useful productivity.

These people have made tension and stress work for them instead of against them.

In learning to use anxiety and stress, they turn their aggressiveness towards productive goals and do not allow the anxiety and stress to become carriers of hostility and arrogance.

If one were to study cases where people have turned anxiety and stress into vehicles for production, we notice that they share one commonality—the correct attitude.

These people know their limitations, but they are not restrained in their capabilities. They reach out for big goals, with the deep-seated belief that each problem can be overcome and that greater strength comes with each victory and with each difficulty.

Napoleon was short and physically weak, yet he compensated for his stature and physical makeup by becoming one of the most famous field generals of all time.

It is said that Abraham Lincoln lost many political races and had many personal setbacks in life. Yet he never gave up and ended up becoming president of the United States and one of the great leaders of the century.

Silva Mind Control had very humble beginnings, was created by people with little formal education, and at first was rejected by most people and institutions. Yet it is now the most widely used method of mental training in the world.

It is true that turning anxiety and stress into useful and productive tools for self-betterment is easier said than done.

However, those of us at Silva have done a lot of research into this and have come up with information that can help mankind make anxiety and stress useful.

For example, we now know that there is a type of substance in the blood that reacts whenever the body undergoes stress and anxiety, causing an imbalance in the blood system. Whenever the anxiety and stress are gone, that substance suddenly disappears from the bloodstream. It seems that the substance disappears when we have relieved the source of stress and anxiety, whether mentally or physically.

At that particular resonant point, fast recuperation takes place. We believe that it takes place at the deepest level of relaxation, so by occasionally reaching a deep level of mind or a slower brain frequency—we can free ourselves from stress and anxiety.

We also have found that doubts—simple, everyday doubts—prevent a person from remaining at that level. When doubts are removed, it is possible to once again reach that level.

It is exactly these doubts that prevent people from turning anxiety and stress into useful tools for self-advancement. We doubt almost everything, and modern society, with its runaway inflation, its catastrophic capabilities, its declining energy supplies, its dwindling faith in God and its materialistic overkill, all are factors that bear upon man's inability to keep doubts under control.

At Silva we have various tools that we use to turn stress and anxiety into productive tools. We have Mental Housecleaning, where we consciously get rid of negative words and thoughts, so that they will no longer breed negative concepts that can harm us.

In this Mental Housecleaning, negative words and thoughts are replaced with positive ones.

Phrases like, "It burns me up," "It makes me sick," "Makes me nervous," are substituted with, "I can fix it," "Better and Better," "I will figure it out."

The Mirror of the Mind and the 3-Scenes Technique, in helping us visualize ourselves in a positive image, provide us with the right path for achieving more positive attitudes, which in turn helps us direct our anxieties in positive, productive ways.

Living in today's world is indeed challenging, and, often traumatic. Yet, knowing ourselves, and using the Silva Mind Control Method, we can continue to live productive lives even though stress and anxiety are very much a part of our daily lives.

Better and Better is more than a slogan that changes negative stress into positive stress, it is a slogan that helps us reach a better way of life!

Note: If you have not taken any of our courses and learned these techniques, you can start learning them for free right now with any of the free training options in appendix A.

33 Here Is How You Can Be More Positive
(1987)

Many people are beginning to realize that the mental pictures you put into your bio-computer brain affect your body, your performance, and your health.

Athletes are now training themselves for greater skills and endurance by picturing themselves playing the perfect game, running the perfect race.

When amateurs tee up on the golf course and take a furtive look at the water hazard to the left, then the wooded rough to the right, they have just programmed themselves for a poorly aimed drive.

Professionals, by focusing only the flag at the hole, program themselves for a perfect drive.

Mental pictures produce demonstrable effects on our body.

Positive pictures produce desirable effects.

Negative pictures produce undesirable effects.

If you have ever been confronted with the fangs of a poisonous cobra, merely imagining that event can cause the adrenalin to flow, the skin to perspire and the heart to pound, as if the cobra were really there.

If you have ever been confronted with a jealous spouse, a snarling boss or an incensed police officer, imagining or worrying about such eventualities can cause the hormones to speed up the body's functions as if it were a real emergency.

Your lungs pump faster. Your blood pressure rises. Your heart races.

And your white blood cells, the body's combat troops in the battle against disease, are suppressed.

The better you are able to concentrate on your fear or worry, the more harm you are able to bring to your body.

For every mental picture, there is a corresponding body reaction.

Try This Simple Experiment

Hold your arms straight out in front of you. Close your eyes. Imagine a heavy shopping bag over your right wrist.

Also imagine a red balloon filled with helium tugging up on your left wrist.

After holding these mental pictures as if they were really happening, open your eyes.

You find your right arm has moved down, your left arm up.

What mental pictures do you energize? Perhaps you fear losing your job, having a serious illness, being attacked at night in the street, being alone in your old age, that something terrible will happen to a loved one.

How your body reacts to these mental pictures, depends on how your past experiences cause you to feel when you entertain these potential future experiences.

The good news is, there is a way to deal with the problem.

For Silva graduates, the way is very simple.

First, remember your Mental Housecleaning.

"Cancel-cancel" all negative thoughts and immediately replace them with positive thoughts.

Then re-program yourself at the alpha level.

If you have trouble dealing with a negative thought or idea, then program it out at level.

How to Reprogram Yourself

First, enter your level and state the problem. Identify the negative thought.

Second, state your goal, that you do not want this thought, but you want the corresponding positive thought, the thought of what you desire. Instead of being out of work you want to be gainfully employed in a job you enjoy. Instead of being ill you will be well.

The third step is to use a trigger to change the thought.

You might program that every time you have the negative thought, you will take a deep breath and as you exhale, you will recall the positive mental picture, the positive thought.

The fourth step is to do what you programmed to do. That is, whenever you notice the negative thought, immediately take a deep breath and as you exhale, visualize the positive mental picture you have already created.

The final step is simply to accept your end results and claim your rewards. Take it for granted, and it is so.

And as you become a more positive thinker in this manner, you will find your life getting better and better all the time as you become healthier, happier and more successful in everything that you do.

Note: If you have not taken any of our courses, you can learn to enter the alpha level with any of the free training options in appendix A.

34 Here Is How to Set Goals to Bring You Prosperity *(1985)*

Are you getting everything you want from life?

Many people aren't, and they ask us to tell them the secret of acquiring great wealth. Sometimes they can't even acquire a little wealth and they don't understand why this is.

There are a lot of people who say they meditate, who repeat numerous affirmations designed to help them overcome any guilt they may have about having money, affirmations to program themselves to attract money, and so forth.

The truth of the matter is very simple. There's no secret at all.

To acquire wealth, you must continue to follow a program that you have probably been following for a long time. The difference is not in finding a new approach, but in perfecting an approach you already know.

Setting Goals

It is interesting to ask people what their goals are, what they are programming for.

Many people want money, of course.

But many others are smart enough to understand that usually it is not money that people want; there is something that they expect to obtain with that money.

It is good to set goals for things you can picture.

Even abstract things can be pictured, like peace of mind, financial security. Exactly what is it that will bring you peace of mind or financial security? When you know what it looks like, then you have a goal.

Right Values

But setting goals for all the things you want to have and programming for them will not insure that you will get all these things.

This was something that was demonstrated to me repeatedly when I used to help people get well by applying holistic faith healing techniques to them. When someone was sick and asked for my help, the first thing I would do was ask them why they wanted to get well. Many people would answer that they wanted to travel, to enjoy life, do things and have things. This was the wrong answer, and I'd talk to them to straighten out their thinking.

Higher Intelligence did not put us here just to have fun and enjoy ourselves. Higher Intelligence put us here to help correct problems and to help convert the planet into a paradise.

Getting Rich

Stop and think for just a moment about how people get jobs. When you got your first job, what happened?

Remember the person who hired you? Did this person give you a handful of money and tell you to come to work the next day and earn that money?

In most instances, we have to work first, then we are paid. We have to provide some service, create some product, and then we are compensated for what we have done.

How much are we compensated?

We are paid what the service or product is worth—not what it is worth to us, but for what it is worth to the one who is paying for it.

The more people you help, the more you are paid.

The more problems you correct, the more you are paid.

The more you help Higher Intelligence, the more you receive of the good things in life.

It's a simple system, and it works.

Taking Action

Now you know the so-called "secret."

Set goals to serve. Set goals to help correct problems.

You can judge the value of what you do by how much desire other people have for the service you provide. And they will let you know how important it is to them by how much they compensate you for it.

While you are serving, keep your needs in mind.

At your level, program these needs; let Higher Intelligence know what you need to keep you going, to keep you inspired and motivated to continue serving.

When you are serving, you will continue to receive everything you need, and a lot of the things you want, too.

35 Taking Advantage of Hard Times
(1982)

More and more frequently we hear people ask about how to use the Silva Method effectively to overcome economic hardships.

People are getting laid off. Major companies are closing down. Unemployment is increasing. The list goes on and on.

Economic hardship is nothing new to me. In Laredo, times have always been hard for the majority of people.

Yet there are always ways to cope, and even to thrive, if you go about it properly. I went about it properly from the time I was very young. And I thrived.

Look for the Good

First of all, remember to always maintain a positive attitude, though it may seem difficult to do at times. The bigger the challenge, the greater your opportunity to practice your own personal "mind control" to stay positive and keep looking for solutions.

I remember a man who called me one night and told me he had programmed for a promotion and a raise, and got laid off. I told him to keep programming. A few days later he called me and told me that another company had hired him, in a better job than what he was programming for, and for a lot more money. This company, he said, would not approach him while he worked for someone else; they thought that would be unethical. Getting laid off was the only way.

Economic pressures have sometimes forced people to look for supplemental sources of income. Sometimes these supplemental sources of income have become full time businesses that made the person much more money than they ever could have gotten working for somebody else.

Program Success

What were the characteristics that made me, as an adolescent, more successful than ninety percent of the adults in Laredo?

First, of course, was my natural ability to use my right-brain hemisphere as well as my left-brain hemisphere. That meant I could think more creatively and more intuitively than ninety percent of the people.

The Silva ESP training teaches you to use your right-brain hemisphere so that you, too, can think more creatively and more intuitively.

Throughout history, there have been people who used both brain hemispheres. They have written books about the techniques they use, but these techniques will work only for those people who function the way they do: by using the creative right-brain hemisphere, as well as the logical left-brain hemisphere.

By practicing your Silva ESP techniques you can develop more proficiency in the use of your right-brain hemisphere. You will develop more confidence in your ability to use the right-brain hemisphere, and you will be more successful. The world has plenty for those who use both brain hemispheres.

Much of the success has been due to my confidence because I would succeed more often than most people, and I succeeded more often because I was using my right-brain hemisphere as well as my left-brain hemisphere. These successes gave me more enthusiasm, and the more enthusiasm people have, the more they will achieve. If you want to make more money, then develop more enthusiasm. But even this is effective only if you are using both brain hemispheres and functioning creatively and intuitively.

The way out of an economic depression is through the use of both brain hemispheres. Practice your techniques . . . all of them. Then all of those "success formulas" from the ten percent who naturally use both brain hemispheres will work for you, too.

And when you are functioning that way, your confidence and enthusiasm will be high and you will achieve your goals in life.

Note: To learn how to put this into practice starting today, choose any of the free training options in appendix A and follow the simple instructions.

36 Teach Children How to Use Visualization and Imagination *(1983)*

Children from seven to fourteen years of age are at a very important point in life. It is at this time that a child can learn naturally to use both the left and the right hemispheres of the brain.

By the time a child is fourteen years old, it is too late to learn by natural means to use the right brain hemisphere.

Up to seven years old, a child uses mostly the delta and theta portions of the brain—that is, the parts of the brain that emit the slower brain frequencies.

By the age of fourteen, a child is using mostly the part of the brain that vibrates at the beta frequencies, from fourteen to twenty-one cycles per second.

It is between the ages of seven and fourteen, when a child is functioning primarily at the alpha brain wave level, that the choice is made regarding the use of one or both halves of the cortex of the brain.

Ninety percent of humanity take the path of least resistance when that crucial time comes; most choose to use the objective half of the brain, the part of the brain associated with objective, physical senses such as sight, taste, smell, touch and hearing.

Very few only about ten percent of humanity—choose to think with the right brain hemisphere

Perhaps many of those were forced to think creatively and intuitively in order to survive. Perhaps, then, what appeared to be a hardship actually turned out to be a blessing.

Take my own life, for instance. By the time I was seven years old, I had made a decision to earn money to help support my family. Perhaps it was through necessity that I thought creatively, that I used my imagination, that I called on my intuitive faculties and functioned clairvoyantly. By doing these things, I was better able to find ways to help support my grandmother, my uncle, and my brothers and sisters.

Therefore, I grew up using both brain hemispheres, which has given me a definite advantage in life.

When I began to research the potential of the human mind, I began to realize that there was something different about the ten percent of humanity who achieve outstanding success; these ten per-centers function differently than the rest of humanity

Is there a way, I wondered, to help the ninety percent who use only the logical left brain hemisphere to learn to do their thinking with the creative and intuitive right hemisphere? The way seemed to be to regress back in time, to re-create the situation that existed at the age of seven. That is, to function at the alpha brain wave frequency—at what we call the Basic Plane Level, or seven cycles per second—and at that level, practice using visualization and imagination.

At the same time, we use very carefully worded statements to program into the bio-computer (the brain) the belief and expectancy to be able to function clairvoyantly.

Thus, in the first half of our Silva Mind Control Basic Lecture Series, participants learn self-programming techniques that help make the left hemisphere stronger; and in the second half—the ESP training, they begin to develop the use of their right hemisphere so that they can function with control and full awareness in the subjective—psychic—dimension.

If all parents will take our training and learn how to help their children develop the use of the right hemisphere prior to the age of fourteen, then all children will grow up to be geniuses; these children will not need our training.

Note: If you have not yet learned this, you can learn right now—and also teach it to your children—with the free training in the appendix.

37 Let's Give Our Children That "Something Extra" *(1982)*

Do people who are the most successful, the most popular, the best athletes, the healthiest and the smartest have something "extra" that most other people do not have?

Is there something that makes a person "lucky" that is possessed by only a few fortunate individuals?

My experience and my research have revealed that there is, indeed, something different about those people who seem to attract success, good fortune, friends, and fame. I know what it is that makes them so successful, and I also know how to impart this same "something extra" to anybody who wants it, including you.

That Something Extra

Approximately ten percent of the people in the world learn, when they are growing up, how to function effectively with both the left and the right-brain hemispheres. The other 90 percent function with only the left-brain hemisphere, the logical, rational brain hemisphere.

To function to full capacity, a person needs to use the creative, intuitive right-brain hemisphere as well as the left hemisphere.

A person who uses the right-brain hemisphere functions clairvoyantly.

This person senses information with psychological (psychic) senses as well as with physiological (objective) senses, and thus has more data to use for making decisions and deciding future courses of action.

A person who uses only one brain hemisphere is limited compared to a person who uses both brain hemispheres.

You Have It

The Silva ESP training portion of the Basic Lecture Series teaches people how to use the right-brain hemisphere to be more creative, healthier and more successful in life.

There are many books on success; they are all written by people who are natural clairvoyants, who naturally developed the use of the right-brain hemisphere. These success books will work for people who use both brain hemispheres, but not for people who use only the left-brain hemisphere.

People who grow up using both brain hemispheres have a lot of self confidence, because they are correct more often than people who use only the left-brain hemisphere.

The earlier a person learns to use the right-brain hemisphere, the more confidence that person will have in school, in relationships, on the athletic field, in the business world. Therefore it is of the utmost importance that people learn as early as possible how to use the right-brain hemisphere, and how to perceive information with the subjective senses.

When we first began researching, we developed methods to help students relax so they could concentrate on their work better. We found that these students could retain information better; we also found that they appear to perceive information impressed on another person's brain.

This ability helped the students do better in school. Of course, this ability carries over to all aspects of life:

- choice of career
- performance in that career
- selection of a lifetime partner to marry
- and all other aspects of life on this planet.

Learn It Early

Everyone has the potential to use the right-brain hemisphere creatively and intuitively. Graduates of the complete Silva Method have learned how to do just this. All it takes after graduation is practice. This is a new habit to develop, so graduates must practice until they build confidence and expertise.

Obviously, the earlier a person learns to use the right-brain hemisphere, the better. This is why we have always offered to let school systems teach our Method to students without paying any royalties to us so long as they make it available free of charge to all students in the school.

We have long had the dream of seeing all school systems teaching our Method, so that all children will grow up confident, successful, lucky and happy, the way about ten percent do now.

If all children learned in school how to use the right-brain hemisphere, then we would raise a generation of geniuses.

This is why I am so pleased that Sr. Naomi Curtin and Dr. George DeSau have developed the pilot project on Guam, to present the complete Silva Method training to all of the students in three schools during the next three years with close evaluation of how well these students perform compared to previous performance and performance of students in neighboring schools where students have not been taught the Silva Method.

Our special thanks to Bishop Flores, Gov. Calvo and all the others who helped make this dream a reality, and a special request that we all join together to program that this spreads to all schools throughout the world.

Then our world will truly be a better place to live.

Note: The course was altered and was not taught in its original form, and the 3-year project was not completed. You can learn the complete training in its original form and can teach it to your children, all for free, starting with the free lessons in the appendix.

38 Why Don't Schools Teach a Memory Course? *(1987)*

As you know we have a good consultant at the PhD level doing research in schoolwork. They pre-test the students and then we come in to do the training for them. Then the PhD's post-test them.

The results in several schools and high schools and in universities were always very impressive.

It is said that people go to school to learn. That means you must retain information. You must remember what you have studied.

How much do you retain after you finished college? Why do you use reference books? Is it because you forgot almost everything and you have to go back to textbooks to recall the formula and the step by step procedures and so on?

We wonder sometimes: If schools are there to teach us, then why is it that they don't have memory courses to teach how to remember?

Teach Students *How* to Learn Before You Teach Them *What* to Learn

Then the first thing they need to do is to train the children to retain information better.

Teach this even at the kindergarten level, or first or second grades. Begin with a memory course. Students are going to have a whole lifetime spent at schools and they must retain information to get better grades. You wonder why schools do not teach memory courses.

There are many memory courses in the field, but they're independent, they're private. You can take any memory courses you want.

But actually it's interesting why we don't have them in schools to begin to teach students how to remember first, before teaching them what to learn.

In order to learn, you must remember what you've learned.

We know the memory courses work. There is no question about it.

Why Do Memory Courses Work?

Because they use mental pictures.

Words don't mean very much. We forget words.

But if you convert words into mental pictures, chances are you will remember the mental picture better than the words.

If you have converted a word into a mental picture, and given it a color and action, that's even better, it is more strongly impressed on your brain cells.

If you convert words into mental pictures, give them color and action and make it ridiculous, then you could remember it even better.

How to Do This

When you are reading or listening to people, try to convert words into mental pictures. Make a mental movie of what you're listening to. Give it action, and you'll be surprised so much you remember.

When a person is talking to you, or when you're reading a book or lesson, convert every word—every word that you can convert—into a mental picture, and give it action and color.

Make a mental movie of all those words. Then you will remember it and explain what you read because you retain mental pictures a lot better than words.

You make even stronger impressions when you give it color and action and make a mental movie of it. That is far better than just remembering so many words.

Use the Strongest Part of Your Brain

You make stronger impressions of these mental pictures when you do this at the Alpha brain wave level. That is the biggest discovery right now.

The brain frequency functions most at three specific frequencies: 5, 10, and 20 cycles per second.

We made a study how strong is 5, how stable is it, how synchronized, how orderly? Then the 10, the 20.

We found that ninety percent of people learn on 20, and it is the weakest, the least energetic frequency of the brain and the most desynchronized, the most unstable frequency of the brain. And this is where ninety percent of humanity do their learning.

It's a wonder that learning is so difficult.

So now people who are learning to slow down the brain waves to the center which is 10 cycles per second, which is the strongest, the most energetic, the most synchronized and stable frequency of the brain, they retain information better, and have better recall ability.

So this is what you need to have in order to pass tests and to be able to get good grades in school.

Specific Techniques to Help You

Now, what else do you need to do to get higher grades in school?

Besides learning to function at 10 cycles, you can use Three Fingers Technique to be able to recall information and to relax when test taking time arrives.

Sometimes students get excited at test time, they may have gotten very high grades throughout the school year, but come test time they "blank out."

They may completely blank out and that ruins the whole thing. They are not going to get a good grade because they blank out when they take tests. They are so tense and full of anxiety that they "blank out."

So if students have learned to function at the alpha level and know about the Three Fingers Technique, they can program themselves, with the Three Fingers Technique, then come test time, all they need to do to use the Three Fingers Technique, take a deep breath and relax, and they will become more comfortable, and will remember everything they need to get high grades.

But they must break that panic function, the panic attack. They can do it by pre-programming themselves before test time with Three Fingers Technique, and since they have learned to be at alpha, they will be relaxed and confident.

(This is transcribed from a recording of José Silva in 1987.)

Note: There are several excellent books that teach memory improvement. You can also learn a memory course in the *Silva Choose Success Master Course* published by G&D Media and available at booksellers worldwide. The same "memory peg system" is also included in a special Speed Learning workshop available at the SilvaESP.com website. You can learn Jose Silva's study and test taking techniques now in the appendix of this book.

39 You Have Many Ways That You Can Use to Communicate *(1998)*

Here's a short quiz:

Q: Why is your body like a radio?

A: Because both are communications devices.

Your body radiates energy, called an aura, just as a radio station radiates electromagnetic waves that carry a radio program.

I spent much of my life repairing radios and other electronic equipment. When I began to learn about the human mind and the body's aura, my experience with electronics came in very handy.

It helped me to understand some of the ways that we communicate, ways that most people don't yet fully understand.

Your body is a much more sophisticated communications station than a radio transmitter. You can communicate with:

- Words
- The tone and inflection of your voice
- Your eyes
- Your body language
- Your hands
- Your aura
- Your mind

The first six kinds of communication that we've listed here are limited by time and space. People have to be able to hear you or see you, or be within range of your aura.

The seventh kind of communication—your mind and your psychic ability—has no limits, as far as we know. You can communicate with anyone, anywhere, instantly, with your mind.

There are plenty of books and courses to help you with the first five types of communication.

Now, I want to talk about the other two.

Your Aura

The human body radiates seven energy fields. The combined energy fields are called the human aura. The human aura is modulated by brain activity. To modulate means to change, to alter in some way. A radio transmitter transmits a "carrier signal."

The information to be transmitted—the announcer's voice, for instance, or the music being played—is combined with the carrier signal and alters the carrier signal.

The radio that receives this combined signal then strips away the carrier signal and is left with only the information that was added to it.

Your aura is modulated by your brain activity. Your brain is modulated by thoughts. Every thought that you have alters—modulates—your aura.

Your Aura Penetrates and Alters Matter

The objective part of your aura radiates out about eight meters—about twenty-five feet—from your body. Anyone within that range can detect your aura.

That's why, when a person who is very upset comes into a room, you can "feel" their presence even before you see them or hear them.

You can influence people around you by your own thoughts. If you are happy and at peace, your aura will reflect this, and will tend to influence other people's auras to be happy and peaceful.

The aura energy penetrates both inanimate and animate matter, causing an alteration in matter.

Inanimate matter retains the alteration.

Animate matter continues to evolve in an altered state.

You can learn more about this in our book *Silva UltraMind Systems Persuasive Thoughts* published by G&D Media and available from booksellers worldwide.

Thought Modulation

There are several different frequencies that the brain operate on:

Beta, the outer conscious level, which is ideal for taking action in the physical world.

Alpha, the inner conscious level (formerly the sub-conscious), the strongest, most rhythmic frequency, ideal for thinking.

Theta, a lower frequency.

Delta, associated with deep sleep.

Thinking modulates the brain at various frequencies: the beta brain wave frequencies, and also at the lower alpha brain wave frequencies.

The energy transmitted when thought modulates the brain at the beta frequency is limited by distance. This energy, a physical energy, can be used either to help or to harm. It can attract animate matter back to normal, or force matter into an abnormal condition. This is what happens when a psychic bends a spoon: The normal is changed to the abnormal, through the use of the physical part of the body's aura radiation. That's why we don't teach or practice spoon bending in the Silva Method; we prefer to change the abnormal to the normal.

When thoughts modulate the brain at the alpha frequency, then distance is no barrier. When doing this, you can help, but you cannot harm. You can change the abnormal back to the normal, but you cannot change the normal to the abnormal with this subjective, spiritual (non-physical) energy.

It takes physical energy to cause physical harm, to change the normal to the abnormal. Physical energy works by repulsion.

Subjective energy cannot exert force against physics. Subjective energy can only work through attraction. It attracts animate matter to return to a normal condition, to conform to the original spiritual blueprint for that particular object.

The modulation is stronger when thought is accompanied by imagination.

The most effective programming is done when thought, accompanied by imagination, modulates the brain at the alpha level, where there is the most energy, and where distance is no barrier.

Examining the Aura

The human aura is made up of seven fields of energy:

The first is spiritual, the genetic, which is controlled 99 percent by the "other side," from the spiritual dimension.

The next three: sub-atomic, atomic, and part of the molecular, are subjective and are controlled from the right brain hemisphere. However, the molecular evolves into the physical, and is partially controlled by the left brain hemisphere.

The final three: cells, organs, and organ systems, are controlled from the left brain hemisphere.

In order to live a normal life, the way God intended, we must learn to control the energy fields correctly, that is, we must use the right brain hemisphere appropriately.

Solving Problems

Most people, approximately 90 percent, cannot use their right brain hemisphere to think with.

In the Silva ESP training, everyone learns, with just a few hours of instruction, how to detect subjective information with their right brain hemisphere, and how to think with both brain hemispheres when they are at the alpha level.

After that you are ready to take action at the beta brain wave level, using the left brain hemisphere.

Once you have access to both sides of your brain, and you have learned how to activate your mind while remaining at the alpha level, then you have tremendous programming capability.

Your thoughts will modulate your aura, so that everyone around you is influenced in a positive direction. This will make your life much easier.

And you are also able to project your thoughts great distances, through the use of the right brain hemisphere, so that you can influence people and events that are not in your physical presence.

By Chance or By Choice?

Your aura is automatically influencing people around you, whether you know it or not.

The question is: What kind of influence is it?

What kind of people do you attract into your life? This can give you an idea of what kind of message you are putting out through your aura.

A big portion of the attraction between male and female comes through the aura.

Have you ever met a person of the opposite sex and immediately felt attracted to them, even though at first glance they would not seem to be your type? This happens to most people. It is the influence of the aura.

When you meet the right person, you *know* it immediately, because of the way you feel. This is the influence of the two auras coming together in a certain way.

Once the boy and girl start dating each other, their auras begin a process of trying to alter the other person's aura. Eventually, both are altered a certain amount, until they are equal and in harmony with each other.

That's why it is important for couples to stay physically close to each other. They should sleep in the same bed.

If one person starts seeing another person, then their aura changes, and it is no longer in complete harmony with their original partner's aura. Then the original partners grow apart.

When you learn to function at the alpha level with the Silva Method techniques, you become more sensitive both at detecting information that can affect your life, and in programming to correct problems.

Unfortunately, 90 percent of the people on the planet live their lives more by chance than by choice. They hope that good things happen to them, but all too often they don't.

People who use both brain hemispheres have the ability to take greater control over their own lives, and to be healthier, happier, and more successful.

If you are not one of the fortunate ten percent who are "naturals," you need not despair. Simply take the Silva ESP training and practice the techniques and you will be able to do all that the naturals can do . . . and probably even more. You can begin right now with the Free Training that starts in appendix A.

It is how God intended us to live—using *all* of the equipment that we were given, using both brain hemispheres, using both the beta and the alpha levels consciously, to detect information and to correct problems.

40 We Are Punished Only by Our Own Ignorance *(1988)*

Some people complain about having bad luck.

Others claim that God is punishing them when something bad happens.

And everybody, at one time or another, has probably pointed a finger at someone else and accused that person of causing their problems.

"If only my wife (or husband) were more understanding . . ."

"If only my boss would give me a chance . . ."

"If only I had a little good luck for a change . . ."

"If only I had gone to college . . ."

I'm certain you could easily add more items to this "If only . . ." list.

We all succumb from time to time, and want to take out our frustrations on somebody else, or on something like "bad luck."

But the truth is, most of the time we are responsible for our own lives. The only thing that punishes you is your own ignorance.

Because of ignorance, you make mistakes.

The way to have more good luck, the way to achieve more success, the way to greater abundance and prosperity, is to banish ignorance and learn the things you need to know to be successful.

You can have what you want to have, do what you want to do, and be what you want to be, if you know how.

Do I mean that you will never have problems? Do I mean that everything will always go the way you want it to?

No, that's not what I mean. We will always have challenges. That's the way the world is.

But as an old friend of mine said once, "I have some problems, but I don't have any troubles."

It seems to me, based on almost half a century of research, and almost three-quarters of a century of living on this planet, that higher intelligence (God) created us to help perfect planet earth.

I have observed, all of my life, that when people are engaged in constructive and creative activities, and are helping to make this world a better place to live, that these people are usually prosperous, healthy, lucky, and happy.

So it seems to me that the first law of success must be that we do all that we can to help correct problems and convert our planet into a paradise.

Anything that corrects problems, without creating any new problems, is doing what higher intelligence wants us to do.

To do this, we must understand that our thoughts are the blueprints for everything.

The past is composed of thoughts that have already been materialized.

The present is the process of materializing thoughts.

The future is composed of conceived thoughts that have not yet been materialized, that are still pending.

Change your thoughts, and you change your future.

Of course, there are certain ways that we must do our thinking. You learn these methods—what you might call Laws of Prosperity—in the Silva training.

You must first learn to enter the alpha dimension and do your thinking at that dimension.

You must also learn how to become sensitive to other people and to your environment.

You must be able to project your mind so that you can become aware of information that you need to correct problems, and project your thoughts of the future to people who can help.

You must take action in the physical world to help materialize these thoughts. It doesn't happen by itself.

It is important to practice working health cases, to develop your sensitivity and your ESP, and so that you can learn how to identify that special feeling that you have when you are at the correct level and you are functioning clairvoyantly.

You must be able to project your thoughts effectively if you want to succeed in correcting problems. It is not enough to just think you are at the correct level; you must *know* that you are at the correct level.

The best way to learn is to get a lot of practice. And the best way to get a lot of practice, with immediate feedback, is to practice working health cases as you do in the final part of our ESP training.

By working health cases, you will quickly learn to tell the difference between just *thinking* you are at the right level, and *knowing* that you are at the correct level.

It is only our own ignorance that punishes us.

Banish ignorance by entering level every day and practicing the Silva techniques, and especially by working health detection and correction cases regularly so that you can develop your skills even more.

This will help you to be right more times than you are wrong in all of the decisions and choices you make in your life.

Note: If you haven't already learned, you can begin right now with the free training starting in appendix A.

41 Here's a Problem You Can End Without Making Any Efforts *(1984)*

There is an enemy in our midst. It probably causes more illness, suffering, and death, than anything else.

It ruins relationships, begets mental and emotional breakdowns, limits learning, spoils success, and causes many more problems.

If you attempt to fight this enemy, to struggle against it, you give it more power. But this enemy can be defeated. Without effort. By relaxing.

The enemy is stress, or more precisely, distress.

Excessive stress is at the root of many of our problems. That is why the Silva Method begins with more than half a dozen stress management techniques that everybody can use.

In fact, the Silva Method is the most powerful and most effective stress management program ever created.

Use Your Mind

To begin with, in the Silva Method we use imagination to bring about a state of physical relaxation.

You imagine relaxing various parts of your body, and through the use of imagination you relieve stress.

With practice, you can learn to relax simply by establishing points of reference. Associate the number 3 with physical relaxation, and when you mentally repeat and visualize the number 3 your body will relax. That's what is known as a "conditioned response."

You can use the number 2 for mental relaxation.

You can cause both body and mind to relax by recalling your ideal place of relaxation.

Once you have done something, your brain remembers the event, so when you recall it to mind, the brain recreates the conditions that existed then. If you recall a place where you relaxed, you will relax again. That's a conditioned response.

Deep breathing helps you relax.

You breath deeply to energize your body with oxygen, then relax as you exhale. It is like a "sigh of relief," you might say. Release the air that you inhaled, and at the same time release the tension in your body.

You can also program yourself, at your level, to use your Three Fingers Technique to trigger a state of relaxation when you are faced with a challenging situation.

When you are relaxed, you can deal with any situation. You need not take out your frustrations on your body in the form of illness, or on other people, or society.

Awareness and Action

Many people do not know they are suffering from distress.

People can experience "burnout" without ever realizing the amount of tension in their lives.

What are some of the signs? Ask yourself some questions:

Are you bored with your job?

Do you lack the enthusiasm you once had? Are your relationships running smoothly, or is there too much friction?

Do you have trouble remembering important things?

Do you dread getting involved in something new?

Do you feel healthy and alive?

Sometimes stress eats away at us so gradually, we do not realize that we do not feel as alive as we used to.

I am in my 70th year, and I still exercise daily and feel vigorous, enthusiastic, and young. There is no need to feel old at 40. If you do, check for excessive stress.

Enter your level for 15 minutes every day, and relax at 10 cycles per second brain frequency. This will take care of stress, and keep you healthy.

If you are too busy to enter level for 15 minutes every day—then it is even more important that you do so. If you are that rushed, then you are under even more stress than usual, and need the time at level even more.

After all, when stress causes your body to break down, you *will* find time to go to the hospital.

When you make wrong decisions because of the pressure you are under, because you can't recall vital information due to excessive stress, then you will find time to correct your decisions.

Do it right in the first place.

A 15 minute investment is a small price for optimum health, superior mental functioning, and gratifying relationships

Note: To learn how to put this into practice starting today, choose any of the free training options in appendix A and follow the simple instructions.

42 Free Yourself from Old Programs by Breaking Your Habit Cycles *(1989)*

The Silva Method gives you freedom.

The Silva Method gives you greater control over your own life.

The Silva Method gives you a way to accomplish what you desire, not just live life as somebody else wants you to live it.

Many people go through life functioning like robots.

Or like mud wasps.

Mud wasps are programmed biologically to do certain things "by the numbers." They cannot alter their programming.

You can watch a mud wasp bring food back to its home.

Before going inside, it puts the food down, looks inside to make sure everything is all right, then picks up the food and takes it inside.

That's how a mud wasp is programmed.

If you alter any step of the program, the mud wasp cannot complete the cycle.

While the mud wasp is looking inside, if you move the food an inch away, you have altered the programmed cycle and the mud wasp cannot continue. It first has to pick up the food and put it back into position just outside the entrance. Then it looks inside, makes sure everything is all right, and turns to pick up the food again.

If you move the food each time, then the mud wasp will never take it inside.

It will eventually collapse from exhaustion.

How many people are programmed in a certain way, and cannot alter that programming?

We all have many habits. And most of our habits are good. We are able to tie our shoes without thinking about how we move our fingers, where each lace goes. We put on a belt the proper way without even thinking about whether it goes around to the left or to the right.

But many people also have habits that are not beneficial.

Smokers do not even realize when they are lighting a cigarette, or what the cues are that prompt them to light up.

Drinking, overeating, procrastinating, gossiping, thinking negatively—these are all habits.

People are programmed to do these things, automatically.

Sometimes we program ourselves, and sometimes we are programmed by other people.

Sometimes other people program us in beneficial ways:

Look before crossing the street.

Say Please and Thank you.

Other times people program us in detrimental ways. We might be programmed that only one form of religion is correct, and all others are wrong. It is interesting that so many different people have been programmed in this manner, for hundreds of different religions.

Each thinks their way is the only "right" way. But the truth is, they are all working towards the same goals.

They just use different words to explain it, different symbols, different names.

Many people just accept their programming like a mud wasp. They have to carry the complete cycle through, without any alterations.

This limits a person's freedom.

It is difficult to be confident if you have been programmed that you are worthless. And as long as you continue to run the program over and over and over again, nothing will change. Like the mud wasp, you will drop from exhaustion before you reach your goals.

But there is good news for human beings:

You can alter your programming.

You can change.

You do not need to drop from exhaustion without ever reaching your goals.

The first step is desire. You must desire to free yourself from the restrictions of your programming, so that you can make informed decisions.

You can increase your desire by dwelling on your goals. Think of all the reasons you have for reaching your goals (stop smoking, lose weight, seek a promotion). Think of how your life will be changed for the better.

Think about why this is important to you.

The next step is to identify the programming cycles, and change them.

Break the cycles.

Stop smoking automatically, on cue. Alter the habit. It will be easier to break your new—altered—habit.

Whatever the habit, whatever the programming, change it.

Break the pattern.

It is much easier to do all of this by programming yourself at the alpha level, of course. That is why we developed so many, techniques in the Silva Method to help you with this.

You can claim the freedom, the control, and the success you desire by taking over your own programming, making conscious choices, and using the alpha level to make decisions and program yourself for success.

43 There May Be Reasons for Failing But No Excuses Will Be Accepted (1989)

It's funny how sometimes people will ask for advice, and then won't accept it.

In fact, it almost seems as though some people are looking for excuses for failure.

I keep telling people over and over again, the keys to being more successful in life, based on my 45 years of research, and a quarter of a century of teaching the Silva Method worldwide:

You have to use the alpha dimension with a sincere desire to solve problems. And you have to be persistent until you get the techniques working for you.

But many people don't want to believe it.

People come to me with the excuse that they don't visualize.

They expect to "see" pictures, as clearly as they see with their physical eyes.

Or at least as clear as a dream.

Well, I don't "see" that way when I am at my level. It is not like seeing with your eyes. It is not as vivid as the images you get in a dream.

Everybody can remember what something looks like. Everybody can think about what something looks like.

Everybody can describe what something looks like, even when they are not looking at the object they are describing.

In other words, everybody can visualize, because doing any of those things listed above is visualizing.

And everybody can imagine. If you think about what your living room's south wall would look like if it were painted a different color, you are imagining.

And later, if you go back and recall what you imagined, you are visualizing.

Imagination is a creative process: to think about what something looks like that you have never seen or imagined before.

Visualization is memory: to remember what something looks like, that you have seen or imagined before.

So the excuse that a person doesn't visualize is no good.

The important thing is that you do it at the alpha level. If you don't know how you can learn right now for free with the Free Training in appendix A.

You can practice memory pegs to make it easier for you to think about what things look like: in other words, to improve your visualization and imagination.

So, forget that excuse. Make sure you are at alpha, and think about what things look like, and you are doing it correctly.

Your Purpose In Life

The second thing I mentioned is to have a sincere desire to solve problems.

Some people program to find parking places. But that usually is not really a problem. Sometimes getting a parking place a little closer to your destination might be necessary to solve a genuine problem, but usually it is merely a convenience.

Someone suffering from a heart attack has a real problem.

A student who is failing a class has a real problem.

Migraine headaches are real problems.

So is insomnia.

A person who is out of work and cannot support their family has a real problem.

Often graduates want to program for things to make their lives more convenient. This is fine, as long as they are also doing all that they can to help correct the real, serious problems on our planet.

We were not sent here for an eighty-year vacation.

I believe we were sent here to help higher intelligence correct problems on this plane of existence, here on planet earth.

When you are helping to correct problems, then you will be compensated appropriately; then you will get the extras you want, that will make your life more enjoyable.

So do not come to me with the excuse that programming doesn't work for you because you haven't gotten all that you want. When you are solving problems that need to be solved, you will get everything you need, and more.

Keep Working

And what about persistence?

How many people give up without making a good effort?

Once your mind knows you are serious, you will succeed.

I remember back in 1967 when Jim Needham attended class. He could not work cases accurately, so I told him to work 100 cases.

He called me a few weeks later and said he had worked the 100 cases but still was not getting anything right.

I told him to work another 100 cases.

A few weeks later he called to say he had done as I told him, but still was missing everything.

I told him to work another 100 cases.

The next time he called, he told me he was finally getting them right.

Jim went on to become one of the best psychics I know.

Persistence pays off.

It did for me. You can read all about it in my autobiography.

There are a lot of tips to help you become an even better programmer. But by far the most important advice is this:

Use the alpha level, with a sincere desire to solve problems, and be persistent.

Then you will surely succeed with your programming.

44 Guidelines for Using Subjective Dimension to Solve Problems (1997)

One of the biggest problems in our new science is terminology. This is true of any new science: There are no words to explain what we have found.

Psychologists surely found this in the early days of psychology, and they invented terms like the subconscious to help them explain what they found. They re-defined other words, and created new words, like ego, superego, and id, to help them explain their theories.

Those words don't mean anything unless you understand their system.

If you accept their ideas, then those terms make sense.

Pioneers in psychology and related fields created their own words and terms to represent what they were doing. That's why we have peak experiences, the collective unconscious, akashic records, nirvana, heaven, and all sorts of other terms. They define what somebody felt was important.

Even a simple word like meditation has many different meanings.

What Is Meditation?

One person's meditation is another person's concentration. Some people say that Silva Method graduates are not meditating when we go to level to work on a project, but if we calm our mind, perhaps we'll go into meditation.

What's that again?

Well, that's alright, because we call what we do "dynamic meditation."

If somebody starts talking to you about meditation, you might want to ask them to define the term for you. Then you will have a better idea of what they are talking about.

You can meditate on anything.

When you meditate on a picture, or on symbols. Calm your mind by concentrating on a picture and you are meditating.

When you meditate on music. Calm your mind while listening to great classical music and you are meditating.

If you concentrate on a project at your level, you are meditating on that project.

What Does Concentrate Mean?

Of course concentration can be tricky too. Comedian Jeff Foxworthy said you may be a "redneck"—a term embraced by working people who are more comfortable in overalls than a tuxedo—he said you may be a redneck if you sit and stare at a can of frozen orange juice because the label says "concentrate."

"Concentrate" is defined differently when you are speaking of orange juice: it means to reduce the volume by removing water.

What we mean by concentrate is to direct your thoughts and attention towards one thing only. This will calm your mind and help you achieve an altered state of consciousness and a lower brain frequency.

And there are many different kinds of meditation, determined by the process used, the goals sought, and what happens when you do it.

For instance, concentrating on a picture, or concentrating on your breath, or concentrating on a word or phrase and repeating it over and over either mentally or verbally is something that is taught in yoga.

Meditating to Correct Problems

That's different from what we do in the Silva Method, and while it can bring about an altered state of consciousness, it is not necessarily the same state of consciousness as you achieve when you use the 3 to 1, 10 to 1 method to enter your clairvoyant level.

We use physical and mental relaxation, and countdowns, to enter a state of dynamic meditation. Then you learn how to maintain a light level of meditation even after you activate your mind so that you can go to work to correct problems. This is active meditation, because you can take action to correct problems.

If you prefer, of course, you can use the deepening exercises—countdowns, physical and mental relaxation, visualizing tranquil and passive scenes—to achieve a deep state of passive meditation. Do this for 15 minutes a day and it will strengthen your immune mechanism and help you in many other ways.

What Is Prayer?

There are other terms that are not always clearly defined, such as prayer.

There are many different definitions—and methods—for prayer.

Here's how I see the process of prayer:

It is the process of making your needs known to higher intelligence, on the "other side," as I like to say. It is also giving thanks when you receive guidance and help from higher intelligence.

We pray by concentrating on our needs and on making higher intelligence aware of our needs.

Solving Problems

The first thing you want to do when working on a project is to concentrate on the project yourself, to meditate on it so that you can solve your own problems.

When you have concentrated and meditated on your project, then it is important to go out and take action.

It is important to use your body as well as your mind. We want to use both dimensions to correct problems.

When you reach a sticking point and do not know what to do next, then you concentrate on making your needs known to higher intelligence. By doing that, at the correct level, you will receive guidance from the other side to help you continue on with your project.

That guidance might come in the form of an idea. You must act on that idea to determine if it was actually information from the other side, or only a fantasy that you created with your imagination.

Verifying Information

How do you determine whether the idea came from higher intelligence, or from your own imagination?

Simple:

By the results that you get.

If the information helps you to correct the problem, then you can take it for granted that it came from higher intelligence. If it doesn't help you to correct the problem, then it was probably your own idea.

In that case, try again:

Do some more deepening, work some health cases, check with your Silva Method lecturer for guidance—do whatever is necessary for you to learn to get to the correct level where you can communicate successfully with the other side.

On the other hand, the guidance from higher intelligence might come in the form of a "coincidence" in the physical world. This is a sign to guide you as to which way to proceed.

Perhaps someone comes and offers you some help. Maybe you read an article that helps you determine what to do next. Maybe your way is suddenly blocked, and you cannot proceed as you had hoped to. As the lyrics to an old song say, sometimes you ask if you can have something or do something and the answer is No.

How to Proceed

Keep in mind that we first attempt to correct problems ourselves. That's what we were sent here to do. Concentrate on correcting the problem yourself first. And when you successfully correct a problem yourself, remember to express your gratitude to higher intelligence for having the ability to correct problems.

When you get stuck, pray for guidance and help in solving the problem. You don't tell higher intelligence to solve it for you; you concentrate on asking for guidance so that you can go ahead and finish the job yourself.

When you have completed the project, pray again to give thanks for the help that you received. Concentrate on the completed project, and concentrate on conveying your appreciation to higher intelligence for the help that you received.

We have a new technique designed specifically for that purpose: The MentalVideo. You can learn it and begin using it tonight with the Free Training in appendix B.

Our Obligation

We have been assigned to do a job here on planet earth, and those who assigned us are there to back us up and help us when we need help.

They are willing to help us when we need it. That's their assignment. They are not there to do our work for us. They are not there to give us things just for the sake of having things.

They give us help based on our performance, on what we have done in the past. If you have a solid record of correcting problems—not just for yourself and your family, but any problems that are given to you—then the other side will provide you with a lot of help.

Promises to help out in the future don't mean much to our helpers on the other side. Anybody can promise anything. They go by your record of what you've been doing with what you already have.

If you have demonstrated by your actions that you meet your obligation to help correct problems whenever you encounter them—

How many reasons do you have for reaching your goal? If you can think of five reasons for reaching your goal, five people who will benefit, then you have a certain amount of desire.

If you go to your level and think of five more reasons for reaching your goal, five more people who will benefit, you have twice as much desire.

At your level, think about the ways that different people will benefit by your reaching your goal. And think about why that is important to them.

This is how to increase your faith.

One More Thought

Be sure you are programming for what you actually want. When you set a goal, think about how it is going to help you to reach that goal, and why that's important to you. This will help you make sure you are programming for the correct goal, rather than one of the steps towards your goal.

For instance, most people don't want money just for the sake of having money. Most people usually have that money mentally earmarked for something, and you probably do too. That's your real goal.

One more thing you can do: remember to always add the this one final thought to your programming:

"This or something better."

47 "Better and Better" Says It All
(1980)

"Better and Better"

This is the Silva Mind Control motto, the goal of our very existence, and I feel there can be no better one.

My commitment to this motto was enhanced recently when my wife, Paula, and I attended Sunday church services at our local parish church. We have belonged to this church for years, ever since our children were mere tots, and I like to worship there every time my demanding schedule allows me to.

While this is not often, I thoroughly enjoy attending this particular church. I enjoy the church not because it is particularly beautiful in an architectural point of view nor because it is elaborately decorated, but because of the people who worship there almost every Sunday.

You see, these people have been my neighbors and friends for years, people with whom I grew up and with whom I have shared experiences as a community. Many of them I find with faces that are markedly more wrinkled than when I saw them last; and some of them I find sitting down with members of their own family—young men and women who seem to have reached adulthood unnoticed before our very own eyes.

Each one of them pursues a different career, some known to me others unknown. And although I do not interact with them very often, except from one side of the church to another when we are gathered for church services.

There, in that church, like in countless other churches throughout the world, are gathered ordinary human beings giving of themselves, at least for an instant, so that they can be more at peace with themselves and their Maker.

"Better and Better"

Isn't this what we are all about?

Aren't we as humans always seeking that impossible dream, the achievement of happiness, of love, of peace with ourselves, our neighbors and our God?

Better and Better"

Not perfect by any means, for we know that perfection itself is merely the never-ending process of self-improvement which each one of us performs at our own pace and direction. Not hypocritical, either, for the very essence of our Method is a sincere desire to help humanity, and to set an example not by words alone but by putting in practice what we teach.

"Better and Better"

Not conformity which settles by the mistaken belief that we have achieved a plateau of performance, but our ardent desire not to be satisfied, to strive for creativity, increase our humanity and involving ourselves more and more in motivating others to do likewise.

"Better and Better"

In a world burdened with insecurity, threatened by chaos, challenged by forces which most of us cannot fully understand, "Better and Better" becomes a beacon to which all of us can turn to, one which, if pursued ardently, can transform all our doubts and fears into mere illusions of the past.

The people in that church were testimonial of people's inner desire to better themselves. It is not an easy task, especially with the constant bombardment of false priorities and warped motivations that are loose in the world.

Yet, amidst these turmoils, "Better and Better" continues to catch our spirit, channel our efforts and solidify our commitment to ourselves and our neighbors, whoever they might be.

"Better and Better"

It is not just a slogan, but a way of life, the anchoring weight of our beliefs in a sea swollen with indecision and insecurity.

"Better and Better"

Can there really be any other three words that captivate our movement so adequately?

48 Mind Research Helps Us Understand Who We Are *(1992)*

When I began my research into the mind and human potential, I came across the term ESP. The initials stood for "extra-sensory perception."

The idea was that people have some kind of an extra sense, besides the five physical senses of touch, taste, smell, hearing and sight. This so-called extra sense has also been called the sixth sense.

However, as I continued my research, I began to question the conclusions that other scientists had come to.

I realized that everything begins with the conception of a thought.

First you conceive a thought; then you act on that thought; and as a result, the thought is manifest in the physical (objective) dimension.

There are many other things I realized.

For instance, where did we come from? Where do we go when we have completed our mission on earth? The physical body is only here for a short time; but physical death is not the end for the individual.

When I learned that people could learn how to obtain information with their mind, information that was not available to their physical senses, then I knew for certain that we are more than our physical bodies.

What are we? I coined the term "human intelligence" to identify the non-physical part of the individual, and the term "biological intelligence" to identify the physical part.

Human intelligence can perceive information from anywhere in the universe. Biological intelligence, on the other hand, is limited.

Human intelligence existed prior to biological intelligence. It will exist after biological intelligence is gone.

Extra Senses

Putting all of this together, it seems to me that the original senses are those of human intelligence—the subjective (non-physical) senses.

If that is so, then the "extra" senses are the physical senses.

Both kinds of senses are valuable to have.

Which are the most valuable?

It depends on the circumstances of course. But overall, the subjective senses would have to be considered the most valuable.

People often try to equate "subjective senses" with the physical senses. They speak of someone with good visualization as a clairvoyant; one who gets information through imaginary conversations is called a clairaudient.

In fact, we have no subjective eyesight, no subjective sense of hearing or sense of smell or sense of touch.

The subjective dimension is not physical; the subjective senses are not objective but are subjective.

The person who receives information—with the subjective senses and then converts that information to a mental picture is called a clairvoyant.

The person who receives information with the subjective senses and then converts it to an imagined conversation is said to be clairaudient.

Who's Talking?

Many scientists do their research in the physical dimension. They speak of the subjective senses as being the "extra" senses.

I did my research in the subjective dimension.

From that perspective, I realized that the physical senses are the extra ones.

You can tell which dimension you are coming from by the way that you talk. When you say, "my arm" or "my foot," you are speaking from the physical dimension; it is biological intelligence speaking.

When you say, "my body," then human intelligence is speaking.

Check it out for yourself:

Enter your clairvoyant level as you learned to do in the Silva ESP training and put your own body onto your mental screen.

You can disassociate yourself from your body. It is one of your possessions, you might say. You can disassociate yourself from the events in your life, somewhat like watching a movie.

When you are wrapped up in the events, you are functioning in the physical dimension; biological intelligence is in charge.

When you can observe the whole picture clearly and picture yourself as a participant in life, you are functioning in the subjective dimension; human intelligence is in charge.

The ideal partnership is to use human intelligence to make decisions, and biological intelligence to take action and implement them.

49 Here's How You Can Ask for Help From the Other Side *(1989)*

There are many ways that you can get help from the other side, to help you correct problems on this side.

That is, there are many ways to use the subjective (non-physical) dimension, to help you in the objective (physical) dimension.

You can develop your skills at this with many of the techniques in the Silva courses.

Establish a Connection

For instance, you can use the To Awake Control Technique, to practice awakening without an alarm clock.

Some people think this is no big deal. But consider it for a moment:

At the alpha level, you are giving an instruction to your human intelligence, in the subjective dimension, to interact with your biological intelligence, your physical body, in the objective dimension.

We included this technique in the Basic Lecture Series primarily to give you a way to practice using your mind to get help.

After you have done this, you are better able to get help from the other side to heal your body, to change your appearance, to improve your personality . . . virtually anything you desire.

Getting Information

Dream Control Step 3 is another technique you can use to get help from the other side.

In the test taking technique, you use the subjective dimension to get an answer from your professor.

Making Changes

The Mirror of the Mind and 3-Scene Techniques can also be used to get help from the other side.

For instance, when you want to change something about yourself, you can create the desired change in the subjective dimension—on the other side—while at the alpha level, and then expect the change to manifest in the physical dimension.

Of course, everything in our ESP training deals with getting help from the other side.

Mediums

Even with all of these techniques available, some Silva graduates like to go to professional psychics, mediums or channelers to get help from the other side.

How can you tell which ones can really help you?

There are two simple tests that apply.

First, see if they can tell you what the problem is, without you having to tell them. This is one way of demonstrating that they have a connection with the other side, that they are connected in a way that could help you.

We do the same thing when we work health cases:

First, we determine the problem so we know that we have the right connection. The second test concerns the correction of problems.

Does the information they provide, help to correct the problem?

Many writers and story tellers are able to say things that are exciting to listen to, things that make us feel good.

But do they help to correct problems?

When I say "correct problems," I mean tangible results, results that you can detect in the physical dimension.

I realize that this may not be the only way to measure value, but it is the best for me. Even many so-called "intangible" benefits can still be measured objectively. Developing more self-confidence is beneficial, as is peace of mind. When this happens, you can see it by the way the person is able to accomplish more and to correct more problems.

Heal Thyself

The best thing of all is to learn to develop your own abilities, and to trust yourself.

Nobody can do a better job for you, than you can.

Practice the techniques mentioned above, and especially practice working health cases, and you will be able to get all the help you need from the other side. You can review these techniques—or learn them if you haven't already learned them—starting in appendix A.

Case working is the most valuable tool you have, because it gives you immediate confirmation that you have established a good connection with the other side.

And of course the MentalVideo is available whenever you need it.

Once you learn exactly how it feels to you, to have a good connection with the other side, and you can establish such connections reliably, then you will be able to get help from the other side whenever you need it to help you correct problems.

50 Activity and Involvement Will Keep a Person Young *(1985)*

As we grow older, we must remember to remain active, especially mentally active. Death means stiff and inflexible and no mental activity within the organism. Therefore, here are some suggestions for older people to help you remain alert and in control as you grow older and better.

Read stories or good books. Read for entertainment, and to get your mind on different subjects.

This is an easy and pleasant way to exercise your mind.

Check up on members of your family regularly, both objectively and (for graduates of our ESP training courses) subjectively. Talk with them and see how you can help. Work cases on them and correct any abnormalities you detect.

If you do not have any grandchildren or nephews and nieces who need help, then help your friends.

How can you help a friend? Wish them well, see if they are doing all right, check with them every so often to find out how they are getting along.

If you are completely alone without family or friends, then you can take care of animals. The main thing is to make certain you take an interest in something, do some useful work.

Get used to using your senses as much as possible. If you see a flower, concentrate on it. Notice how beautiful it is. Study the details. View it from different distances: near and far. When you hear sounds, concentrate on them: crickets, footsteps, whatever.

Use your sense of feeling, too: is it cold? Is it smooth? Is it rough? Concentrate on your sense of smell. Concentrate on the use of all the physical senses. Keep your mind active, because if you do not keep your mind active doing something, it will atrophy, and might become senile.

While you are analyzing things, use your imagination too. Compare your present experience with past experiences. Make changes in whatever you are perceiving, and think about how it would be. Keep your mind active, keep your brain working.

The working brain draws more nutrition, more blood circulation to the brain neurons. Working neurons require more energy to work with. And work means imagining, visualizing, thinking, analyzing. So a working brain receives more nutrition, is better fed, and the neurons won't die on you, and you won't become senile.

Too many people tend to stop thinking, stop imagining, stop experiencing life, and the neurons weaken, atrophy, and eventually die.

So use your senses, use visualization and imagination, and remain interested in your friends, relatives, nature.

Another way to exercise the brain is to recall past experiences when you were more active physically. Recall running, playing sports, or whatever physical activities you were involved in when you were younger. Recalling these experiences vividly will help keep your brain young, and help you maintain a youthful outlook on life.

Of course, older Silva graduates should practice entering level the same as younger graduates. In fact, since they often have more time to practice, they can get in even more practice than the recommended three time a day, fifteen minutes each time.

When you practice using visualization and imagination at the alpha level, you are practicing where there is the most brain energy. Keep your mind active at the ten cycles-per-second alpha level, which is the strongest portion of the brain.

Remember to exercise your mind, to look for ways to help correct problems, to help younger people with your experience, to help everyone just by being there and being interested in them, and you will remain young in spirit and will stay in control of all of your physical and mental faculties for as long as you live.

When we are useful and active, and have a purpose for being here on the planet, we will have a good, healthy, lengthy life.

51 Keep Getting Batter and Better by Increasing Your Awareness *(1991)*

We are walking brains.

It is sometimes easy for us to think that the body has a brain, but in reality it is just the opposite: the brain has a body.

The brain needs to have information, so it has biological senses to bring it this information.

When the brain needs to see, it uses eyes.

When the brain needs to hear, it uses ears.

When the brain needs to know what something feels like, it uses nerves.

The brain needs nourishment, so it uses the senses of smell and taste to help it find the proper substances.

By doing all of this, the brain is able to function in the physical world.

But that is not all that the brain does.

The brain also has a connection with the subjective world.

The brain can detect information with subjective senses.

When the brain needs information from the subjective world, it gets this information by using the mind.

The mind is the sensing faculty of human intelligence.

Human Intelligence

What is human intelligence? It is what is called the soul or spirit in religion, consciousness in metaphysics.

So there are biological senses of the body that send information to the brain, and subjective senses of human intelligence that send information to the brain.

The biological senses of the body are called sight, hearing, smell, taste and touch.

The subjective senses of human intelligence are referred to as the mind.

We perceive the subjective information as visualization and imagination.

All of the information from both dimensions is transmitted to the brain.

It is the brain that transfers information from one dimension to the other.

It is the brain that makes it possible to conceive something in the subjective dimension and manifest it in the physical dimension.

When you are centered, with the electrical energy of your brain pulsing at ten cycles per second, this transfer can take place.

Objective information comes through the left brain hemisphere.

Subjective information comes through the right brain hemisphere.

At ten cycles per second brain frequency, you can have awareness in both dimensions.

Practice developing all your senses, the mental and the physical. Exercise your brain. This will help you correct more problems.

Increased awareness will help you become more aware of information that you can use to solve problems, and this will help reduce the amount of stress in your life.

52 Prosperity Comes with Practice
(1982)

A lot of people want to know how to program for "prosperity." There are many kinds of prosperity: our health can prosper; so can our relationships; we can experience great joy in living; we can have the deep satisfaction of knowing we have solved many problems and served many people.

It seems like most people equate prosperity with material success. Money. We have lecturers who conduct workshops on prosperity. And write books about prosperity . . . and money.

As I see it—and I've been fortunate to be prosperous in all areas of my life—there are four main things you need to consider in any "prosperity programming." Those are: clairvoyance, confidence, enthusiasm, and work.

We are all born to be prosperous.

We are all born natural salesmen and saleswomen. We are all born confident. We are all born clairvoyant. We are all born with an attitude of enthusiasm and a willingness to work.

In the process of growing up, many people develop bad habits that tend to neutralize one or more of the characteristics they need for success and prosperity in life.

Affirmations and Actions

Many of the prosperity programs I read about advise the use of affirmations to neutralize the bad habits and improper thinking that have neutralized the person's natural inclination to succeed. Some of these programs tell you to pretend you are carrying around a lot of money, perhaps to use play money and pretend it is real money.

This is to help get your imagination working better.

All this is valuable, and can be put to use effectively by Silva graduates who know how to program at level, using the imagination.

This is part of the first requirement for attaining prosperity and wealth: clairvoyance. You must be able to create, in the subjective dimension, the thing you desire in the objective dimension.

You must have desire, belief and expectancy in your project. If you do not really desire prosperity, you will not make the effort to achieve it.

You also need belief. Confidence. You must have confidence in the project or service you are providing, and confidence in yourself.

You must be able to create, in the subjective dimension, the thing you desire in the objective dimension.

You will achieve wealth only in proportion to the services you provide. If you desire a million dollars, and you have a need for a million dollars, you can get it easily by providing ten million dollars worth of service to humanity.

To find the right kind of service to provide, you can use your clairvoyant level. Go to your level, and ask what you should be doing with your time here on earth. Follow the answer you receive. When you are really at your level, and receive answers, you will know you can trust those answers.

Then you will have the confidence in your services and yourself that you need to succeed.

At that time, set definite goals for yourself, and you are ready to start marching towards those goals.

Why Some Succeed

I was once a speaker at a program where W. Clement Stone, head of a major insurance organization and author of several books on success, also spoke. Mr. Stone has accumulated great wealth, and encourages his employees to use his methods to do the same.

There is one big difference in W. Clement Stone, however: he is a natural clairvoyant, who learned to use and to trust his intuition at a very early age. This is easy for me to detect in him, because the same thing happened to me.

With the Silva Method, you can learn to find and use your clairvoyant level. The next step is to practice, so you will build the confidence you need in the use of your clairvoyant level. In fact, having confidence in yourself and what you are doing is extremely important. This activates the "expectancy" factor that is so important to your success. If you program affirmations, select affirmations that will help build your self confidence.

Once you have learned to use your clairvoyant level effectively, and you are confident in yourself and your ability to make correct decisions, the other two steps become very easy.

When you have sufficient desire to succeed, and confidence in your ability to effectively use your clairvoyant level, then you will start to work enthusiastically, expecting to see results.

And you will see results.

After that, your progress depends on your generating more enthusiasm, and in your developing more confidence in your clairvoyant level. And that will build your confidence, which will build your enthusiasm . . . and you will have a self-reinforcing mechanism that will carry you to success.

53 We Must Meet Our Obligations and Help Relieve Suffering *(1982)*

Good health is important in living a prosperous, productive life. It is the exceptional person who achieves much, who achieves their full potential, when wracked by the pain and energy-sapping effects of illness.

When a peoples energy and attention are drawn to their ailments, then they lose some of what they might have devoted to achieving their goals in life.

This is why one of the foundations of our System is consideration to techniques to help recreate and preserve good health.

And this is why much of my life has been devoted to helping people overcome their physical ailments.

Several years ago, I decided to stop performing holistic faith healing techniques on people, other than members of my own family, and instead show others how to use the techniques, both for themselves and for others.

That decision is paying big dividends now.

Our new one-evening workshop on Holistic Faith Healing is both popular with the public, and effective in correcting health problems.

Doctors who have attended these workshops have been amazed and astounded at the results they have seen.

They are even more surprised when they find they can achieve the same results themselves.

In these workshops, we show people how to use the Silva Rapid Hand Vibration Holistic Faith Healing Technique. We have all those who are suffering pain stand up, and then we have all those who want to be faith healers select a person to work with.

We then guide the people who want to be healers, showing them exactly what to do.

Under our guidance, they follow the simple instructions, and even though this is often their first attempt to do anything like this, they always get positive results to a degree.

After the healing applications, which take just a few minutes, we ask the subjects who had been suffering pain to tell us how much, if any, the pain has decreased.

For many, the pain is gone entirely.

For others, it is only a fraction of what it was before.

In many instances where there was limited movement due to injury, the subjects find they now have an increased range of movement in the affected area. When healing, healers concentrate on removing the cause of the problem, as well as the pain.

In most instances, the subjects continue to improve for the next twenty-four hours. Pain decreases even more, and the range of movement increases. To insure that they continue to heal, we make sure the subjects understand how to use certain basic techniques that they can apply to themselves.

Of course, it is very valuable if the subjects are Silva graduates, who know how to enter their alpha brainwave levels and program themselves for perfect health.

In addition, they are taught how to use the Alpha Sound tape recording to eliminate any abnormal conditions.

The natural state for human beings is perfect health. And while it is true that there is often something in the person's lifestyle and thought processes that invites illness, still it is difficult to change your way of thinking and become more positive when you are suffering from illness.

Our Silva techniques are very powerful and effective in helping people regain their natural state of perfect health.

We hope many more people take advantage of the opportunity to regain good health.

And we hope that they repay their debt by then helping others who might be suffering, so that we can reduce and eliminate pain and suffering on our planet.

It is our job and our intention to help the Creator in helping solve the problems of those on this planet who are suffering.

It is our obligation to work for our Creator in helping solve the problems of the creation.

We have an obligation to do all we can to eliminate suffering of the Creator's creatures.

This is an important step in converting this planet into a paradise.

Note: Before his passing, Mr. Silva asked us to make videos of his Holistic Faith Healing Techniques in order to make them available to more people. You can obtain those videos now on our SilvaESP .com website at a special discount. When you check out, submit coupon Code: MM15.

54 To Achieve Success, Follow This Plan
(1982)

How do you spell success?

Is it by the amount of money you earn? By the number of friends you have? By how many problems you solve? Or by what other people say about you? Or the size of your family?

There are many areas where we can measure our success. It is important to have successes in many areas to live a full and happy life.

The measure of your success is the measure of how many problems you solve. And to help solve problems, you must be strong. The more successful you are in several important areas, the more problems you can solve in all areas.

You can solve more problems when you are strong financially, when you are strong physically, when you are strong mentally, and when you are strong spiritually.

Building mental strength is often the best way to help yourself build strength in other areas, for if you can not control your mind, your thoughts, your imagination, then how can you ever build the desire, belief and expectancy to grow strong in the other areas? If you have weak mental capacities, then the first obstacle that arises might knock you off the track of your goals.

You can strengthen your mental faculties, of course, by practicing the Silva techniques. Go to your level at least three times a day for five, 10 or 15 minutes at a time. Practice what you have learned. If you haven't learned yet, you can learn right now with the Free Training in appendix A.

How to Build Success

Success breeds success. The more you succeed in any area, the more you will expect to succeed, and the more you expect to succeed, the more you will succeed.

So how does one start succeeding?

First of all, you have to make attempts. The more time you try something, the more your chances of success. It is not idle dreams, but it is action that solves problems. It is not the person who comes up with ideas who succeeds and solves problems; it is the person who acts on those ideas who solves the problems.

Once you succeed at something, it will be much easier to succeed again.

There is a special feeling you get with success, a unique feeling of success. There is no other way to get this feeling except by success. Use this feeling to help you achieve future successes.

We used to think that we eventually reached success with a ladder of failures.

We know now that we reach greater success with a ladder of lesser successes. It is a lot easier to move from lesser positive to a more positive, than from a negative to a positive.

Remember how the brain works. Remember mental housecleaning from the first segment of the Silva Mind Control Basic Lecture Series. Your bio-computer, or brain, bases its decisions about the appropriate action to take on data that had been put into it. In other words, whatever has gone into your memory bank will be used for decision making. All of your experience, and all of your thoughts will contribute to this process.

So when you have a success, recall that success. Think about it. Imagine it over and over. Dwell on it. Recall that unique feeling of success, and you will be well on your way to another success.

Is it worth the effort it takes to build a ladder to great success? It certainly is.

Just remember, there is more health, wealth and happiness in success, that overshadows failure, that outshines failure in every way.

And of course, there is a lot more money in $u¢¢e$$ than there is in failure.

55 Time to Begin the Second Phase of Human Evolution *(December 1987)*

The door is now open for humanity to take the first step into the second phase of human evolution on our planet, and you, as a Silva graduate, have played a big part in opening that door.

We found the key to the door during our twenty-two years of research. It is a key that, I think, has been lost for 2,000 years, and we were fortunate enough to be guided by Higher Intelligence to find it.

What will we find when humanity marches through that door?

A New World Awaits

The many benefits you have received by using the Silva techniques are only a tiny sample of what humanity has to look forward to.

You already know that the shape of your inner thoughts can influence the appearance of your outer body.

You have already experienced how you can use your mind to cause your body to relax, to stop feeling pain, to give up addictions.

In our ESP training you have already learned to communicate with other people with your mental senses, and you know that you can help others correct their problems by projecting to them mentally, from a distance.

You have even had a taste of what it is like to experience all of the elements of your environment directly, thorough mental projection into the kingdoms of inanimate matter, plants, and animals, as well as humans.

You have unlocked the "Secret of the Ages" and much more: You have put your knowledge to practical use.

You are able to do the things that other people read about with awe, when they read about the masters who have lived on the planet.

All of this that you have done has helped to open the door so that humanity now stands poised to take the first step in the second phase of human evolution on our planet.

What the Future Holds

When enough people have begun the journey, we will experience a world completely different from what we now know.

The second phase of human evolution is the evolution of the human mental faculties. We have developed a marvelous body that we can use while living on planet earth.

Now we need to develop our minds.

Science and logical thinking have produced a lot for us, a lot of good things, and a lot problems.

In fact, we seem to be creating more problems than we can solve.

Every time we cure one disease, it seems like three new diseases are discovered.

Every time we improve our political systems, our systems of government, it seems like people find even more ways to abuse the system.

Ronald Reagan is the first United States President in a quarter of a century to serve two full terms in office. What better evidence could you find that it is no longer enough to depend only on our physical senses and our logic and our science and our educational institutions.

A New Breed

Our new world of the future will be filled with people who use creativity and intuition, who use their mental senses, to find new solutions that we don't even dream of today.

The new fully-functional human we will see in the second phase of human evolution on our planet is likely to be as different from the human of today, as animate matter is from inanimate matter.

You have opened the door to that.

But despite all you have done, we have only just begun.

We now need to encourage humanity to step through that door, to begin that journey to the second phase of human evolution.

You have a very special, and a very unique, opportunity.

And an obligation.

Those of us who have arrived at the door have an obligation to show the way to others. This is our job. And when we are doing our job, we will be rewarded with health, prosperity and happiness.

That is my wish for you during this holiday season, for the year ahead:

May Higher Intelligence bless you and help you become healthier, wealthier, more successful, and happier. God Bless you.

PART 3
SOME PERSONAL REFLECTIONS

by José Silva Jr.

My father was very observant, pragmatic, and curious, and those traits helped him accomplish many things—some good and profitable, some not.

He observed people to see what they wanted and needed, and when he could figure out a way to provide it to them, he did.

Not all of his ideas turned out as well as he hoped, but that didn't bother him—he just found another way to fill people's wants and needs.

A Six-Year-Old Child Learned the Secret of Making Money

My father was just a small boy of four when his father was critically injured in a terrorist action during the Mexican revolution.

When he was six, feeling a strong need to help his family, he hit the streets of Laredo to earn some money. His career began at ground level, at the very bottom: his first job was shining shoes.

When he saw that people purchased newspapers every day, he began selling newspapers to his shoeshine customers. His uncle even taught the child how to keep records so he would know which customers wanted shoe shines, which wanted newspapers, and which wanted both.

When he overheard two businessmen complaining about how hard it was to find someone reliable to clean their offices, José popped up and volunteered.

It was a way to earn more money: Find a need and fill it. It is such a simple concept that even a six-year-old child can understand it.

When he heard of an elderly woman who needed someone to run errands for her, he volunteered for that, and earned more money,

A few years later, when he heard people complaining about the trouble they had shopping for household items, he came up with another idea: He traveled to San Antonio, brought back merchandise, and sold it door-to-door.

He earned a lot of money doing that, so next he put a crew of kids to work, walking up and down the streets, knocking on doors, making it easier for people to shop.

My father kept finding more ways to earn money.

Self-Improvement Pays Unexpected Dividend

He never attended school as a student, not even one day. But that didn't keep him from an education:

He asked his sister and brother to help him learn to read and write. And he'd visit a barber shop and read comic books for practice.

The pictures helped him understand what the words meant.

One day at the barber shop he picked up a booklet to read. It was a course on how to repair radios. The explanation of this brand new thing called radio began to make sense to him, so he asked the barber if he could borrow the book.

The barber refused. But that didn't keep him down. He rented the course from the barber for a dollar a lesson. And he had to agree to take the test at the end of each lesson, and sign the barber's name.

The barber got the diploma and hung it on his wall.

My father came out of the deal with a radio repair business. Another ground floor opportunity in 1928.

A New Opportunity During the Worst of Times

During World War II he was called to serve in the army.

He sold all of his electronics repair equipment, converted all of his assets to cash for his family, not knowing if he'd survive, or if he'd ever see Laredo again.

He came home safely two years later with a new subject to study: psychology.

Psychology led him to hypnosis and he now had a new way to help his family, his friends, and their friends.

Pretty soon his name was coming up all over town, but not always in a good way. People fear what they don't know, and many feared hypnosis. They even feared what he might learn about the human mind.

Pioneers are often criticized, condemned, even killed. He was threatened with legal action, and the church considered excommunicating him for what they *thought* he was doing. Now of course the church is one of his biggest supporters.

He persisted through all of the difficult times. During his first quarter century of research, he learned more about the mind and how it works than anyone else in history.

He conducted research on my brothers and sisters, but not on me. He called on me to record those sessions in a big Roberts reel-to-reel tape recorder. I was watching—and recording—history in the making.

When he saw that many people wanted to learn what he knew about the mind, he created a course, and eventually his courses were being taught in 100 countries worldwide.

Guided By Coincidences

How did this man who never attended school as a student do this?

That is another interesting coincidence:

In 1947, as he was rebuilding his radio repair business, officials in Laredo were starting a new college: Laredo Junior College. They wanted to offer an electronics course, so they asked him to develop it. When officials from the Veterans Administration came to evaluate it, they declared it the best in the entire state of Texas.

During the next two decades—from 1969 until today—his research and the world famous course that has grown from it have helped millions of people worldwide change their lives for the better.

His courses are offered throughout the United States and in 100 other countries. It is taught in more than twenty languages.

And countless spin-off and knockoff courses, that trace their roots back to the research that José Silva conducted in Laredo, help even more people.

What Made Him Different

Is there something different about my father that helped make him so successful?

Not really.

Circumstances guided him, at a very young age, to function in a way so that he used more of his brain, and more of his mind, than the average person.

There are others who have done that, used more of their brains and more of their minds, than the average person. These people help other people, usually for a fee.

And that's the biggest difference between José Silva and the others.

My father taught everyone who wants to know, how to do what he does, how to use more of their brains and their minds, to be more successful in every area of life.

He taught it in his courses.

He taught it in his books.

He trained thousands of instructors to teach people what he knew, to teach people how to do what he does.

And now, twenty-four years after his passing, we are continuing his mission and carrying on his work exactly the way he asked us to.

How did he measure his success?

Not by how much money he made.

He measured his success by how many people don't need his help anymore.

56 You Can Get More Done When You Make Every Minute Count *(1989)*

How many times have you heard someone say, "I wish there were more hours in the day so I could get everything done"?

You usually hear that from people who don't do very much.

The people who are getting things done just get out and do what needs to be done. The truth is, each day has a certain number of hours, and we all have equal access to those hours. What we do with those hours is what makes the difference.

The people who want more hours in the day would only become more frustrated if they actually got the longer days they think they want, because there would be more opportunities and therefore more things left undone.

Just Do It

The key is to use time wisely, to make every minute count.

That does not mean that you have to work all the time. I don't work all the time. But I do what needs to be done, when it needs to be done.

I've known people who worry so much over how they are going to finish a big project that they never begin the project.

As the old saying goes, a journey of a thousand miles begins with one step.

You cut down a forest one tree at a time.

Faith can move a mountain, if you wheel out one load of dirt at a time.

When I first started my research on the mind and human potential, if I had known then how much work I would wind up doing, I would never have continued.

In fact, I did stop a couple of times.

So what kept me going?

I simply made every minute count.

Solve Problems

I did not conduct research just to see what would happen. I conducted research to find better ways to correct problems.

I wanted everything I did to lead to some practical results, to something that would help people lead healthier, happier, more successful lives.

As I saw people benefiting from my research, I continued working.

And when I became tired and discouraged and wanted to stop, I received messages from higher intelligence to keep on going, to continue my research.

You do not have to conduct research into a new field of science in order to make every minute count.

For years, I conducted research in my "spare time" while I continued to work full time repairing radios and television sets.

When I was fifty-two years old, I began a new career: I began to devote full time to teaching people my method.

And in my "spare time" I began to work with electronic circuits and invented several electronic instruments that people can use to help them correct more problems.

When I see something that needs to be done, I do it. Not every idea works, but enough ideas work out to make it worthwhile.

You Are Important

Whatever you do, it is important. Your job is important. Do the best you can, and make every minute you spend on your job count for something.

If I had spent my life looking for something worthwhile to do, I would not have accomplished what I did.

Instead of searching for something worthwhile, instead of searching for more hours in the day, I invested myself into doing the best I could at whatever I did.

When I shined shoes for a living, I did the best job I could.

When I cleaned offices, I did the best job I could.

Do not let life pass you by.

Get in the game, go out onto the playing field, make your contributions.

Do this, and you will lead a healthy, happy and successful life.

57 I Have a Reason For Optimism: More People Are Solving Problems *(1989)*

When you read the news, it seems that problems are outperforming solutions.

It sometimes seems as if every solution brings with it a greater problem.

Many products—from automobiles to aerosol sprays—make life easier, but pollute and damage our environment.

Does this mean that we are doomed to extinction because our problems will eventually overwhelm us?

I think that we can overcome our problems. I believe that we can convert our planet into a paradise.

But not if we use only the tools of the physical dimension.

We need to also use the tools of the subjective dimension.

It is important to use logic and reason to correct problems.

But even before logic and reason become useful to us, we must use insight and intuition to know which direction to go.

Once we use insight and intuition to determine which way to go, then we can use logic and reason to help us get there.

In other words, we must be balanced.

That is why the Silva training is so important—not only to us as individuals, and to our families, but also to the world.

Physical medicine can take care of emergencies and keep a person alive until the person's body is able to heal itself. The mind can speed that healing process.

We earn our living in the physical world, but first we must go within and determine what our specific role in life is.

We make decisions daily involving our loved ones and other people we come into contact with.

We should make these decisions at the alpha level, using the right brain hemisphere. Then we implement those decisions with the help of the left brain hemisphere.

We must be balanced.

Right now, too few people are balanced. Too few people are able to function consciously at the alpha dimension, to use their right brain hemisphere and utilize the subjective dimension for solving problems.

The ten percent who can function in both the objective and the subjective dimensions cannot solve all of the problems that the 90 percent are creating.

Many people write to me and request that I solve more problems.

They ask me to go to my level and heal them.

They ask me to program and solve various problems that plague humanity.

I used to heal people. Through the years I have healed hundreds of people personally, using the holistic faith healing techniques that I teach.

I have even tackled bigger projects and carried them through to success.

But I am only one person. There is only so much I can do.

That is why I am on the path I am on.

I was guided to develop a method to teach everyone how to use holistic faith healing techniques, and how to work on the big problems that plague our planet.

For a serious case of cancer, it is necessary to use the holistic faith healing techniques on the person three times a day for six weeks. This takes time; there are only so many people I could help.

But by training thousands of holistic faith healers who can each go forth and help those who need help, many more people will be saved.

A problem like AIDS will require a great deal of research and work by many people to find a solution.

I am training people as fast as I can—and I am training instructors to go forth and train people to function in the subjective dimension—so that these people can seek solutions.

I have been assigned the task of training people so that they can use the subjective dimension, as well as the objective dimension, to correct problems. This task is not finished yet, and I've been told to continue with this task.

The best way we have of solving problems is for all of us who know how to work in a balanced manner, who know how to use both the subjective and the objective dimensions, to work as hard and as fast as we can to find solutions to problems.

I am doing my part.

I am training people as fast as I can.

Now you must do your part.

Use what you have learned.

Practice working health cases and develop your skill. Practice so that when you need the techniques, they will work for you.

Working together, we can solve the problems that plague us.

Please go to level today, and every day. Work some new health cases at least once a week.

Become proficient at all of the Silva techniques.

Let's solve those problems.

58 Prayer Is More Effective When Done at the Alpha Level *(1989)*

A minister had an interesting report after he had learned the Silva Method and practiced it for several months:

"My prayer seems to be much more effective now," he said. "I have been a minister for twelve years," he continued, "and I was never really confident that my prayers were doing any good.

"But now I pray, and I usually see results in a very short time.

"Do you have any idea why that is happening?" he asked.

The Alpha Connection

Success in communicating with the other side is a direct result of functioning at the alpha level.

It is something like this:

We use our objective senses to communicate in the objective dimension. That is, we use our eyesight, our ability to talk and listen, our senses of touch, taste and smell, to communicate with one another physically.

But to communicate with the other side, the physical senses are useless.

The other side is the place that we came from when we were born, and is the place that we go back to when we leave this planet. The spiritual dimension cannot detect our physical dimension directly.·

Spiritual means non-physical. So we must find a way to make a connection with the spiritual dimension, and convert our information from a physical form to a spiritual form.

The Kingdom of Heaven

To use a Biblical term, you must first enter the kingdom of heaven: To put it into scientific terms, you must reach a mental state that is connected with the mental—subjective dimension as well as the physical—objective—dimension.

If you attempt to communicate with the other side while you are functioning only in the physical dimension, you will not make the connection.

When you enter the alpha level, you make a connection with the subjective dimension.

As long as you remain centered—in alpha—you can communicate between the objective and subjective dimensions. If you go to far either way, you will be stuck in one dimension or the other.

The Correct Language

Once you have established the connection with the other side, you must communicate in a manner that spiritual beings (like God) can perceive. In the Bible this is described as functioning righteously.

How do you do that? What is the language of high intelligence?

The universal language, used throughout the universe, is visual.

Different countries use different words and sounds to express meaning. If you don't know the words or the sounds another person uses, you can't communicate with them verbally, but with mental pictures, you can communicate with anybody—provided, of course, that they also function at alpha.

With mental pictures you can communicate with the other side, with high intelligence. You can even communicate with animals this way, and with plants, as Cleve Backster has demonstrated.

You can communicate effectively even if your mental pictures are dim.

You can communicate effectively even if all you are able to do is to think about what things look like, provided that you do this at alpha.

The people who are the most effective at prayer—and who are the most effective in any endeavor—are the people who mentally picture their goals at the alpha level.

The keys to effective communication—to effective prayer—are: first, enter the alpha dimension and second use mental pictures (think about what things look like).

Do this, and your message will surely get through.

59 At Ten Cycles Brain Frequency, You Can Alter the Environment *(1988)*

The ten cycles brain frequency seems to be a universal health producing frequency.

This seems to be one of the most important reasons that functioning at ten cycles brain frequency, as you do when you enter your level the way you are taught in the Silva training, helps you stay healthier, and also helps you become an effective healer.

Scientists have found that the space between the earth and the ionosphere is pulsing at ten cycles per second, and no one knows where the generator, or the point or origin, is in relation to the universe.

There appears to be a correlation between the ten cycles pulsing and the interaction of magnetic, electrical, and chemical energies.

Healers, when tested while healing, are found to be operating at the ten cycles brain frequency.

This means that the healer's brain, the generator, is discharging or pulsing at the ten cycles frequency, radiating· human energy, called the aura, to the patient.

The aura energy penetrates life matter—the patient—causing an interaction or stimulation between the magnetic, electrical and chemical energies within the patient.

When the stimulation is stopped, and while the excitation of matter is gradually decreasing, it appears that natural laws attract the resettlement of energy in matter to conform to the original natural healthier life form.

This would indicate that the complete process is therapeutic.

Human Programming

People who have the ability to function consciously at ten cycles brain frequency find it easier to adapt to any environment or circumstance because they have the ability to program either themselves or the environment.

When we speak of the programming faculty of a human being, we mean the ability of a person to alter the state of matter.

Matter is altered through the interaction of the magnetic, electrical and chemical energies stimulated by the radiation of human energy, the aura and the projection of thought.

It is in the programming faculty of human beings, and in the knowing that only human beings have a programming faculty, that we are assured of having been created in the image of our creator.

It is in this programming faculty that we most resemble our creator.

Our creator has the faculty of creating throughout the whole universe. We, created in the image of our creator, have the faculty of creating throughout the planet earth.

Our understanding now is that inanimate matter has no programming faculty. It cannot program itself, or the environment. We can say that inanimate matter is helpless against environmental influences.

We can also say that plant cell life has no programming faculty and cannot program itself or the environment. Plant cell life is also helpless against environmental influences.

Animal cell life has no programming faculty and cannot program itself or the environment. It is also helpless against environmental influences.

Since the body of a human being is made up of animal cell life, it too is helpless against environmental influences. Cell life is considered to be biological intelligence.

We believe that what has been created in the image of our creator is our human intelligence.

It is our human intelligence that has the programming faculty, with which we can program anything on this planet.

We can program on this planet what the creator can program in the universe.

Through our desire, belief and expectancy, and with the use of visualization and imagination, when functioning at ten cycles brain frequency, we can alter conditions in matter, near and far.

This is what we in the Silva Method call programming.

Having the programming faculty is what makes the adjusting to any environment or circumstance possible for human beings.

Note: You can learn to function at 10 cycles per second brain frequency with the free training in appendix A.

60 We Can Help the Creator by Creating, Not Destroying *(1989)*

It is sad to see people killing each other in the name of the creator.

The creator creates; the creator does not destroy.

Isn't it interesting that so many people are willing to kill other people, and also to give their own lives, for the belief systems that they hold?

This is done in the name of patriotism, in the name of religion, and also for ideas like freedom of speech.

It is particularly sad to see violence in the name of religion, for God is a creator, not a destroyer.

My own church has been guilty of violence. During the crusades people were tortured to death if they would not embrace the Catholic religion.

For years in Northern Ireland, Protestants and Catholics routinely killed each other.

Farther East, Hindus and Sikhs kill each other.

Jews continue to battle for the survival of their religion.

And now the Moslems seem to have reached that phase in the development of their religion when they feel compelled to go to war, killing those who disagree with them.

In every religion we find people who are completely convinced that their own view of God is the only correct view. That has been programmed into their bio-computer brains since infancy.

It seems to me that whoever could create us, must have a higher level of intelligence than we have.

Our intelligence is finite; it is limited. Yet with our finite minds we attempt to describe something that is infinite . . . at least it is infinite from our point of view.

Perhaps each religion has part of the picture, but not all of it.

It reminds me of the story of the blind men who were asked to describe an elephant.

The only way the blind men could learn about the elephant—with their finite senses—was to feel it.

The one who felt the leg said that an elephant was like a tree.

The one who felt the elephant's body said it was like a large wall.

Those who felt the trunk, the ears, and the tail, each had his own idea of what an elephant was like.

All of them were correct. But they each had only a part of the picture. While each was correct in a limited way, none had the whole picture.

And each one thought that all of the others were wrong.

Would it make sense for them to kill each other over their experiences and their belief systems?

Would it not make more sense for them to combine their knowledge and learn more of the truth?

As long as we keep trying to describe God based on our own limited experiences and finite minds, I believe we will fall short of the mark.

We were made in the image of God, and the image is never as clear or as sharp as the original.

We have God-like attributes, but God is more than we are. At least that is what makes sense to me.

It seems that religions always want to create a vision of God in the image of man, to give God human-like characteristics, instead of the other way around.

We live in a finite, physical world, so religious leaders describe everything in a finite, physical manner to make it easier for us to understand.

Look at the physical models we have for heaven and hell, even though at death we leave the physical body (and physical dimension) behind—ashes to ashes, dust to dust.

Do I have the correct answers?

I believe that I have found *some* answers that are correct for us at this time and in this place.

I base that belief on the fact that the things I accept as truth and reality have been demonstrated to be able to help us correct problems on earth, to relieve suffering, to heal the sick, feed the hungry, house the homeless.

I also know that knowledge and wisdom accumulate, which means that our descendants will know more of the truth than we know.

When we study all religions, as I have; when we study various mental disciplines as I have done—from psychology to hypnosis to yoga and more; when we experience all that we can of life and learn how to use those experiences to correct more problems, perhaps it is like knowing about the elephant's leg and body and trunk and ear and tail. Perhaps we know more than our ancestors knew.

But we still don't really know what the whole elephant looks like.

We only know in part—several parts perhaps, but not the whole picture.

My prayer is that we all use what we know to help correct problems, to be creators here on earth to help perfect the creation of the creator.

Let us stop destroying, let us stop killing people because they have a different part of the picture, and let us each work in our own way to relieve suffering of all kinds.

61 Eliminate Limitations and You Will Enjoy Better and Better Success *(1987)*

In the basic Silva training, we learn techniques to help correct health problems. In the Ultra Seminar, you learn a variety of ways to help yourself and others overcome health problems.

It would seem that there could be no argument with better health. Yet, we occasionally run into criticism on an ethical, moral or religious level.

Lessons To Learn

Some people feel that illness bears within itself a lesson to be learned and if we heal ourselves, we deprive ourselves of a learning experience.

Similarly, if we help someone else to heal, we deprive them of a learning experience.

Others say that the mind power we use to heal comes from the devil, and still others that we are trespassing on forbidden ground.

Answers Offered
We find in Jesus' teachings the answers to all of these challenges.

No, we are not trying to covert anyone to Christianity, but neither do we desire to be pressured into accepting someone else's viewpoint.

Our viewpoint is that our Creator is perfect and all-encompassing and that there is no power that is not His.

Abnormalities are created by humans going contrary to nature.

Corrections of those abnormalities are working with nature.

Who Has the Power?
When Jesus healed, religious leaders of his time said he was in league with the devil.

Later, St. Paul spent a good portion of his ministry trying to get people in the churches he established to quit bickering about who had the most power, who was best and who was most right, but to get on with the task assigned by Jesus: to heal the sick, raise the dead, cast out demons and teach others to do the same.

The Proof Is Obvious
Jesus said, "By their fruits ye shall know them."

We are dedicated to correcting problems and making this planet a better place to live.

If our fruits were bad, we would not last.

We have lasted. We can all live longer and happier lives using more of our mind.

This is ethical.

This is moral.

This is religious.

Still, ours is not a religious movement, nor is it a movement into the "occult."

There is nothing secret about our organization, nothing dramatic, no rituals, no initiations.

The Silva Method simply seeks to acquaint people with the potential of the whole person and how, by using more of the mind, they can get rid of limited ways of thinking and unproductive habits and move on to better and better levels of creativity, enjoyment and success.

62 How You Can Determine What to Do With Your Life *(1991)*

One of the most significant things I've learned in more than four decades of research into the mind and human potential is this:

The creator set up a whole system of automatic self-correcting and self-regulating mechanisms. We can allow these automatic mechanisms to harm us, or we can use them to help us.

Let me explain what I mean by automatic mechanisms:

How We Receive Help Automatically

Look at how your body can automatically adjust for different temperatures.

When it is hot, your body perspires to cool the body.

When you need nutrition, your body sends a hunger signal.

There are more than two thousand such automatic mechanisms.

There are automatic mechanisms that involve all aspects of our lives. They let us know whether we are doing what we are supposed to do or not.

For instance, if you do not eat, the hunger signals will increase. When you eat, you feel satisfied and content.

Warning Signs

Sometimes the messages are more indirect. For instance, we know that sex is very pleasurable. As long as we use sex to bring new souls onto the planet, we will continue to enjoy it.

But look what happens when people start using sex strictly for pleasure. They began to contract sexually transmitted diseases (STDs).

A few decades ago, syphilis and gonorrhea were fatal. Then scientists developed penicillin and all a person had to do was to go get a shot and they could then go right back to using sex only for pleasure.

A decade ago herpes was a major problem. A lot of people who had many sex partners instead of just one, and who used sex for pleasure rather than for reproduction with those partners, wound up suffering.

But despite what was happening, people's behavior did not change. People ignored the automatic self-correcting mechanism.

Then came AIDS, another deadly STD.

Please understand: I am not saying that God is punishing us for being bad. What I am saying is that the creator set up a system to help us know what we should be doing from what we should not be doing.

Utilizing Automatic Mechanisms Effectively

There are ways that we can gain added value from some of these automatic mechanisms.

Early in my research when I was studying hypnosis I learned that I could cause a person to produce a blister even though they had not been burned.

In other words, I fooled the body's healing mechanism into creating an imaginary injury.

That brought up a question: Could I also influence the body's healing mechanism to aid in the correction of a real injury?

The results are in several of our courses as well as in the Free Training in the appendix of this book.

Glove Anesthesia grew out of that early research. Instead of waiting for the body to automatically ease the pain and stop the bleeding, we program ourselves in a way that we can accelerate the process.

When you apply Glove Anesthesia to yourself, your body reduces the pain and often stops the bleeding or hemorrhaging. And the healing process is often accelerated.

Glove Anesthesia is designed to use on yourself. But we have extended the concept of influencing the body's healing mechanism to aid in the correction of health problems.

Helping From a Distance

By using mind-to-mind communication, we can help others at a distance. We call that "case working."

In the Ultra Seminar and our Holistic Faith Healing home study course we have many techniques for influencing the healing mechanism of our own body and also the bodies of other people.

If we will only observe the effects that we cause, we will be able to make intelligent choices about our future actions, and we will have better lives when we do those things that help us.

How to Earn More Money

People often ask me how they should program themselves to obtain more money.

Here's what I have observed:

When people concentrate only on themselves, they get very little.

When they help to correct problems, to relieve pain and suffering and make our world a better place to live, then they prosper.

It seems that the message here is that the creator wants us to help correct problems. When we do that, we are compensated.

Again, I am not saying that we are punished by God when we cause problems, and rewarded by God when we correct problems.

Maybe that is what happens; or maybe it is just an example of the automatic self-correcting mechanism at work.

It seems to me that higher intelligence has also set up another pretty good system, one where we can originate a call and be heard and get help when we deserve it.

This system, like all of the systems that the creator has established, is a good one for us to use.

63 Silva Techniques Give You 3 Ways to Improve Your Genius Ability *(1999)*

We began our research in order to find a way to enhance the educational process, to help students do better in school.

How can we do that?

We found that when a person learns to enter lower frequencies of brain, consciously, then they will find larger amounts of brain energy to make impressions with.

So at the alpha we have more brain energy—it's a less complicated frequency, a more fundamental frequency, where we can function, and we can use that energy to impress information that can be recalled.

Therefore, recall will be a lot easier when we impress information that's stronger.

It is not a matter of just reading a book that counts, or reading as many books as we need that counts. What matters is how much we recall of what we read.

When we can impress information with more brain energy, making a stronger impression on neurons, that makes for easier recall.

We can impress information a lot stronger at the alpha than we can at the beta. Which means that we can recall information impressed at the alpha, a lot easier than we can information impressed at the beta.

So for educational purposes, the Silva Method can be tremendous, because we can learn to function consciously at the alpha to make use of a greater amount of brain energy to make stronger impressions of what our senses detect. That will help in recalling this information a lot easier.

It will also help by enhancing your IQ factor.

You can do away with distractions, you can have superior concentration, and of course, you will have superior understanding . . . all simply by programming to do so, at the alpha level.

We know that we need to impress information on brain cells in order to have something to use.

But once it's there we must be able to use it, by becoming aware that it's there. We can become aware that it's there when it has been impressed strongly, more so than when we have made weak impressions.

So we *can* enhance the IQ factor, because how much information you remember will help you do better, IQ factor-wise.

Use Other Peoples Brains As If They Were Your Own

Another reason why it is excellent for educational purposes is because here is subjective communication.

In the beginning, we thought that our intelligence, human intelligence, could only sense information on its own brain cells.

At the alpha level, you can detect information on your own brain cells, *plus* any information on any neurons, wherever they are.

That's subjective communication.

If you are able to become aware of information impressed on some other brain, then you can make use of that information, or those experiences, as though they were your own.

You do not need to be limited to your own impressions on your own brain cells, because you can now become aware of information impressed on other brains, along with becoming aware of their experiences.

You will be using other human being's experiences as your own, which means:

Now it is not just a matter of reading books and storing information at the beta; it is not just a matter of storing it strongly, and impressing it strongly at the alpha. But also, how you are to *use* this information.

We know that you can improve your IQ factor by recalling information previously impressed. Now, not only at the beta but also at the alpha.

You can also improve the IQ factor by sensing as *how* to use this information, and using the experiences of others in determining how you are to use your own information.

By subjective communication you can find means and ways of using that information in a superior manner.

Which means, IQ factor-wise, it is not just having more information and recalling more information that will make a difference. It is how we use this information; how wisely you apply the use of this information.

By exposing other brains to your awareness, their experiences to your awareness, you are now in a position to use what information you have, along with their information and experiences, very wisely.

This is wisdom.

Wisdom

Accumulation of information, which reaches a level of having knowledge, applied wisely, is wisdom.

You have two dimensions to store information:

You have the beta senses, to store information at the beta region of the brain.

You have the alpha senses, to store information at the alpha region of the brain.

You have subjective communication to become aware of information impressed on other brain cells, which means other brains of other human beings, wherever they are, and to become aware, to sense, how they have been using this information, and use it as your own.

And that is wisdom.

(This information was transcribed from a recording that José Silva made in 1969 for Silva instructors, published in 1999 after his passing.)

64 How Research and Testing With the EEG Lead to Breakthroughs *(1996)*

After reading about Sigmund Freud and the work he had done, we began to search for ways to help our children get better grades in school, and be more successful in all of their activities.

We began to seek ways to improve their minds. As we had success with this, we began to search for the specific factors that were producing the positive results.

In order to help us determine exactly what was going on that was leading to success, we set up projects in the following manner:

Problems were presented to subjects while they were connected to an EEG with a digital counter in the output.

We were training them with various mental exercises, including hypnosis in the beginning. Later we abandoned that for superior methods.

Some subjects, while trying to analyze and answer the problem question, would cause the digital counter on the EEG to indicate 10 cycles per second frequency.

However, the majority would indicate 20 cps while doing the same thing—attempting to analyze and answer the problem question.

This attracted our attention since the average brain frequency range of humans is between 1 and 20 cps.

We observed that when people enter normal, natural, deep sleep, the sleep-and-dream, cycles indicate a movement between 1 and 20 cps on the average.

However, when people are awake, the average brain frequency is 20 cps.

So it seemed unusual to us to observe that approximately 10 percent of our subjects would cause a 10 cps output when analyzing and solving problems.

Since 10 cps is the center of the normal brain frequency range, we began to call those people who did their thinking at 10 cps "centered thinkers" and those who did their thinking at 20 cps "eccentric thinkers."

We then realized that our mental training exercises were teaching our subjects to learn to control their brain waves consciously.

Doing the "Impossible"

At the time, university scientists were saying that it was impossible for people to consciously control their brain wave activity. They challenged us to prove it at the University of Texas Medical School and also at Trinity University, both in San Antonio, Texas.

We were successful in showing them that our trained subjects could enter the alpha level at will and could even activate their minds while at the alpha level, so as to analyze and solve problems. These results were published in a scientific journal in England in 1972.

Since then, it has become accepted knowledge that people can learn to consciously activate their minds at the 10 cps alpha frequency as well as at 20 cps beta.

People receive many benefits when they function consciously at 10 cps alpha.

We have observed that they are healthier because they rarely get sick with psychosomatic health problems.

They are safer because their intuition functions at this level and they rarely get into accidents

One of the most outstanding benefits of being a 10 cycle thinker is that you can use your intuition at that level, and can be more times right than wrong when making decisions, which leads to greater success in life.

All of these factors contribute to people being more successful in life.

We always believed that the 10 cycle alpha level would be the ideal level to solve any kind of problems, especially since the alpha level is the strongest, the level with the least impedance to neuron discharge, and the most synchronous. Thinking should be faster, thoughts and ideas should be more clear, and insight should be better.

Able to Help More People

Despite all of the benefits that were being received by people who used our method, some people were concerned that borderline psychotic patients could be thrown into psychosis when entering the 10 cycle alpha level.

In order to demonstrate that even borderline psychotic patients would not be harmed in any way, we set up a test project with a team of psychiatrists, Dr. Clancy McKenzie, and his associate Dr. Lance Wright.

At first they proceeded very cautiously, sending only one patient at a time and monitoring that patient very closely.

Eventually they began to send groups of patients.

Finally Dr. McKenzie decided that they should recommend that all of their patients use our method to learn to enter the 10 cycle alpha level, and use our techniques for problem solving.

Dr. McKenzie reported that none of their patients became psychotic or was harmed in any way, and virtually all improved. He has provided us with many reports of patients using the alpha level to gain insight and, as a result of this insight, having tremendous breakthroughs and dramatically shortening their recovery time.

He has written of many patients who programmed themselves at the alpha level to have a dream that contains information to help them correct their problems. When they gain insight on their own in this manner, they readily accept it and act on it, according to Dr. McKenzie. He said that he has found this to be one of the best ways for them to hasten their recovery.

Real World Results and Replication

Since that project was conducted, we have gone on to verify through many research projects that the Silva Method can help everyone who wants help and will use the techniques. We have conducted research and verified the many beneficial results with groups such as:

- High school students (Effects with Three High Schools).
- Alcoholics (The Alcoholic Study).
- Executives at a major corporation (RCA Records).
- Single mothers on welfare (The Ottawa County Project).
- Adolescent girls in a Catholic high school (Hallahan High).
- Average people (The Albuquerque Report).
- And of course mental patients (The Consciousness Movement and the Mental Patient).

The research confirmed that regardless of how much or how little success a person has had, they can achieve even more success by learning to activate their mind at 10 cycles alpha.

Now we no longer need to settle for only 10 percent of people being centered, and able to think at 10 cycles alpha, while 90 percent are eccentric, and think only at 20 cycles beta.

Now everyone can learn to center themselves at alpha, activate their mind and analyze and solve problems, and be more successful in life.

What we have accomplished is to convert the sub-conscious into what we call the inner-conscious level.

Now everyone can learn to use the sub-conscious, consciously.

Note: You can learn to enter the powerful alpha brain wave level in the appendix, so that you can enjoy all of these benefits.

65 We Have Finally Solved Life's Biggest Mystery *(1990)*

We now have the answer that people have sought for ages.

Throughout history, people have wanted to know what separates the average person from the person who goes on and rises to super success.

It takes a certain amount of talent, of course, to become super successful. But it is obvious that that's not the answer. A couple of years ago, advertising genius David Ogilvy wrote that he had recently taken an IQ test. It revealed that his IQ was a little below average, he reported.

Ogilvy added he was glad he did not know about his IQ when he was young, or he might have remained a chef and never gone into the advertising business.

Likewise, it is not hard work that causes a person to rise from success to super success. We all know people who are workaholics, but who are not superstars.

Hard work is a necessary ingredient.

But there are a couple of questions that arise:

What gives some people the energy to work that hard?

And why does that help them rise to superstardom, but not other people?

The importance of timing is often cited, and also just plain old fashioned luck. Some people get those "lucky breaks" that help them rise to super success.

The truth is, opportunities come to everyone, although some people do seem to get more than others. And some of the most successful superstars seem to get more bad breaks than the average person, yet they somehow rise above their obstacles to achieve their great success.

In my own life you can see examples of this.

I grew up without a father, and without ever attending school as a student. These were bad breaks that I overcame.

Why?

What was it about me that made it possible—perhaps inevitable— that I would rise above those obstacles?

I got my share of good breaks.

What perfect timing, that I studied a course in radio repair when radios were brand new. I got in on the ground floor.

For as long as people have been around to ask, they have asked the same question: Why?

Why him and not me? Why her instead of someone else?

Now we know the answer. And we are trying to teach it to everyone on the planet.

I like to quote a phrase from the ancient literature, a phrase that helped me understand the answer to the big question.

The phrase goes like this: First enter the kingdom of heaven, and function within God's righteousness, and all else will be added unto you.

There are three parts to that statement. Here is what my research, and my experience and observations, have found:

The super successful people are all able to do their thinking at the alpha brain wave level, where they have access to both the logical left brain hemisphere, and the creative and intuitive right brain hemisphere.

When alpha thinkers have a goal, they are more inspired to strive hard for it, because the alpha thinkers are using more of the brain to reinforce that goal. That gives the alpha thinkers more energy to do the necessary work.

The alpha thinkers also remain healthier, because at alpha you strengthen your immune mechanism. This allows you to work harder.

The alpha thinkers are more intuitive.

This accomplishes several things:

It attracts more "good luck."

It guides you to take advantage of those lucky breaks when they appear.

The alpha thinker has access to more information, because the alpha thinker can obtain information through the subjective senses as well as through the physical senses. Therefore, the alpha thinker makes more correct decisions than the average person.

The next part of that statement deals with functioning within God's righteousness. To me, that means that we were put here on earth to help correct problems, to perfect the creator's creation.

When you use your abilities correctly—to correct problems— then you qualify for the third part of the formula: All else will be added unto you.

To put it simply, the average people find what they are good at, and they use their talent to succeed.

They work long and hard.

They build contacts and network with other people to help them get what they need, and make better decisions.

This accounts for 90 percent of the people on the planet.

The super successful people, the top ten percent, do the same things as the successful people.

And they have one more ingredient in their success formula:

The superstars do their thinking at the alpha level, they strive to solve problems, and while doing this, they keep in mind what their own needs are . . . and a little bit more.

That's the "secret."

They follow the formula that I mentioned above.

That's what every Silva graduate is taught to do.

If you will do the things the successful people do—work hard, use your God-given talents, and so forth—and follow that simple formula, a formula that is attributed to Christ, you will rise far higher than the average person.

Note: You can learn how to enter the powerful alpha brain wave level and use it to solve problems and achieve solutions in the appendix of this book.

66 Remember the Real Purpose of the Silva Method *(1991)*

What is the main purpose of the Silva Method Basic Lecture Series?

People receive many benefits from the BLS (as we call it), depending on what their needs are at the moment.

A lot of people in the world today are under a great deal of stress. One of the benefits they receive from the BLS is to reduce the stress and tension in their lives.

People find it difficult to keep up with the rapid pace of change: for instance, to remember all the things they need to do. The BLS helps them to cope and accomplish their needs.

There are those who find the information in the BLS valuable in making decisions.

Others use some of the techniques in the BLS to help them get rid of bad habits, and start good habits.

The list goes on and on. Just look through the table of contents in your student manual to get an idea of the many benefits you can receive.

The Main Purpose

So back to the original question: What is the main purpose of the BLS?

The main purpose is to get people reconnected to the dimension that they came from when they were born and will go back to when they leave the planet, so that they can get help to solve problems in this dimension while they are here.

We call that dimension "the other side."

Why do we want to be reconnected with the other side?

Because the dimension we call the other side contains the highest level of intelligence that reigns over the entire universe. When we need information to correct problems on this side, we need to be connected so that we can solve more problems.

When there· are problems to be solved, and you are not getting them solved, then you need to do your thinking on the center of the brain frequency spectrum, which normally functions up to 20 cycles per second.

This means you will function at 10 cycles per second alpha, where you are able to use either brain hemisphere to think with. You can think with the logical left brain hemisphere, or the creative and intuitive right brain hemisphere.

How We Help Ourselves

You can use the subjective (mental) dimension to help yourself. You can program yourself to perform a task better, to be more confident, to change habits, to find a new job or a new car, and much, much more.

You can analyze problems while at your level, using the subjective dimension.

While sleeping, your mind can scan all of your brain cells as you go through your normal sleep and dream cycles during the night. You can often find the solution to the problem in this manner.

Sometimes, though, we do not have enough information or experience to be able to develop a solution.

That's when we need help from the other side.

How We Get Help

When we need to solve a difficult problem, we can consult with entities assigned to help us from the other side. They will then become aware of all thoughts that relate to us and to our activities.

When we ask for help from the other side, they are in a position to analyze our situation and help us. They will check and learn what else is happening, or is planned, or has been conceived but not yet manifested, and can guide us so that we will make the best decisions, the best choices, and will take the best possible action.

There are many benefits to this. We will be better at making decisions relating to other people, and doing our jobs.

Our helpers on the other side can survey the big picture and determine, for instance, what is causing excess stress—distress—in our life and guide us to correct the cause of the· problem.

They will guide us to whomever and whatever can help us correct problems.

How to Get the Help You Need

How do you get this help from the other side?

First, you have to do your job here on planet earth.

What is that job?

Solving problems and improving living condition on the planet for yourself and others.

As we say in the very first Beneficial Statement in the Course: "Your increasing mental faculties are for serving humanity better."

The better you are at solving problems, the easier it is to get help when you need it.

We get calls here at the office from Silva graduates who ask us to solve their problems for them. Many of these graduates have not practiced, have not repeated the Course, have not participated in graduate groups and helped other graduates.

We advise them to practice what we teach in the Courses. Then they will find it easy to get help from higher intelligence.

Using the MentalVideo

I learned long ago that I cannot solve everybody's problems.

But help is available to you. Higher intelligence has seen to that. All you have to do is ask.

You can use the MentalVideo Technique to communicate directly with higher intelligence at night while you sleep, to make your needs known.

This is what makes the Silva Systems different from all other self-improvement programs.

We show you how to actually get the help that higher intelligence will provide for you, to help you correct problems on this side and help to convert the world into a paradise.

Note: José Silva wrote this in 1991. We have updated it with new information he received from higher intelligence in 1997 that resulted in the MentalVideo Technique

You can learn the MentalVideo Technique right now in appendix D.

67 Are Russians More Advanced in Psychic Phenomena *(1981)*

It has just become a matter of public record that the US Defense Department has allowed the expenditure of funds for the study of psychic phenomena and how they can be used in defense strategies.

As was perhaps expected, the public outcry against such studies was great, and the Defense Department was immediately taken to task for spending time, effort and money in what people thought to be a waste of everything.

But is it a waste?

The reason why psychic phenomena were being studied for defense purposes was simply because of reports that Russian scientists have been doing it for years, and that Russia has become a leading reservoir of knowledge in this field.

In essence, the problem that the Defense Department faces is one of fixed values and a suspicion of anything that cannot be proven immediately in laboratory tests. In the United States, people pride themselves on being "rational," and "pragmatic." If something cannot be proven or if it does not work immediately there is no sense of continuing. For something to be accepted, it must first of all be "understood."

Yet, despite all of this rational tradition and love of "what works" the chief problems in the country are those that are not "understood" and those which stem from things that cannot be clinically "tested" and scientifically "isolated."

The brain, for example, is generally conceded to be the body's most wondrous organ, one that holds the key to our very existence. The tremendous powers of the brain are generally accepted.

But are they "understood?"

Why do placebos work?

What power—and from what origin does it emanate—does the brain possess over other organs of the body that it can eliminate pain simply by some form of "message" the brain provides when it believes some form of medicine has been ingested when in reality such was not the case?

Why does soft music put us in melancholic moods?

Why do we cry?

Why do we dream?

What prompts the brain to provide us with mysterious "hunches" that, if followed, may prove to be right?

Why do we react differently to similar experiences?

Why do color schemes affect the way we think or feel?

Why can some people adapt to even hostile environments when others are incapable of doing so?

All of these questions deal, in one form or another, with "unknown" variables. While medical science offers explanations which are satisfying, the total reason why we do these things has never been given.

There are many things about the human mind and the natural order of things that we still have not comprehended. Instead of impeding the quest for this knowledge, we ought to encourage it.

Whatever our human intellect holds in store for us, we can use for the betterment of humanity. We should never be afraid to unlock it.

Note: The Russians were having the same problems getting support for psychic research as we were, according to Dr. J. W. Hahn, our top consultant. The story about the CIA Psychics broke a decade later and confirmed it.

68 These 7 Subjects Provided Silva Method's Foundation *(1988)*

The study of seven different subjects went into the formation of the Silva Method.

Credit should be given to each of these subjects in contributing to the Silva Method as it is today.

1. The study of the Bible, Old and New Testaments.

Every time we came across something in research that appeared to be beneficial to human beings, and we thought that it should be added to and made a part of the Silva Method, before adding it to the Method, we made sure that it did not conflict with the Bible's Old and New Testaments.

2. The study of the beginning of all religions, and the creation of churches and their buildings: when, by whom, and under what conditions.

Later, because of research in psychometry, I became interested in studying psychometry and church buildings. Here is why:

The human being walks around surrounded by a globe of energy called the aura, that reaches out in all directions to a distance of no less than twenty-five feet (about eight meters). Everything that this human energy field touches is programmed automatically.

By programmed we mean that the aura alters at some depth the state of matter in relation to our thoughts and experiences.

The walls of a church are saturated with thoughts of thousands upon thousands of people who have entered the building with the thought of communicating with our creator.

You may or may not believe in the rabbi, priest or minister; they come and go. But the building stays and continues to host thousands upon thousands of people who radiate and continue to program every bit of mortar, wood and steel with the desire to communicate with our creator, making it easier for those of us who follow, to find the channel of communication with their creator.

Many of my ideas came to me while in my church.

3. The study of the writings and instructions given by a Jewish Rabbi named Jesus and called Christ. He is the Jewish Rabbi who is given credit for the founding of the Christian church.

In studying Christ's sayings and comparing them with our research findings, we found very close similarities. This helped us to develop techniques that helped people.

4. The study of the greats in mind science and research, such as the magnetizers, mesmerizers, and hypnotizers from the past, to the psychologists, psychiatrists and hypnoanalysts of the present.

The one who impressed me the most as a researcher in the field of the mind was not one of the best known. His name is Phineas Parkhurst Quimby, who lived from 1802 to 1866.

Here was a man who became attuned to the same message of passing on to humanity, Christ's discovery that human beings can and should function on more than one plane with full awareness.

5. The study of psychology, hypnosis, parapsychology, electro-encephalography, and electronics.

The study of psychology helped us understand human beings better.

The study of hypnosis helped us become better acquainted with the power of our phenomenal minds.

The study of parapsychology helped us to know what others had done in the field and how they did it.

The study of electroencephalography helped us to distinguish the difference between the brain, the mind, and human intelligence.

We have come to accept human intelligence to be what religions call soul or spirit, and different from animal intelligence.

Animal intelligence is also known as cell or biological intelligence.

We also have come to accept the human brain as a biological computer that can be programmed by human intelligence to function automatically, to function semi-automatically, or to function manually through programming.

As for the human mind, we do not consider it to be a thing, but a faculty of human intelligence, existing in what we consider a non-physical dimension, attuning itself to a certain region of the brain that exists in the physical dimension.

Since everything has to do with electro-chemical-magnetic energy interaction, the study of electronics was very helpful.

6. The study of so-called unorthodox medicine, such as faith healing, psychic healing and spiritual healing.

This research has been very exciting, interesting and beneficial.

The most impressive thing is to see a healer use an unorthodox method of healing to correct one of the so-called chronic, incurable, or irreversible health problems, such as arthritis, diabetes, glaucoma, cancer, leukemia, allergies or migraine.

We have seen so much done with the use of unorthodox methods that we wonder when someone is going to establish a branch of medicine that encompasses all unorthodox methods of healing to take care of the chronic and "incurable" cases.

Since the very beginning of our work on the Silva Method, we have included all of the common elements that use the patient's own belief systems and mental attitudes to enhance the healing process.

This makes a Silva Method graduate an ideal patient, one who will respond more quickly to all types of treatment.

7. The study of ontology.

This led us to understand that we are representatives of Higher Intelligence.

We call the creator, or God, Higher Intelligence. We believe it is our obligation, our mission, to take care of creation on our plane of existence. We are just now becoming aware that we can do on our plane of existence, what the creator does in the whole universe.

We believe that Higher Intelligence needed someone to take care of this part of creation, so we were created for that purpose.

In order to take care of our mission, we must place at the top of our list of items of importance the correction of all problems.

We think that a problem is anything that keeps the flow of the creative process from reaching perfection.

For us in the Silva Method, we believe that God is the highest of intelligences because God can solve all problems.

We believe that persons who solve many problems are closer to God.

Keep in mind that when we cause a problem we are against God, because problems hurt the creator's creation.

We believe that a coincidence is a mechanism through which Higher Intelligence helps us from another dimension, when we ask for help from the right dimension, in the right manner, for the right thing, at the right time.

The Silva Method will help us find the right dimension, and help us learn to ask in the right manner, for the right thing, at the right time.

69 Researcher From the Past Guided Us In Our Work *(1988)*

During my twenty-two years of research that led to the development of the Silva Method, I studied what had been done by the greats in the field of mind research.

The man who impressed me the most was not one of the best known of the so-called greats.

His name was Phinias Parkhurst Quimby, who was born in 1802 and who made his transition in 1866.

Here was a man who became attuned to the same message that I did, of passing on to humanity Christ's discovery that human beings can and should function on more than one plane with full awareness.

Dr. Quimby appears to have gone through everything we experienced in our research, with only minor differences.

But these "minor differences," from another point of view, do make a great difference.

For example, the coincidence of Quimby finding a naturally developed psychic, Lucius Berkbar, and observing what Lucius could do with his mind, must have been the most important stimulating factor that caused Quimby to continue with his research.

It appears that Quimby's objective was to become a healer, using Lucius for the detection of problems in subjects, and for recommending a medication.

It also appears that later Quimby himself, in an unknown way, became a clairvoyant, and healed people with what he called "The silent method."

It was apparent that Quimby valued very highly the faculty of clairvoyance in Lucius.

It was through our study of Quimby and Lucius that we became aware of the great value of clairvoyance.

But there is quite a difference between using a subject that has a naturally developed faculty of clairvoyance, and using a subject whose faculty of clairvoyance we had to develop. It took us nine years to develop the first trained clairvoyant.

We believe that it is one thing to apply healing to a person whose health problems you become aware of through the physical senses, and another thing to apply healing to a person whose health problems you become aware of through the use of the psychic senses, through clairvoyance.

We believe that the best thing is to detect the problem clairvoyantly, to insure that you would be the best level for correcting the problem through the use of psychic healing; when you do this, the healing would take place at the same level where you detected the problem.

During our research on Quimby, we found one of Quimby's patients (who later became a student of his) with a familiar name: Mary Baker Eddy, founder of the Christian Science Church.

We found several names in reference to her, such as Mary M. Patterson, Mary Baker Grover, Mary Baker, G. Eddy, and finally Mary Baker Eddy.

We also found several names in reference to the Christian Science work, such as Science of Man, Mental Science, Science of Health, and finally Christian Science.

In the past 100 years, the Christian Science Movement has developed into a massive operation. This growth indicates that people like what is there, so Mary Baker Eddy must have done the right thing at the right time.

Better still, Mary Baker Eddy was a good student and must have learned her lesson well, and applied it well.

She must have been Quimby's star pupil to have been the only one to do what she did with Quimby's research findings.

The Silva Method confirms that Quimby was right in his discovery of the scientific method of what we now call scientific prayer healing.

Healers using our method of prayer healing, where they first detect the problem clairvoyantly, usually do better than healers who are told what the health problem is beforehand, as was the case with Quimby's pupils.

We believe that our system will carry humanity forward even more than Christian Science, because we are teaching more than what Mary Baker Eddy got from Quimby: We teach our students how to develop clairvoyance.

Our students learn to detect health problems clairvoyantly, even at a distance. This is apparently what Quimby learned to do for his own use just before his transition.

The Silva ESP training trains people to become clairvoyants, to function like Lucius and like Quimby, so that they can use their clairvoyance to become healthier, more intuitive and productive, and more successful problem-solving agents on this planet.

70 Do It Yourself and Correct the Cause of the Problem *(1993)*

When I first began my research, I read about how Freud had used hypnosis.

Although Freud had some success with hypnosis, he also learned that the great rapport that is established could also lead to trouble—he became romantically involved with one of his patients.

Nevertheless, I started experimenting with hypnosis. It turned out that I was a very effective hypnotist.

I believed that a person's IQ was simply a measurement of their ability to solve problems. The more problems you solve, the higher your IQ. So I began using hypnosis to search for ways to improve my subject's ability to recall information, so that they could get more right answers and solve more problems.

I had some success with this. But at the same time, I. realized that there were some severe limitations:

The deeper I took the subjects into hypnosis, the less they remembered (the more they forgot) about the hypnotic session.

At deep hypnotic levels, they could answer questions, but they could not ask questions.

At deep hypnotic levels, they could reason inductively, but not deductively. When I gave them a problem to solve, they could not remain at those deep levels and reason deductively to find a solution to the problem.

The subjects gained something by using hypnosis, but they also lost something, they gave something up.

My Hypnotized Subject Began to Take Control

Eventually, after many hypnotic sessions, one of the subjects began to function differently: She told me what I was going to ask her . . . before I asked!

I had been reading poems to her the day before, and I wanted to find out if she remembered the poems. But I added a twist: I planned to ask her to recite them back in a different order than the order that I'd read them to her.

Before I asked her to read the first poem, she told me which one I wanted, and proceeded to recite it. Then she did the next, and the next, and the next.

Actually, she started with the second, then the third, then the fourth. She got them in the right order, but was one ahead of me.

The event surprised me so much that I shifted my research and began to investigate two new areas:

1. Subjective communication: her seeming ability to "guess my mind."
2. How she seemed to have developed the ability to become mentally active while under hypnosis to ask questions, to reason deductively.

With continuing research, I eventually developed a method so that people can actually learn to use the untapped power of the mind without having to give anything up.

Silva Students Are Always In Control

From the beginning, when you attend the Silva training, you gain greater awareness. You do not give up any control or any awareness to the lecturer or anyone else. You are always in control.

From the beginning, you are able to direct your attention where you desire it, and *you* are able to use your mind to relax your body.

Here is a major difference between hypnosis and the Silva Method:

In hypnosis, the hypnotic operator would direct your body to relax by saying, "Your scalp will now relax."

In the Silva Method's Standard Conditioning Cycle (the Silva Centering Exercise) you are instructed to "Release and relax all tensions and ligament pressures and place your scalp into a deep state of relaxation. . . ."

Notice the difference?

In one instance, the hypnotic operator is taking charge of your body, while in the Silva Centering Exercise, you yourself are gaining greater control.

The Benefits of Being In Charge

This is not just done as a safety factor, to keep you from falling under somebody's spell.

There is a very practical advantage, and it is what makes our Method so successful:

When you enter deep levels of mind by yourself—without being directed and managed by a hypnotist—and you apply the formula type techniques yourself, then, the results you get will be much better.

Take the Headache Control Technique for instance.

I learned, while practicing hypnosis, that I could give a suggestion, before I brought the subject out of hypnosis, that they would not have a headache, and sure enough they would not have a headache.

By doing this, I was able to relieve a subject's headache.

But I was not able to bring the headache problem to an end. The subjects would continue to get headaches.

In the Silva Method, you learn how to get rid of your own headache, without the aid of a hypnotic operator.

Even Greater Benefits

But that's not even the best part.

That's not all: When you continue to get rid of your tension and migraine headaches with the Headache Control Technique, "the body forgets how to cause them, bringing to an end the migraine problem, without the use of drugs."

The best part is: Even though the technique does not address the underlying tension that is causing the headaches, the problem is still eliminated. There are no substitute symptoms. The tension and stress does not surface in some other form.

It is as if the tension itself is eliminated, rather than just the headache.

How can this be?

Here's how.

Even More Benefits

When you enter level on your own, and you apply the formula-type technique yourself, then your mind will do whatever is necessary to eliminate the cause of the problem.

Not just the problem—but the *cause* of the problem.

Drugs can reduce or eliminate a headache, but not the tension that causes the headache.

The same is true of hypnosis.

The implications of this are far reaching.

Whether you want to eliminate headaches or other pain, heal an illness in your body, eliminate a bad habit, improve your memory, become more creative and intuitive, enhance your ability to think and reason and to come up with good solutions to problems—whatever you want to accomplish, when you enter your level on your own and do the programming yourself, you will get much better results than using somebody or something else to do it for you.

Hypnosis, when used properly by people who are properly trained and qualified to use it, can be helpful in certain situations.

Hypnotherapists can sometimes help with deep rooted problems that the subject cannot reach on their own. But you need therapists who know what they are doing, or it can quickly become an unpleasant experience.

On the other hand, you can use the Silva Method for any kind of problem at any time without any fear of running into any kind of problem or unpleasant situation, because *you* are in charge.

You are not going to move into any areas that are uncomfortable for you.

In fact, when you use the Silva techniques and follow the five steps that are used, in one form or another, in all of our problem solving processes, results can come very easily.

Five Steps to Success

First you identify the problem that you are having now. Then you identify the solution, the goal, that you want now.

You don't necessarily have to go back into the past, or worry about why you have the problem. If that information will help, then you will become aware of it. Then make your plan, work your plan, and expect results. The formula is covered in more detail in your student manual, so I won't dwell on it here.

The Silva Method is unique. It accomplishes what no other method has ever done: It puts you in charge of more of your life; it puts you in charge of your mind and your own thoughts and mental processes.

When you control your own mind, then you control your own life.

That's why our method has been so successful. It doesn't just work for a few people:

It works for people in ninety-four countries;

It works for people in twenty-seven different languages;

It works for people of many different religious beliefs;

It has been helping people change their lives for the better for more than twenty-five years, and millions of people say, "Thank you, Mr. Silva, for showing me how to change my life for the better."

And I tell them, "Congratulate yourself, because you did it."

Note: You can learn many of our techniques in the appendix of this book.

71　While Others Treat Symptoms, You Can Correct the Cause Of Problems　*(1986)*

You have a kind of intelligence within you that will correct problems even when you do not know what causes the problem or bow to correct it.

All you have to do to use this intelligence to correct problems is to enter the proper level of mind—the alpha level—to identify the problem, give the proper instructions, and have faith that it will be corrected.

Let's take some examples.

If you have a tension or a migraine headache, first you enter your level and identify the problem.

Then you give the proper instructions—the program you will follow as you count yourself out.

If you desire that the problem be corrected, believe it is possible, and then claim your desired end result, it happens.

Correcting the Cause

That takes care of the symptoms. But what about. the cause of the problem?

Since you are performing the process yourself, this special intelligence within you automatically corrects the cause of the problem. This is why there are no substitute symptoms for the stress that is causing the tension and migraine headaches.

Your inner intelligence has taken care of the cause of the problem.
An outside agent usually cannot take care of the cause for you.

Drugs do not treat the cause of the problem. Nor does a hypnotist.

But when you apply the corrective procedure that you learned in the Silva Method, then your own inner intelligence takes care of the outer manifested problem by correcting the inner cause of the problem.

Other Solutions

You also learn how to take care of habits and addictions in the same manner.

To eliminate a bad habit such as smoking, or drug addiction, enter your level every day and program that on a certain date, thirty days from the date of your initial programming, you will be a non smoker, or a non addict.

When you do this, you are literally claiming a new lifestyle for yourself, and this inner intelligence will take care of whatever is causing the problem.

You can program yourself with the Mirror of the Mind or the 3-Scenes Technique and achieve the same results in any area of your life.

If you want to change your personality, enter your level, identify the problem, give the proper instructions, and have faith—desire, belief and expectancy. You will get your results.

Period.

Understanding the Cause

Sometimes it may help to understand the cause of the problem, to understand the prior programming that has brought about a limiting belief system for instance.

But generally, this is not necessary.

You understand everything at some level. All you need to do is to give your inner intelligence the proper instructions, with desire, belief and expectancy, and you will correct the problems you want to correct.

Remember that the key is doing it yourself, and doing it from the proper level of mind—the alpha level.

Practice, and soon you will begin to take for granted the kind of successes you once thought of as miracles.

Note: You can learn the Silva problem-solving techniques in the appendix.

72 A Prophet Who Inspired the Silva Research *(1985)*

We had a wonderful visit shortly before Christmas with an organization that has been a pioneer in the field of parapsychology and research of human potential. It is an organization that all Silva graduates will find interesting and can learn from.

Forty years ago I first became aware of the founder of this organization, although I had no idea at the time that my research would lead me into the same area that made him famous. It turned out that, to a certain extent, his life served to inspire me and guide me in the development of the Silva Method.

When I was in the army in 1945 I was assigned to a camp near Bowling Green, Kentucky, the birthplace of Edgar Cayce.

Since I had become interested in psychology, I was curious about what this man had done. This contact made me aware that things such as clairvoyance were possible, and it influenced my research later on.

In my early research, I was working with hypnosis. When my research subjects began guessing what I was thinking about, I recalled that it was a hypnotist that had cured Cayce of a serious throat affliction, and after that he became an excellent clairvoyant.

Thus the "coincidence" of being assigned to that particular military base just as I was becoming interested in the human mind turned out to be a very significant factor in the process that resulted in the development of the Silva Method.

Later in my research, I had some contact with representatives of the organization that grew out of Cayce's experiences: the Association for Research and Enlightenment, Inc. (ARE). But we had some misunderstandings, and did not continue working together.

At the time, both organizations were so busy studying, researching and promoting their own works that they had little time for one another. It may have been a mistake to have allowed this situation to exist for so long.

Edgar Cayce was known as the "Sleeping Prophet." He was one of the great clairvoyants. While at deep levels of mind, he could detect illnesses in people and recommend corrective action. "The Edgar Cayce Readings" are still studied by many, and are still helping people.

He led the way and established standards that other clairvoyants strive to match. His son, Hugh Lynn Cayce, deserves tremendous credit for helping to make so many millions of people around the world aware of the Sleeping Prophet and his abilities.

While in Virginia Beach in December to conduct a Holistic Faith Healing Workshop, I took advantage of the opportunity to visit ARE headquarters. There I met with Charles Thomas Cayce, grandson of Edgar Cayce and now the president of ARE.

We had a very enjoyable and informative afternoon together and parted with a mutual respect for each other.

Tom Cayce is a nice, pleasant individual, easy to get along with. He is easy to communicate with, very pleasant to talk to, and we had a nice conversation. He was very receptive to hearing me out on the misunderstandings we'd had with some of the individuals associated with the Cayce organization in the past.

I'd visited ARE previously, and had seen the old buildings.

Now they have new buildings and a new look. It is all very attractive, and something they can be extremely proud of.

Tom Cayce said he was going to learn the Silva Method, and we agreed to let our graduates know about the benefits the ARE has to offer. It feels good to know we will be helping each other.

Edgar Cayce was, indeed, a prophet—in many ways. Not only was he able to help tens of thousands of people directly, and millions more through his example, but he also served as a symbol of what is to come in the future when all of the inhabitants of our planet develop their clairvoyant abilities.

73 If the Government Wants Remote Viewers *(1996)*

What do you think the United States government thinks of psychic ability?

The Central Intelligence Agency (CIA) was willing to spend $11 million (some say it was actually $20 million) to see if psychics could help in the espionage game.

We could have told them that thirty years ago. As a matter of fact, we did!

On my birthday, August 11, 1965, I decided to give the US government a gift worth millions of dollars.

I wrote a letter to President Lyndon Johnson offering to give the government all of my research, free of charge.

I had invested more than $500,000 of my own money and time, so it was not exactly a small gift that I was offering.

At least they were polite enough to answer me. But they gave the wrong answer!

"There is much yet to be learned about the activities of the human mind," the letter from Randal M. Robertson, Associate Director of the National Science Foundation said, "and there are many unsettled questions about hypnosis and about paranormal activities. There does not seem to be any specific need at present for the assistance you have offered."

Many Benefits of Right Brain Thinking

Can you imagine, if President Johnson had known how to use his mind to get more information and make better decisions, he might have been able to prevent the deaths of so many human beings in Vietnam, and might not have had to give up the Presidency and return home a broken man who died shortly after.

The government might not have seen a need way back then, but the public did.

People at the grass roots level have embraced the Silva Method. Today the Silva Method is being taught in 103 countries and territories around the world, in twenty-nine different languages. We have more than 1,000 instructors carrying the work forward.

And graduates in every language say, "Thank you for showing me how to change my life for the better."

The CIA and the Pentagon got good results for their millions of dollars. Some reports say the psychics were correct fifteen percent of the time, well above chance levels.

On the Larry King Live television program one of the people involved in the project said that in one instance the psychics located all twelve submarines that they were asked to find.

As you know, Silva graduates are often 100 percent accurate on the cases they work. But not always. Their overall accuracy is about 80 percent, much better than the CIA's remote viewers.

Instead of spending $20 million, they should pay us a few hundred dollars each to train their own staff people to use their clairvoyant ability. They are the experts in their own field, and they could do amazing work . . . if they would.

Regardless of what the government does, we'll continue with our own work.

In this field, our track record is much better than the government's!

Remote viewing is just one of the many techniques taught in the Silva Method. We are leading the way into the second phase of human evolution on this planet.

The Second Phase of Human Evolution

What do I mean when I say, The second phase of human evolution of this planet?

Everything indicates that we have completed the first phase; it is apparent we have advanced as far as we are going to advance objectively.

We have mastered space, the sea, the plants and animals, the earth itself.

What we have not mastered is our own human nature.

We are using our human abilities incorrectly and causing terrible damage to our world and its inhabitants.

Research indicates that we have been created to take care of the planet at this dimension. This means we should protect and supervise its development.

This is a huge responsibility. Yet we humans are still fighting each other and destroying more than we are creating. Many want to gain at someone else's expense.

Others are becoming millionaires while poisoning the planet's air and water.

We mature adults are causing the problem.

Why?

Not Yet Fully Developed

The only logical answer is that most humans are not yet fully developed. They do not know how to use the alpha brainwave level to think with and to obtain information that they can use to make better decisions and correct problems.

There are thousands of seminars to help develop the left brain hemisphere—from motivational seminars to winning friends and influencing people to NLP to computer sciences and on to the "challenge" courses like mountain climbing, high ropes courses, fire walking, and more.

All of those left brain courses, for the physical senses, are fine, but what about the subjective, intuitive right brain hemisphere?

This is where the Silva ESP training comes in.

We now have a method to guide humans through a series of mental projection exercises into inanimate matter, plant life, animal life, and human life, in order to develop the subjective, intuitive right brain hemisphere.

We must develop the right brain hemisphere, as we have already developed the left hemisphere, if we are to have any hope of correcting the problems on our planet.

It will be like being born again. Following our biological birth, we have spent our lifetime developing our left brain hemisphere and our physical (biological) senses.

Now it is time to start anew and develop our right brain hemisphere and our subjective senses.

Then we will think with the right and act with the left. We will function in a balanced manner, as nature intended, and we will find solutions for the problems that are killing us and our planet.

There are three main areas we need to concentrate in at this time:

• Health
• Family relations
• Business

This applies to everyone, regardless of race, religion, creed, or national origin.

All indications indicate that humans have reached the saturation point in left brain development. An indicator of this is that many "developed nations" now have run out of reserves, are faced with increasing debts, with future generations facing the prospects of a lower quality of life.

Learning to use the infinite capacity of the right brain to solve problems is what we call the second phase of human evolution on the planet.

This will help us to know one another better. It will help us to get all that we need for ourselves without taking anything from anyone else, without hurting anybody. It will end the desire to fight and kill one another. It will convert our planet into a paradise.

Thank you for helping to spread the word about the Silva Method and how your loved ones and friends can learn to use the untapped power of their minds to correct problems. Remember that we can train a group of people to specialize in medicine, business, electronics, agriculture, industry, and in all other fields.

Call on us for any help you need.

Thank you.

74 Develop Superstar Qualities to Bring You More Success In Life *(1985)*

What makes a champion? What are some of the star qualities you see in highly successful people?

What goes through the mind of a superstar during training? While practicing? In competition when success or failure hangs in the balance?

There are several characteristics that are common to the stars in athletes, business, industry, science, art and other endeavors.

Champions are persistent and dedicated. They are able to control and direct their physical and mental energies.

And when they make decisions they are more often right than wrong.

The Most Important Quality

The most important quality I've observed is persistence. You can achieve any kind of goal you set for yourself if you make it the most important thing in your life and sacrifice everything else for it. There are people who do that. But that is not necessarily what I'd call success. Achieving a single limited goal at the expense of everything else is usually not worthy of a person's whole life.

To achieve success, you not only reach your goal but you are also able to take advantage of the benefits that come along with your accomplishment.

To achieve success in life takes as much persistence as reaching a single goal. Perhaps more.

To reach your goals, you must make them more important than anything else. Any time something else comes up that seems important, you should analyze it at your level and put it in its proper perspective: second to your primary goal.

Sometimes things distract you from your primary goal. At that time it is important to relax, enter the alpha state of mind and analyze it. If you want to be a champion, you have to stick to your major goal, whatever it is. All else must be secondary, regardless how attractive it may be at the time.

How can you use this quality of persistence to become successful in all aspects of life? Let's consider a busy executive with many important tasks.

If executives value their health as being important to help them reach their primary goal, then they must program themselves to do the things they needs to do to maintain their health, vitality and energy so they can get what they want out of life.

To put this idea into practice, first determine just what you must do: how many hours per week must you exercise if you are to reach your goal?

Then set up a schedule, and do not let anything interfere with that schedule. The time that you set aside for exercise is just as important as your primary goal. If you sacrifice one exercise session to deal with some other problem associated with your primary goal, you are not helping yourself, for you will suffer in the health and fitness area.

Use a holistic approach: Determine your primary goal. Then determine the ingredients necessary to help you reach that goal. In addition, analyze why you want to reach that goal; when you do this, you may find goals that are really important to you, goals that will spell success in life for you.

There are always several ingredients involved in reaching goals. All of these must be taken into consideration.

If you cannot demonstrate discipline in the various ingredients that go into your formula for reaching your primary goal, you are not likely to have the discipline necessary for the big things when they come along.

Here's How to Proceed

You must be healthy both mentally and physically. The best way to make the necessary decisions on what to do is to spend some time in quiet contemplation and meditation.

To achieve your goals, program yourself at an alpha state of mind. Whenever you deviate, reprogram yourself at alpha and correct your ways. Make the correction immediately, as soon as you notice a tendency to deviate. Avoid developing bad habits.

Meditation brings mental health. Physical exercise promotes physical health. The two together will boost you towards your goal.

You can learn to reach an alpha state of mind by learning the Silva Centering Exercise with the free training in appendix A.

To help you in the areas of athletics and fitness, we developed the Silva Star Athlete program.

The various audio recordings will help you improve your concentration and your performance, improve your visualization and imagination, make better decisions, recover from injuries more rapidly, improve your nutritional program and more.

Set your goals. Take time to learn and use the alpha level to help you make correct decisions, and to program yourself to achieve such goals.

And persist. Do this and you will succeed.

Note from José Silva Jr.: My father was a professional athlete, a successful businessman, an author, scientist, and the creator of the Silva Method and the Silva UltraMind ESP Systems, used by millions of people worldwide since 1944.

Please see the appendix for a special offer that you can use to obtain the Silva Star Athlete workshop and other Silva courses.

75 How Knowledge Once Saved Me From Injury *(1982)*

Ignorance does not exempt us from suffering. Knowledge helps us to escape suffering.

The more we know about our world and how it really is, the less we need to suffer. The more skills we have learned and practiced, the less we need to suffer.

I learned this lesson early in life, and it has helped me ever since. I've always been both curious and observant, with an inner compulsion to know more about life and the way things are. This is how, at the age of seven, I learned that a company needed its offices cleaned, but was having trouble finding someone to do it. Because of this knowledge I gained through listening to people talk as I shined their shoes, I got a contract to clean their offices, and earned very good money doing it.

Later, as a teenager, I learned how ignorance could hurt me . . . physically. I got into a fight, the first of my life.

Although I knew I was stronger than the other boy and could tear him apart if I could get my hands on him, I never got my hands on him. He knew how to box, and his superior skill won out over my superior strength.

The next day, I signed up for boxing lessons. I became a very good boxer, and for five years traveled with a boxing club for matches in various cities. I was never knocked out. Outside of the ring, I have never started a fight.

After I stopped boxing, I was not in another fight for almost ten years. Then, while working to repair a coin operated machine in a noisy bar one Saturday night, a man who had a mean reputation, and who outweighed me by at least a hundred pounds, decided he wanted to fight me.

I told this man I was fixing the machine so he could use it. I had left my supper to do this for a good customer of mine, and I wanted to get back home and eat. But this bully, who weighed about 230 pounds to my 130 pounds, picked me up bodily, carried me outside and threw me down. Then he told me he was going to knock out all my teeth, and was going to beat me up so bad even my own mother wouldn't recognize me.

The first time he came at me, I just backed away to see if he knew how to box. If he did, I was going to run in the other direction. I made sure he did not back me into a corner. The second time he came at me, I backed away again, just to make sure.

The third time he came at me, throwing punches, I beat him to the punch. Every time he would swing at me, I beat him to the punch. He never hit me. Eventually we wound up in the middle of a busy intersection, both of us covered with his blood, and my big opponent afraid to swing at me because he got hurt every time he did. I never hit him unless he swung at me first.

My knowledge of boxing certainly saved me from a lot of suffering, and possibly saved my life. That man would have hurt me very badly if he could have. He wanted to. I think it is foolish to pay fighters millions of dollars to punch each other in the face for an hour! That was not my reason for learning to box.

Since that time, I have had no more fist fights. But I have continued to learn and acquire knowledge and to put that knowledge to use to solve problems and relieve suffering on this planet.

It does no good just to acquire knowledge. To have any value, knowledge must be applied. And the correct application of knowledge is to solve problems.

And the more you practice solving problems, the more skill you will obtain (your talents will grow) so the more effective you will be at solving problems.

76 Here's How to Get Feedback to Improve Mental Ability *(1986)*

Practice provides feedback.

No skill has ever been learned by humans without feedback.

We learn to walk by trial and error. The error—a fall—provides information to the brain and the error is avoided in the future.

In learning to talk, our ears give us feedback.

Similarly, learning to play a musical instrument is possible only with practice, during which we receive auditory feedback.

The mind as healer thrives on feedback.

You relax and picture positively. You fail to activate the healing process. Again you relax and picture positively. This time you heal.

You have learned through feedback.

Perhaps you relaxed in a different way the second time, or perhaps you imagined more clearly, or perhaps you spent more time.

Whatever you did differently then becomes part of your improved skill, thanks to the feedback that practice provides.

We know that true prosperity comes from living a balanced life, from functioning effectively in both the objective and the subjective dimensions.

We learn to function effectively in the objective dimension through practice and feedback.

We learn to use our sensing faculties to provide us with information so we can make correct decisions.

We learn the most effective ways to take action in the physical dimension to bring us the results we desire.

We must also learn to use the subjective dimension just as effectively, to bring us information and to learn the most effective ways to take action.

What is the best way to develop our skills in the subjective dimension?

That is: What is the best way to practice and get feedback in the subjective dimension?

The Best Way

The best way is through working health detection and correction cases after you complete our ESP training.

When you work health cases, first you practice using your subjective senses to get information.

Then you practice taking subjection action, and the result of your action provides feedback that you can use to keep getting better and better in the future.

Why is case working such a good exercise to develop your skills in the subjective dimension?

There are several reasons.

First, since you are working on real problem cases, there is a greater chance you will be accurate.

It is always easier to program for a necessity than a luxury.

So practice first on serious problem cases.

Second, the feedback is immediate, so you will learn more rapidly.

When you work a case with an orientologist who has the information about the subject, then you will get feedback as soon as you give a complete report on the subject, while you are still at your level and still have the subject on your mental screen.

This allows you to establish points of reference immediately.

Third, this will build your confidence like nothing else can.

Get together with an orientologist one evening and work a dozen health cases.

When you have several "hits" on each case, and you get all of the positive feedback, you will begin to feel very confident.

Then later, when you are ready to program for a raise or a better job, a new car or your ideal mate, a better self-image or a dream vacation, you will be much more effective.

You will be more effective because you will not just *think* that you are functioning correctly. You will *know* you are functioning correctly and effectively.

Seek the feedback. Practice.

And you will succeed.

Note: If you have not taken the Silva ESP training yet, you can start now with the free lessons in the appendix.

77 Let Your Light Shine and Achieve Something Significant *(1990)*

Light cannot be overcome by darkness.

Success cannot be overcome by challenges.

Truth cannot be overcome by negativity.

The good works that you do cannot be overcome by detractors.

Light always banishes darkness.

Persistence overcomes challenges and success follows.

Truth eventually wins out over negativity, cynicism, criticism and doubt.

No Such Thing as Failure

Light cannot be overcome by darkness, because there is no such thing as darkness. There are just different degrees of light.

Darkness does not exist. The only way to have darkness is to take away light.

There is either light, or no light.

There is no such thing as failure.

You either succeed, or you are on the road to success.

You might quit, and that could be considered failure. But as long as you continue to try, you are not a failure.

Successful People Overcome Challenges

Some of the most successful people began as apparent failures. But they did not stop, they stayed on the path until they achieved something significant.

Albert Einstein failed math. But he did not quit.

Helen Keller could not see, hear, or speak. She was an unmanageable child, and no one could even communicate with her. But one person believed in her, and began to communicate through the sense of touch. Eventually Helen Keller became a world famous author, and a sought after speaker. She stayed on the path until she achieved something significant.

Abraham Lincoln went broke in business, was defeated for election repeatedly, and finally was elected President of the United States by politicians who thought that they could control this simple backwoods lawyer.

Abraham Lincoln spoke truth, and did what he believed he should do, and is generally regarded by historians as the best President in the history of the United States.

Light cannot be overcome by darkness.

Nobody Praises Critics

People have criticized my research on the mind and human potential ever since I began.

The church criticized what they *thought* I was doing, but when they found out what I was really doing—how my work was helping the creator's creatures—they became big supporters.

Many neighbors criticized me in the early days. But light always overcomes darkness, and eventually my neighbors began to come to me seeking my help. Of course I helped them.

Have you noticed that nobody has ever erected a statue to a critic?

When people criticize you, when they express doubts about your ability to succeed, when they dump a lot of negativity on you, just remember that light cannot be overcome by darkness.

Remain centered. Let your light shine. Use truth as your ally. Persist. Stay on the road to success, and you will be successful.

Light cannot be overcome by darkness.

78 Here's How Skeptics Become Believers *(1986)*

It is interesting how things that are new seem to go through certain stages. Looking at history and learning its lessons can be quite valuable to you. Let's look at what happens with new discoveries.

In the beginning, everybody says it is impossible, there is no such thing. Then later on they say, well, there could be something there. And finally they say that everybody should know it, they knew it all the time.

It was many years between the time Edison developed practical systems for generating electricity and the time that people started putting it to practical use.

Or consider the invention of the airplane. It allowed people to realize one of humanity's greatest dreams: the ability to fly.

At first, most people believed it was impossible. Even today, there are still people who have never flown, people who say that "If God had meant man to fly, he would have given him wings."

That is foolish, of course: God gave us the capacity to find a way to fly, and that's far better than God simply doing it for us.

When World War I came, a practical use was found for the airplane: observing enemy troop movements.

Then another use was found: using an airplane to shoot down an enemy airplane that was observing your troop movements.

But after the war, there was no use for the airplane—at least, the majority of people thought there was no use for airplanes. Most pilots gave up flying and went into work they thought would be profitable. As one World War I pilot said, "Everybody knew there was no future in aviation."

But a few visionaries continued to believe. With their imagination, they realized the tremendous benefits to humanity that the airplane could bring.

Now, of course, almost everyone can see those benefits: Air travel is the fastest, safest way that people can use.

You can send packages almost anywhere in the world within 48 hours thanks to airplanes.

Even our knowledge of the world has improved tremendously thanks to airplanes: Aerial photography has shown us much more about the planet we live on than we could learn on the ground.

The pattern of history is being repeated with the Silva ESP training.

At first they called us "psycho-ceramics"—crack pots. The "intelligent" people insisted that nobody could develop ESP (enhanced intuition). And even if they could, what use would it be?

After enough people started doing it, then a lot of interest developed. During the 1960s and early 1970s, many, many people came to our lectures to learn what this was all about.

But the ability to use clairvoyance, consciously and with controlled awareness, is something that is so new that many people have not yet realized just how much can be done with it.

I use it every day. You can use your clairvoyant ability to sense other people's needs so you can help them, and can establish better relationships. You can do this in your home, on the job, and in social situations.

You can obtain information regarding career decisions, entertainment, and to help other people.

You can program for virtually anything you desire, so long as it is not harmful to anyone.

At this time, the possibilities are limited only by your own imagination. And you can use the Silva training to expand your imagination; you can use the Silva training to come up with thousands of additional ways to use the Silva techniques.

In some ways it is like flying your own airplane: The more you practice, the better you get, the more confidence you have, and the more you will want to do it.

It some ways it is better than flying: Flying costs you, but it doesn't cost you anything to use the Silva techniques. Instead, you profit from using them.

Take time now to enter your level and become one of the vision-aries who will find so many uses for your clairvoyant abilities that you will serve as an inspiration to others.

Close your eyes, take a deep breath, and while exhaling, men-tally repeat and visualize the number 3 . . .

Note: If you haven't already learned, you can get started right now with the free training in the appendix.

79 Doubters and Skeptics Are Now Among Our Biggest Supporters *(1991)*

Twenty-five years ago we went to Amarillo, Texas, to teach our Method to a group of artists. Back in those days, there were not many people who believed in our work.

Art teacher Dord Fitz believed, and so did the seventy-five art-ists who signed up for our lectures.

Dr. N.E. West believed. He is the one who told Dord Fitz about us, after we went to Wayland Baptist College and spoke to Dr. West's psychology students.

Dr. J. W. Hahn believed. He was director of the Mind Sci-ence Foundation, and was open minded enough to believe that somebody outside of his organization could actually come up with something.

Most influential people in 1966 didn't believe.

Dr. J.B. Rhine didn't believe. He had conducted research on ESP at Duke University for decades. He didn't believe that a person without a doctorate—or even a college degree—could come up with anything important.

Most medical doctors didn't believe. They called us frauds.

Most educators didn't believe. They stuck to their guns, telling students to "study hard" but not telling them how, not telling them what to do with their minds in order to remember something, and to solve problems.

Most in the news media didn't believe. If we were lucky, they ignored us; otherwise they criticized us and called us frauds.

Most religious leaders didn't believe. They often acted as if they were the only ones who could say anything about the spiritual dimension. They often indicated that science had no business there.

Most business managers didn't believe. They continued to use their tools of manipulation and control, and a quarter of a century passed before they began to realize that they could get better results by becoming more sensitive to the needs of their employees and customers.

Most authors didn't believe. They wrote about many irrelevant things, and hawked their own beliefs.

But there were some people who believed.

The public believed. Many people agreed to look at what we had to offer. We always offered a money back guarantee if they didn't learn how to do everything we said they could.

And once the public believed, and learned that we were correct, and that we were telling the truth, then something interesting began to happen:

Some doctors began to believe, and encouraged their patients to learn how to use their minds to help heal the body.

Some educators began to believe, and learned how to teach students *how* to study, and *how* to learn.

Some writers began to believe, and started reporting on our work.

Some religious leaders began to believe, and began to teach their congregations how to pray more effectively.

Some business people began to believe, and their profits increased when they applied the Silva techniques.

Some scientists began to believe, and are demonstrating in their laboratories that there is more to reality than what you can see, hear, smell, taste and touch.

Twenty-five years ago we stood virtually alone. We had Dr. Hahn, Dr. West, Dord Fitz, and a few other loyal supporters.

Today we stand proudly with millions of people who have learned how to change their lives for the better with the Method we authored here in Laredo.

We stand with believers from eighty-eight countries, speaking twenty-one languages.

They come from all fields.

There is a whole field of medicine called psychoneuroimmunology that continues the research we started in 1944.

Conferences are now held for business people to learn how to use intuition in business.

A ten year scientific research project at the Newark College of Engineering in New Jersey proved that the most successful business people have the best intuition.

Many books today are written about the mind and human potential.

John Mihalasky wrote about the Newark College of Engineering project in the book *Executive ESP*.

Dr. O. Carl Simonton detailed his work with cancer patients, who program their own recovery, in his book *Getting Well Again*.

Shakti Gawain, whose mother was a Silva Instructor in the early 1970s, details the power of visualization in her book *Creative Visualization*.

Cleve Backster's exciting research into primary perceptive capability in plants is detailed in Dr. Robert Stone's book *The Secret Life of Your Cells*.

Publishers are seeking us out for more books all the time. We have already written books on the ways that business managers can use more of their minds, and on health and healing, co-authored with Dr. Stone.

Our newest book, due out in January, is *Sales Power, the Silva Mind Method for Sales Professionals*, co-authored with our Newsletter editor Ed Bernd Jr. The Putnam Berkley Group is publishing the book, and Harper Audio the audio cassette.

We have come a long way in twenty-five years. We'd like to share our joy with you, the people who believed, who made it happen, at our Silva/Silver Anniversary Convention in Laredo in August.

We begin with a welcome party on Friday evening, August ninth, and continue with the Convention all day on Saturday August tenth and Sunday August eleventh, which happens to be my seventy-seventh birthday.

You can join a lot of other believers at the Convention. The Holiday Inn, Convention headquarters, is already filled up with those who have pre-registered.

Please send your registration to Ruth Silva at our office as soon as possible, while rooms are still available at other top quality hotels.

We have outstanding Silva lecturers, graduates, researchers, authors and others from all over the world already registered for the Convention.

At this Convention, we will review the Silva Legacy, and how you can benefit even more from our method.

In my closing comments Sunday afternoon, I will give you a sneak preview of what we foresee for the future of the Silva training, our planet, and humanity.

Come celebrate this special milestone with us.

80 Please Help Bring Benefits of Our Research to the World *(1991)*

I believe that our main purpose for being here is to help correct problems and convert the planet into a paradise.

That's why, at the age of fifty-two, I closed my electronics repair shop and started a new business.

It was more than a new business: It was a commitment.

I wanted to help people all over the world learn to function at an altered level of consciousness in order to reconnect to the "other side," to the place where we came from when we were born and will go back to when we die.

I had learned, through twenty-two years of research, that when people are connected to the other side, then a lot of additional help is available to them: They make better decisions, they are more creative, they are healthier, luckier, more successful.

Now, twenty-five years later, you might say that I've been pretty successful at reaching my goal: The Silva Method is offered in eighty-eight countries. We have almost 500 lecturers worldwide, lecturing in twenty different languages.

Today the Silva Method is the oldest, largest, and best mind development program in the world. It is also the most imitated.

But this is not enough to satisfy me.

Even though millions of people have benefited from the Silva training, there are billions more who need to reconnect themselves with the other side so that they, too, can take advantage of the help that is available to them if they just learn how to establish and use that connection.

That brings us to what I call the Second Phase of Marketing of the Silva Method.

Second Phase

When the Silva Method first began to grow, I developed a formula that would help everyone become reconnected.

That formula is: $1 + 2 = 5$ billion.

What I mean by that is, if every Silva graduate will personally bring two other people to the course, and those two will bring two more, then within ten years, all 5 billion people on the planet will have learned to function at an altered level of awareness in order to be reconnected to the other side.

It is time to intensify our efforts to reach that goal.

I cannot do it myself.

Long ago I learned that I could heal people, but I could not heal everybody. There are too many people.

Then I realized that if I could train enough people to be healers, so that we could have a healer in every household, then I *could* help everybody.

Since then, I have concentrated on teaching other people how to do the things that I do, to teach them what I have learned. I do not solve other people's problems: I teach them how to solve their own problems.

I need your help to reach the goal of helping everyone on the planet.

First, practice the Silva techniques every day.

We need you to spread the word to other people so that they know about the benefits of our mind training courses. You need to persuade them to learn and use them.

You also need to help others, as well as yourself.

The more problems you correct, the more your abilities will increase.

A lot of exciting things are happening as we enter the second phase of marketing:

Major publishers are publishing books and tapes about our work.

We are creating several specialized workshops, seminars and lecture series to bring the Silva techniques to more people.

We will soon implement a nationwide public relations effort in the United States.

We are introducing the Silva Systems to new countries almost every month. Recently we presented our first Basic Lecture Series in the Soviet Union.

We see the growth of the Silva training accelerating.

Please help us by telling your friends, your loved ones, your associates about us. Encourage them to read a book, listen to a recording, attend one of our courses including the new specialized programs for business people, athletes, salespeople, or employees.

Twenty-five years ago, many people were skeptical about our claims and we had to keep proving ourselves over and over.

That hurdle is now far behind us. Now we can concentrate on teaching people how to be better problem solvers.

Let's work together to spread the word, to help everyone get reconnected to the other side.

That way, we can make my dream come true: To convert our planet into a paradise.

81 Happiness Comes From Doing What You Were Sent Here to Do *(1994)*

We hear from a lot of people who tell us that the Silva techniques have helped them change their lives for the better.

In some cases, the changes are very dramatic.

We've been observing this for more than four decades, and it still excites us to see people get so much benefit from the Silva Method.

Someone asked me recently about the biggest benefit I've gotten from all of the research that I did and all of the findings that have come out of that research.

My Biggest Benefit

There have been so many ways that I have benefited.

I have been able to help my family. I helped my brother Juan overcome a serious health problem after he had gone to doctors all over the world without obtaining any relief.

Entire student bodies have been trained with the Silva Method. The two thousand students that we trained at Hallahan High School are all grown up now.

Our work is finally being accepted, and that is very gratifying to me, to be proved right after so many years when other scientists referred to me as a "psycho-ceramic"—a crack pot!

But the thing that brings me the greatest satisfaction is just the knowledge that my research and my efforts are helping people.

There Is No Comparison

All of the successes are important. There is no way to know how important a particular success is to an individual.

Developing the ability to get up and speak in front of a group of people may be just as important to one person as overcoming a terminal illness is to another.

Looking from the outside, one may look much more important than the other. But to the person involved, it could be a different story.

Fulfill Your Mission in Life

I believe that we were all sent to planet earth for some purpose. When you figure out what that purpose is, when you figure out what you are supposed to be doing with your life, and then you do it, that will bring you fulfillment and satisfaction.

To me, it is very simple. Those things that bring true satisfaction and joy are the things we were meant to do.

Nothing brings more satisfaction, joy and fulfillment than accomplishing something constructive and creative. Just look at children and how pleased they are when they get good grades.

That's why it brings me so much satisfaction to know that my efforts are helping other people.

That's my mission in life.

I continue to work to bring the Silva instruction to more people because that is what brings me the greatest satisfaction.

Since it brings me so much satisfaction, I know it is what I am supposed to be doing.

Total Perfection

We figure this is the way it is because we always want the best: the best quality, prettiest, and so forth.

In addition to this, we must be prepared to supply the best, and to look for the best for others also. This means progress.

We are here to perfect conditions wherever we are, to perfect whatever needs to be perfected.

The ultimate would be total perfection.

But until we get there, we don't know what we need it for.

Enter your level.

Ask what you are supposed to be doing.

You will get answers. Act on them.

Continue to strive to take part in constructive and creative activities to help make this a better world to live in, so that when we move on, we shall have left behind a better world for those who follow.

That's your assignment—not from me, but from higher powers.

We have some wonderful tools to work with in the Silva courses, tools and techniques to help us get any information we need to solve problems. But still it seems that some things are beyond us.

I have spent some time at level trying to figure out an answer to a question, an answer that will make sense to me. So far it has eluded me.

It is a question that many other people have asked:

Who created God?

Creation of Life

It is said that one being created all forms of life, human beings and all other kinds of creatures. It seems that this one being has organized and set up a framework, a hierarchy.

It seems that we have a hierarchy of levels, a hierarchy of dimensions, to supervise the entire universe: the development of the galaxies within the universe, the solar systems within the galaxies.

But then again, we go right back to the starting point: Who created God? Who started it?

Supervision of Life

People say that God is in charge of us, of our lives.

It seems that whoever was smart enough to create all that we have in our world, in the universe, was also smart enough to create a system that would regulate itself most of the time, without needing the intervention of the creator for every action.

When we need to eat, we become hungry. When we have eaten enough, we feel satisfied and are no longer hungry.

When the body needs to repair itself, we become tired and go to sleep.

When the body is done with its repair job, we wake up.

We know that when we are being destructive, we have more problems in our lives. When we are being constructive, we have fewer problems in our lives.

God does not need to watch us every minute of every day. God created various guidance mechanisms to steer us in the right direction. It is up to us to pay attention to those mechanisms.

Chain of Command

It is only when we stray beyond the prescribed course that we need supervision from a higher authority.

That's when higher intelligence gets involved.

We receive help from a level higher than ourselves, from a higher form of intelligence.

What supervises that intelligence? A higher, higher intelligence?

Ultimately, we come right back to the same question: Who created God?

What Is the Answer to the Question?

I don't spent too much time trying to figure out the answer.

When the time comes that the answer will help us to solve more problems, then we will learn the answer.

It is important to keep asking the question, to keep searching for more information we can use to solve problems and to perfect the creation.

That way, when the time is right to learn the answer, someone will be asking the question.

That someone who is seeking the answer in order to solve more problems and to help convert our planet into a paradise may be the one who will find the answer.

Note: If you have not yet learned the Silva techniques, you can begin right now with the free training in the appendix of this book.

82 Daydreaming Will Help You Function More Like a Genius *(1994)*

Why do most people lose the ability to use their right brain hemisphere?

The focusing faculty of the eye is largely responsible. Ninety percent of humanity do not develop correctly because, between the ages of seven through fourteen, they are more attracted to seeing new things.

The physical world holds great attraction. When young people spend all their time focusing on the things of the outer world, then they do not develop in a balanced manner. The left brain hemisphere learns, but the right hemisphere is idle.

When looking at things, people must focus their eyes, and focusing requires that the brain function at twenty pulsations, which is left hemisphere thinking.

The people who develop incorrectly are people who never have the need to visualize with their eyes closed.

Learn to Daydream

These individuals, or their parents, are not aware of the value of visualizing with the eyes closed to detect information with the faculties of the right brain hemisphere at ten pulsations per second and· thus become clairvoyants.

Those who do visualize and imagine with their eyes closed are called daydreamers, They are ridiculed by both parents and teachers, Daydreaming, they claim, is a waste of time.

Recently, NASA sent a memo out to the staff exhorting them to daydream more as it enhances inventiveness. Three cheers! Now if educators will encourage daydreaming. . . .

Help Your Children

Now parents have the opportunity to help their children, between the ages of seven and fourteen, to develop both brain hemispheres equally, so that they will be geniuses.

Children seldom go in the direction we point, but they readily follow in the direction we go. Use your Silva techniques for the good of yourself and for the good of your genius child.

If you don't use it, you lose it.

The ideal age of the child to work with is between seven and fourteen, during the second seven-year anabolic life cycle.

The overall average predominant brain frequency of a child between ages seven and fourteen, when eyes are closed or defocused and turned slightly upward, is between seven and fourteen cycles per second, centering on ten cycles per second.

How to Practice

Get the child to practice visualization by closing the eyes, turning them slightly upwards in relation to their face, and recalling and describing in full detail and color, people, places, and things that they have seen.

This should be done for fifteen minutes, once a week, preferably on Sunday.

Get the child to explain what they have seen on television or at a movie. The child should explain the movie in full detail and color with eyes closed and turned slightly upward. They are not to explain the plot, but to describe what they saw, what it looked like, in full detail and color.

On the last Sunday of each month (we will assume you are practicing on Sunday), tell the child to practice imagination.

Practice Imagination

With the eyes closed and turned upward slightly, the child should alter any images they have seen.

For instance, if the child has seen someone with a green sweater, then mentally change that sweater to red, and create a mental picture of the same person wearing a red sweater. The child could imagine that person entering their home and coming out wearing a red sweater instead of a green one.

This kind of practice—practicing visualization for fifteen minutes for the first three (or sometimes four) Sundays and practicing imagination on the last Sunday—should be continued for one year, Start when the child turns seven years of age and continue until they are eight.

Then when the child is eight, practice every other Sunday until the child turns nine.

After that, practice on one Sunday, then skip two Sundays.

Continue this schedule until the child turns ten.

After that, practice one Sunday, then skip three Sundays.

Continue this until the child becomes eleven.

Thereafter, practice once a month until the child becomes fourteen years of age.

Case Working

When the child reaches eight years of age, by this time they have practiced visualization for one year. The parents, who have developed their own clairvoyant ability through the Silva ESP training, should then introduce the child to case working, as practiced in the Silva ESP training.

This is the natural way for children to develop their clairvoyant ability.

Once they have developed this ability to communicate subjectively, they will receive many benefits:

They can communicate subjectively with their body and keep it healthy.

They can communicate subjectively with other people and avoid conflicts, and obtain information they can use to solve problems.

They can communicate subjectively with higher intelligence on the other side and get guidance and help to correct any problem.

Do this for your child, and they will not need to take the Silva ESP training.

Best Way to Develop Their Ability

It is best to start with human health cases as these are the easiest to do. Later, you can give business, political, social, or personal problems as cases.

The reason that health cases are the easiest for all of us to do is because human survival is our mind's number one priority. It is easiest to be clairvoyant when the problem is related to life and death.

Similarly, the hardest projects are those that are irrelevant to survival, problems that nobody is worrying about—like will it rain three years from today.

Every case should involve a meaningful problem of some sort. The mind does not want to waste time on situations that are not problems. The more a person is concerned or affected by a problem or the more a person is suffering or is life-threatened by a problem, the better the problem is for the child to work on at this stage.

It would be inadvisable to refer now to psychic ability or clairvoyance. Children do not like to be different from their peers.

They do not hear other children talk about psychic ability, the psi factor, or clairvoyance, so their motivation could be impaired.

But all children enjoy guessing. Guessing is acceptable. So doing cases become guessing, and the child is measured in "guessing ability."

Measuring Progress

When the child does a case and the child's first guess is correct, score 100.

When the child is correct on the second guess, score eighty. If right on the third try, the score should be sixty; on the fourth try, a forty, and on the fifth try, a twenty.

Figure out the average and keep a record. You will notice that the average will increase with practice.

As the child's guessing factor improves, then start selecting more difficult projects. A project can be made more difficult by giving less information to the child about the case.

For instance, don't give the child the name of the person. Instead just say, "What is worrying the person that I have a picture of in my mind?" Later you can say, ". . . the person I am thinking of?"

When the child guesses wrong, never tell the child that they are wrong. You want to encourage successes.

Note down their response and tell them to try again. Give them a multiple choice case and see if they can guess right on the second, third, or fourth guess.

It is important that you remember this: When the child has eyes closed, never say that he or she is wrong. This lowers the child's self-esteem, expectancy, and other genius factors.

When the child is right, get the child to go over the feeling that was associated with the correct guess.

Important Points

The child should be between seven and fourteen years of age.

Have the child explain what they have seen in full detail and color with eyes closed.

Use only problem cases where people are suffering.

Never, never say "wrong" when the child's eyes are closed.

Work ten cases and average out the results to observe the child's development.

Reinforce the correct guesses by reviewing them. Also have the child recall the feeling associated with the success.

At first, use multiple choice problems where people are suffering.

Reward the child for doing well.

Sponsor competitive games between children to encourage their practice.

Exercising the psi factor, which is the ability to guess correctly, is a priority activity.

83 Here Is How You Can Improve the Silva Method Results *(1988)*

There are many dedicated and concerned Silva graduates who come to us with ideas, and tell us how we can use the Silva Method to serve humanity better.

We read their letters, we talk to them on the phone and in person. Their suggestions are all excellent:

Create special seminars for use in schools.

Donate time and resources to help the elderly population.

Implement programs in prisons to help these unfortunate people get on the right track.

Develop a system to help deal with the AIDS epidemic.

Mobilize people to work towards world peace.

You get the idea. These are all good suggestions, and we'd love to see them all implemented.

Getting It Done

Let's talk for a moment about how things get done.

When I began my research back in 1944, there was nobody I could talk to or work with who could help me.

I got it done because I cared, and took action to make my goals come true.

I saw a need, and I did all I could to find solutions.

That's how things get done.

When Everybody says Somebody should do it, we usually find that Nobody does it.

Our Goals

I conducted twenty-two years of research. Then in 1966 at the age of fifty-two, I closed my electronics business and took a chance on a new career. I began lecturing to groups of people who wanted to learn techniques to help them solve problems and live healthier, happier, more successful lives.

For the last twenty-two years, I've stood before every group who would hear me, teaching them the Silva Method.

I built a business so that I could duplicate myself and serve more people.

Now millions of people have learned the Silva techniques from the thousands of instructors I've trained.

We are reaching a lot of people, and teaching in English and Spanish and French and Korean and Chinese and a dozen other languages.

In order for me to tackle any new projects, I'd have to take my time and my company's resources away from what we are doing.

I'm not willing to do that, because I believe that what we are doing now is very important.

What's Next?

Have you wondered why I am training so many people as fast as I can?

I am doing that so that those of you who learn the Silva Method can go forth and correct problems and help convert our planet into a paradise.

It's your turn.

I've invested forty-four years.

Now what are *you* willing to do?

Contact our staff here at headquarters when you need guidance. I have people who have studied with me and who can answer most of your questions.

When they are not sure of the answer, they'll come to me. Many of our instructors are willing to help you.

There are members of our alumni association, the Silva International Graduate Association (SIGA) who are eager to help.

How to Proceed

There is no magic in what I did.

You, as a Silva graduate, have better techniques and more mental abilities than I had when I began.

I never attended school, never sat in a classroom as a student. I had to learn to read and write and run a business in the "school of hard knocks." And I had to learn mental techniques on my own, the same mental techniques I taught you in the Silva training.

In those ways, you have a big head start over me.

The question is, do you have the ingredient that is indispensable to success?

Persistence.

You've got to be willing to begin, and to stay with it, no matter how many hardships, no matter how many wrong turns your efforts may take, no matter how many people criticize you.

I persisted.

And because I did, we are now training thousands of people every month to solve the problems on our planet.

Action Counts

It is time for all of these problem solvers to get to work.

We do not need them to offer us suggestions; we need them to solve problems.

We know what needs to be done as well as anyone else. We don't need ideas; we need *action*.

When you are as willing to pay your dues as I was, then you will see your dreams come true.

We will know by your actions how serious you are in your suggestions, how dedicated you are to the project you propose.

Do not call on us to do it for you, because we have other commitments.

But we'll be glad to help you do it.

The best time for you to begin is . . . now.

Note from José Silva Jr.: Yes, my father *was* persistent . . . stubborn. There are many ways you can help right now:

Send people to our website to get authentic products authored by my father and not changed by anyone else after his passing. Send them to SilvaNow.com to get started immediately with our Free Introductory Lessons.

Even better, join his Save the Planet Project and center your children and other family members and friends yourself. Use the Silva Centering Exercise script in appendix A.

You can also send them to SilvaESP.com where they can get a discount on any of the Online Learning Courses with the discount code: MM15

We will all benefit.

84 Use This Advanced Technique to "Anchor" to Positive Programs *(1985)*

Q: We have been using a technique to "anchor" our feelings of desire, belief and expectancy with physical triggers.

That is, we recall a feeling of great desire, and then anchor it by doing something like pulling on an earlobe, or rubbing a knee. When we repeat this during our daily programming, it seems to give us better results with our Mirror of the Mind Technique. Do you have any suggestions along these lines?

A: (by José Silva) The first thing to remember is that you should not alter what you have learned in the Silva training until you have been successful with the technique.

Once you are successful and confident, then you can start changing the formula, but not before.

If you start changing the formulas before learning to use them successfully, then you will just become confused and won't know what works or what to do.

In the Silva courses, our formulas are impressed at the right dimension for the right purpose. Once you have succeeded and developed your confidence, then you can alter the formula any way you want, but you must develop that confidence first or else you will become so confused that even our formula will not work for you.

Points of Reference

Actually, anchoring is just a method of establishing points of reference.

You have to have experienced it before and established points of reference, then you can depend on it. But you must have experienced it successfully first.

We use mental points of reference in the Silva courses. Remember how we say to recall a previous success as you start to do your programming.

Once you have used our formula and gotten a feeling of success, then the feeling of success is what you attach as an anchor, rather than pulling the earlobe or rubbing the knee.

To increase your desire, keep repeating what you desire mentally or verbally. Keep on thinking about it over and over and over, mentally or verbally. Keep talking about it. The more you talk about it, the more it goes through your mind, the stronger it gets.

When you dwell on it enough, it becomes obsessive. If you keep going, your desire can become so strong that it possesses you.

When you have built up that much desire, then you will get it.

Having Faith

You also must have belief and expectancy.

You increase these the same way:

Keep repeating your belief, know what you believe in and think about what you believe in, repeat it mentally and verbally, and you will increase it like you do your desire.

The same with expectancy.

These three elements have to properly blend to provide the faith that will materialize your desired end results. If you have only one of these elements, you might overdo it and become obsessed. You need a balance.

If you just desire without believing and hoping (hope is the same as expectancy), it is false faith. You must have all three.

Once you have really developed your faith—faith is desire, belief and expectancy—then you no longer need to continue going to your level to program them.

The confidence is there.

The feeling of success is there. You have it made.

If you feel you must use these physical triggers to anchor your faith, then you have not really developed your faith yet.

Subjective Triggers

Rather than anchoring with physical triggers, anchor with subjective ones, with experiences of the mind, not of the body.

That means, your feelings. Feelings are only of the mind.

You feel the body through the mind. We feel everything through the mind. So it has to be done in the mind first.

The subjective is always first.

We must first think of something, then we do it. The use of physical anchors is superficial. We've been familiar with that since very early in our research.

Everything must be done in the subjective dimension first, the mental dimension. This is the only and the correct thing to do.

Sometimes people think that since they have recently become aware of physical triggers, this is something new. What is actually new is the use of mental points of reference, mental anchoring to achieve our goals.

When you are anchoring in the objective, you are not practicing functioning in the subjective, which is where we can really benefit. So you will make must faster progress and develop much more competence and ability by practicing subjective techniques.

We have the Three Fingers Technique to use when your mind is on something else, such as reading or listening to a lecture.

But when you go within, go to your level to program, you do not need this.

You can do it all mentally, at the fundamental dimension, the dimension where it should be done first.

When you work with physical triggers, you are working with the left brain hemisphere. The mental projection exercise that we do in our ESP training are done with the right brain hemisphere. This is what 90 percent of the people on this planet were not able to do before the Silva ESP training was developed.

Most people were not able to use the right brain hemisphere to detect and store subjective information.

If you first do a program with the right brain hemisphere, it will happen on the left hemisphere also. But if you do it with the left brain hemisphere, it will not happen on the right hemisphere.

The right brain hemisphere is attached to a fundamental dimension, where everything should be done first. So we think you will be much better off to practice the Silva ESP techniques the way you learned them in our ESP training.

85 We Need People to Help People Who Need Our Help *(1992)*

During my research into the mind and human potential, I learned many healing techniques, and I learned how to apply them very effectively.

Eventually I began to realize that it might not be necessary to be there in person to heal someone.

Perhaps I could correct problems at a distance.

As I began working with this approach, it seemed promising.

But I wanted to make sure that I wasn't just fooling myself, so I set up a special test.

The Test

I selected ten people here in the Laredo area who were very sick.

Some were given only a short time to live. Others were told they would never overcome their disease.

I decided to work on those people, and see if I could actually help them. If I could help one person with such a serious illness, this could be a coincidence, I thought. But if I could help two of them, I'd know it was beyond coincidence, and I was really onto something.

It was not necessary to work on each person every day. Once I corrected the problem in the subjective dimension, I expected it to manifest in the physical dimension. When I was at my level and happened to think of one of those people, I would reinforce the correction I had made.

If they had regressed any, I would correct it again.

The Results

This was not a short term project that I could just work on for a few weeks and forget. It was a project that could take a lot of time. I made a commitment to myself to work on these people for as long as it took, until they got well, or passed on.

One of them responded. That encouraged me.

Then another one got well.

Then I knew I was really on to something, that I had come upon a method to help people even when I could not be with them in person.

There were still eight more people, so I continued to work on them.

When I felt that one of them needed some help, I would program them while at my level.

Eventually, over the next three years, all of them recovered.

Every single subject got well!

The Next Step

A gift like this should be used. I felt an obligation to help people.

But there was a problem: I am only one person, and I could not find enough time to help everybody who needed help. There was no way that one person could heal everybody in Laredo, much less in the whole world.

So I began to experiment to see if I could teach other people how to do what I did.

As you know, we were able to come up with a method to teach anybody how to use more of their mind to detect and correct problems.

This seemed so promising that I made a decision to stop healing anyone except my own family members, and to invest my time in teaching other people how to heal.

If I can put a healer in every household, then I *can* help to heal everybody in the world.

We Need Your Help

We receive calls here in Laredo almost every day from people who have health problems and need help. Some of the calls come from Silva graduates who need help for themselves.

Sometimes they have been practicing, sometimes not.

Other calls come from Silva graduates who seek help for loved ones or friends. Some come from people who have read one of our books, and some from people who have heard of us from a friend.

We do what we can to help them, but again we receive so many calls that we are limited in what we can do. Often we work the case once, then use the Alpha Uni-Mold, which is a technique for helping a lot of people at once.

We need more people to help us help people who need help.

We need healing hot lines around the country and around the world so that we can refer people to someone in their local area who can help them.

We cannot do it all by ourselves.

Several years ago I helped a group of graduates start the Ecumenical Society of Psychorientology. But the leaders of the organization' gradually drifted away and now it is inactive.

I cannot do everything myself.

We need some leadership from among the millions of Silva graduates worldwide.

I realize that most people have jobs and families and other interests. So do our employees in Laredo. So do I. We are doing what we can, but we need your help.

If you are willing to start and manage a healing hot line and to help some of the many people who call here asking for help, please let me know and we will refer these cases to you.

If you appreciate the benefits that you have received from the Silva Method, then perhaps you will want to offer to help others who are less fortunate.

I believe that this is what we were put here for. I've worked hard all my life to help people. Now it is time for others to help. Please write to me if you are willing to help.

Note from José Silva Jr.: There are not as many in-person courses as their used to be. Instead we meet up online. When you tell other people how they can learn to unleash their genius mind, and they learn our System, then you can work together to multiply your abilities and how much you can accomplish. Spread the work on social media and in person and everybody will benefit.

PART 4

IDEAS CAME FROM MANY SOURCES

by José Silva Jr.

Ideas came to my father from many sources:

- The Sleeping Prophet Edgar Cayce and how he was using a level of consciousness equivalent to light sleep, lighter than hypnosis or yoga or other meditation systems.
- Bible verses and Sunday sermons that seemed to hold messages related to his research into the mind and human potential.
- Out of the mouths of children, who just tell you what they are experiencing with censoring themselves the way grownups do.
- Observing holistic faith healers gave him the idea for the 3-Fingers Technique and others.
- Dr. J.B. Rhine pointing out that he had not pre-testing his daughter and then dismissing his findings didn't stop him; instead it taught him the proper way to conduct scientific research.
- Even his dreams helped him, like the one that led to lottery ticket that paid him $10,000, about two years salary in 1949. It was enough to persuade him to continue his research.

In just a moment we'll continue with more inspiration, ideas, and techniques you use to help you write your own success story.

First let me introduce you to Dr. N.E. West of Wayland Baptist College, the first professional person to invite my father to share his exciting new research with a broader audience.

86 The Educator Who Introduced José Silva to the World *(1986)*

(At the 1986 Silva Method International Convention in Laredo, Dr. West told his version of his first meeting with José Silva, an event that eventually led to public recognition and acceptance of the Silva Method.)

by Dr. N.E. West

I first met José Silva in August 1966. At that time I was teaching at Wayland Baptist College in northwest Texas.

I received a telephone call in June of 1966 from a man of whom I had never heard, saying his name was José Silva, that he had a parapsychology research project that he had been conducting in Spanish, that he had some students who had proved to be very well equipped to do this kind of work, they were graduating from a junior college in Laredo, that he was looking for senior college scholarships where they could continue their parapsychology work and also get senior college training, and wondered if I could help in any way.

I was skeptical, as most psychologists are skeptical, and said that "What you say is interesting, but I must come and visit you."

We came in August of 1966, met at the motel dining room.

He invited us to his office. I went over for three hours, from seven until ten, and stayed until five in the morning.

By that time I was quite impressed.

There were three things that impressed me about him.

First was his sincerity. Most of us in the scientific world deal with charlatans a lot, but a man who is sincere may be wrong, but he is not a charlatan.

Second, he gave some demonstrations of what had been done with students to improve their learning skills.

As a professor, I was very much concerned with what we call under achievers: students who have the ability but somehow or other do not have the skill. That impressed me tremendously.

The third thing, he performed some other demonstrations that convinced me that he had the kind of ability that he had talked about.

Going back home, I talked with Dord Fitz in Amarillo, who has an art institute. Dord thought this would be a good thing to present to art students. So between the two of us, we arranged for José to come to north Texas, to speak at our college, to our classes, and then I went with him to Amarillo.

You know the story of the Amarillo episode, where after the lecture 90 people signed up for a course that did not exist.

I'm a kind of a mid-wife. I'm not very important—I just helped to deliver.

87 Start the New Year By Serving As a Planetary Peace Keeper *(1984)*

How can we help bring peace to our planet?

One place at a time. One person at a time.

There are wars and rumors of wars in many places. Fighting men are sent to keep peace, and are killed.

How can we fight against war?

We have read that we should turn the other cheek. But if we are not as highly developed as Christ, can we do that and survive?

Does anything that I do really help bring peace to the planet?

You Do Make a Difference

You do not have to do something that would win a Nobel Peace Prize to help bring peace to our planet. You can begin with yourself, and become a peaceful person yourself. This will lower the level of tension and stress in the environment where you function, and many people will be affected.

How do you become peaceful?

Your first step is to enter your level two or three times a day, for at least five minutes each time.

Once a day, you should stay at your level for fifteen minutes.

It is at this inner, spiritual, dimension that you have greater understanding. You have greater understanding of what you need to do on this planet, how you should function.

This reduces your stress and anxiety, gives your life direction, gives you a sense of purpose.

It is people who are frustrated and unsure who become belligerent. Those who know where they are going, and know they have the strength, the inner resources, to achieve their purpose have no time for confrontations.

Serve Humanity

Once you have achieved a degree of peace within yourself, you will be much more effective in helping others achieve peace. It is much like the idea of each person lighting one candle, to eventually light up the world.

Your peaceful aura will be a shining example to all you meet.

Then, at your level, program for peace throughout the world.

Not all at once, but one place at a time.

It is much like healing: you must be aware that there is a problem, and correct each problem, one by one.

We will heal our planet in the same manner.

Project to each trouble spot, one at a time, and create a feeling of peace. Work cases on each trouble spot, and correct whatever you detect as a problem.

The more practice you have working health cases, the more effective you will be at working other kinds of cases, so practice health case working at every opportunity.

For far too long, humans have been hurting one another, like beasts. It is time we brought forth our humanity, our spiritual nature, our divine heritage, and stop being destroyers, but become creators.

Remember the messages we have been given.

If you only think a destructive, hurtful thought about another person, even though you do not act upon it, you are still upsetting your own state of peace.

And when you speak a harsh word, "even unto the least of these," you are hurting the cause of peace on your planet.

You have more control over your own actions than you do over the rest of the world, so begin with yourself. Be peaceful, considerate, loving, in every little way, and you will find you will be a more effective peace-maker in a big way, too.

Note: If you have not yet learned to enter the alpha level, or have not completed any Silva training, you can start now for free with the instructions in appendix A.

88 Silva Tools Can Help You Cope with a Changing World *(1992)*

How are you coping with all of the changes that are taking place in the world?

There are changes on a global scale, as Eastern European countries open up to democracy and to a market economy. The cold war has ended, and enemies have become friends.

There are great changes taking place in many nations, including the United States.

There are recessions, there's high unemployment, people are dissatisfied, crime seems to be getting worse, and our leaders seem to be at a loss to do anything to help.

There are many changes taking place on a personal level, too, as people realize that the ultimate goal of life is not the accumulation of as much money as possible. There are other things that are more important, such as family, and spiritual growth.

Some changes, as you can see, are good. Others not so good . . . at least not yet; sometimes we have to be made aware of problems before we can correct them, and this can be painful.

How Change Affects Us

Whether the changes are good or bad, they have one thing in common: They cause tension and stress.

Human beings are creatures of habit. We like to know where we stand. We like to know what is going to happen next. We like to know that we can count on people, that they will do what we expect them to and not confound us with unusual behavior.

Surprises cause the heart to beat faster. Surprises cause us to gasp for breath. They also cause our muscles to tense, and they also trigger the release of adrenalin for quick energy. Because where there's change, we often have to react to that change to avoid being hurt.

We are talking about stress. Change causes stress. And stress—when it builds up and becomes distress—hurts you by overloading and weakening your immune mechanism, impairing your mental ability (such as your ability to make correct decisions), and speeds your body's aging process.

Coping With Change

How are you coping with all of the changes that you are faced with?

It is especially important for you to enter your level every day—I recommend three times a day, for 15 minutes each time if you can.

Spending 15 minutes at alpha will help to counteract the stress syndrome, make you feel better, and make you more productive. The more stress you have in your life, the more important it is to do this.

While you are at your level, you can think more clearly. You have access to more information, so you will make better decisions.

At your level, it is easier to get the "big picture," and to put all of the changes into perspective.

You've gone through changes before, and survived. Many times you were better off after the changes.

We can't avoid change. It is a fact of life, and as long as we are in the world, changes will take place.

What You Can Do

Even though you can't control many of the changes taking place, you can do two things:

First, you can control your reaction to changes. Enter your level, use your Silva tools to program yourself, and to program for the lifestyle you desire.

Second, change yourself. Join the movement taking place all over the planet, the movement towards the second phase of human evolution on our planet.

How to Help Humanity

All over the planet, people are joining us in learning how to center themselves, so that they can get help from the other side, to help them correct problems in the physical world.

You already know how to do this. Use your techniques . . . every day. And bring your loved ones and friends to the Silva training.

Let's all work together for changes that are going to help transform the planet by encouraging everyone to become centered, so that they can get help from the other side and will therefore be better problem solvers.

That's the kind of change we can all enjoy.

Note: You can learn techniques to help yourself deal with change and stress, as well as techniques to help correct the things that are causing stress, with the free lessons in the appendix of this book.

89 More Abundance Can Be Yours When You Program Correctly *(1988)*

You can have whatever you want to have, if you have a positive mental attitude.

You can do whatever you want to do, if you have a positive mental attitude.

You can be whatever you want to be, if you have a positive mental attitude.

Suppose you want to have a lot of money, make even more money, and be wealthy. How do you go about it?

I've read books that say you have to have the right attitude about money if you want to have a lot of money.

The authors of these books are very quick to tell you what *they* think are the right and the wrong attitudes about money.

Many people, these authors point out, seem to think that money is bad, that people get rich by taking advantage of others, that wealth and power automatically corrupt so they should be avoided by pious souls.

Or people think that they don't deserve money, or are not smart enough to make it.

It is true that people tend to place many limitations on themselves.

There may be many reasons for the existence of these limiting belief systems—but that is unimportant.

There may be many types of limiting beliefs—and that is also unimportant.

What is important is overcoming these limitations.

These so-called prosperity books give you many formulas and many affirmations to use to learn to like money, to believe that money is good and that you will use it for good, that you deserve it, that you don't have to be any smarter than you are in order to make it.

The trouble is, when you do this you are still focusing completely on the negative. You are still concerned about your negative thoughts concerning money, and on your lack of money.

If you study carefully what the authors did in their own lives, you will find that their actions are different than their words.

The Origin of Beliefs

To explain what they do, and what every successful person does, let me use an illustration you have probably heard before:

The story involves trained fleas at a flea circus.

How do you train a flea? First you have to make sure the flea won't escape.

To do this you put the infant flea into a jar, a put a piece of clear glass on top of the jar.

When the flea jumps, it hits its head on the glass on top of the jar. Well now it doesn't take long even for a flea to figure out that it will get fewer headaches if it doesn't jump so high.

That lesson sticks, and later even when there is no cover over the flea circus to limit the height of their jumps, the fleas still will not jump more than a certain height.

Now let's suppose we wanted to teach the flea to jump higher. What would you do: Would you point out the limitation, and try to persuade the flea to go beyond it?

How far beyond it?

What's there?

Why should it go?

You see, the more you focus on the old limitation, the more you reinforce the old limitation.

Every time you point out the spot where they used to hit their heads, you reinforce their aversion to jumping any higher.

Creating Resistance

The same holds true when you focus on your old limiting beliefs.

The more affirmations you use about how good money is, and how much you deserve it, the more the old limiting belief system fights to stay alive.

Pressure creates resistance.

The more force you use, the more you strengthen whatever you are fighting.

Lift heavy weights and your muscles grow stronger.

They grow stronger from your own energy, the energy that you exert to lift the heavy weights.

The more you use affirmations to fight your limiting belief systems, the stronger the limiting beliefs become. They draw their strength from your own energy, the energy you are using to fight them.

Reverse Your Approach

In the Silva Method we have another approach, an approach that avoids giving strength and legitimacy to the limiting beliefs.

In the Silva Method we set a goal, a desirable and worthwhile goal, and strive for that goal.

That is what our visualization/imagination techniques are all about, the Mirror of the Mind and the 3-Scenes Technique. Yes, first acknowledge the problem, then move on to the solution and never go back to the problem. From then on, concentrate on the solution that you created in the subjective (mental) dimension.

What kind of goals are we likely to achieve?

Goals that help correct problems on our planet, and help to make our world a better place to live.

If you build a better mouse trap, you will be helping a lot of people who need to get rid of mice. That's a desirable, worthwhile goal.

And the best news is, you will be compensated for your service.

Instead of putting energy into fighting your own belief systems, put your energy into correcting problems, achieving worthwhile goals.

Oh, yes, keep in mind what your needs are, and a little bit more. That's what I do.

I do not program for money. I program to provide service, and I keep in mind what my needs are, plus a little bit more.

I use my abilities to correct problems. I use my abilities to help people. I use my abilities to provide goods and services that people want, that will help people. This has proven much more effective than programming for money.

When you study the lives and the actions of the authors who write the success books, you will find that this is exactly how they made their fortunes. They gave a lot, and they were compensated in proportion to what they gave.

As we say, it is easy to get a million dollars, if you need it:

Just give ten million dollars worth of service to humanity.

Oh, there is one other thing to say about that:

It is not the amount of work that you do, it is the value of your work to humanity that counts.

Just building that better mousetrap is not enough. You also have to sell it to people, so that they will benefit from it.

Remember, it's the little things that count, the little extras you do. If you want to get a little bit more, always remember to do a little bit more without seeking payment.

So enter your level, determine what you can do, then use your Silva techniques to help you do it. Provide as much useful service as you can, keep in mind what your needs are (plus a little bit more), and you can become wealthy.

Note: If you haven't yet learned how to center yourself at the alpha brain wave level and use our techniques to unleash your genius mind, you can start right now with the free lessons in appendix A.

90 Some Questions to Ask When Business Is Not Doing Well *(1986)*

Would you like a sure-fire method to develop an action plan that will help you make the right business decisions and turn them into action? Would you like to have a way to remove doubt about what you are doing?

A Silva graduate called recently seeking help, because her fledgling business was faltering even though she was programming with techniques from the Silva courses, and was working many long, hard hours in the shop.

After consulting José Silva, who has started a great many businesses since his first shoe shine business sixty-five years ago, we came up with the following:

Seek Guidance

In a situation such as this, it would be a good idea to go to your level and find out exactly what you should be doing.

Whenever you are in doubt, check it out at level.

In this situation, since the business is not increasing the way you desire, and you are obviously concerned about it—that is, you are beginning to have doubts that you will succeed despite all that you are doing—check it out at level.

How to Program

The ideal way is to program, when you are in bed and ready to go to sleep, that you will wake up automatically at the ideal time to find out what course of action you should take. Do your programming while sitting up in bed, then when you are finished, stay at your level, lie down and go to sleep.

When you wake up automatically during the night or in the morning, then sit up in bed, lower (bow) your head slightly (about 20 degrees) and turn your eyes up slightly (about 20 degrees), re-enter your clairvoyant level and consider various alternatives. Decide the best course of action for you to take at this time.

It is best to select one of two choices. That is, give yourself either-or choices. For instance: Should I continue with this business, or let it go?

Continue Working

If your answer is to continue with this business, then you could ask whether you need to concentrate more on subjective work (programming) or objective work (improving your sales ability, for instance).

Continue in this manner, selecting the best of two choices, until you develop a plan of action.

Also determine exactly how you need to program to get the results you desire.

Then, after you develop your plan of action, continue to program and work for twenty-eight days, a full moon cycle. Twice a week, program yourself to wake up automatically at the ideal time for your programming, and do your programming.

When you program in this manner, it will be three or four days before you program again. Watch for improvement during that time.

Evaluate Your Progress

If there is no improvement, then when you program the next time, be sure to acknowledge that, "The last time, I did this for improvement, and business didn't improve." Then alter your programming, or your attitude as you program, and monitor the results for the next three or four days.

Acknowledge the failure, and try something different. Try a different direction, and say at your level, "This time it will work."

As soon as you begin to get some improvement, then thank the system for the improvement and follow that direction; continue to program in the same manner to get even more improvement.

More Guidance

If, after programming for three weeks in this manner, you still do not see any improvement, then on the fourth week you can use the MentalVideo to present the case to Higher Intelligence and ask for a clear indication that will show you how to proceed.

If you are not yet familiar with the MentalVideo technique, there is a complete explanation in appendix D.

Eliminate Doubt

It is important to seek guidance whenever you are in doubt, when you feel like you are hitting your head against the wall and do not know what else to do.

We always advise that when you've given an honest effort to open a door but it just won't open, then before you get all bloody banging your head against it, back off and look around to see if there's another door.

You might find another door.

Or you might even discover that the door you've been pushing on so hard actually opens towards you.

Or you might find that you need to give it just a little more time.

Of course, you might find that you should seek some other goal.

Every time you are in doubt, remove the doubt by re-thinking it.

Re-think the options and select the best option.

When you follow this procedure and are certain that you are doing what is absolutely right for you, then you can put the power of all your confidence and certainty into your programming and your efforts, and if you have sufficient desire, belief and expectancy, you will surely succeed.

Note from José Silva Jr.: Ninfa Arteaga of Lubbock, Texas, who asked this question, called just before we went to press to tell us that the recommendations worked.

She said that she programmed and awakened automatically at the ideal time, then asked what she should be doing. The next day, she met someone who had an idea but lacked certain resources.

She provided the missing resources.

Her business improved 99 percent the following month!

91 Here's How to Clear Your Mind So You Can Receive Guidance *(1989)*

Have you ever entered your level, asked a question, and not gotten an answer?

Have you ever sought guidance at your level, only to come up blank?

Do you use your alpha decision making ability to its full potential?

To make sure that you get reliable answers whenever you need them, you must make certain that you know exactly how to switch your mind from "transmit" to "receive."

This is important in the third cycle of the Test Taking Technique, as well as other techniques such as the elimination technique to come up with the best answer.

In the test taking technique, you are instructed to project an image of your professor's face onto your mental screen and ask for the answer that you need.

Then clear your mind, and start thinking again to figure out the answer.

Here is what that means:

When you ask a question, your mind is in a transmitting mode. It can only transmit—it cannot receive.

Before you can get an answer, you must change to a receiving mode.

Once your mind is in a receiving mode, then you can receive your answer.

In Mental Housecleaning we point out that the mind cannot be "empty." When we cancel-cancel an unwanted thought, then we must immediately replace that thought with a thought of what we desire.

If we cancel-cancel a negative thought but do not replace it with a positive thought, then the negative thought will continue to stay right there an fill the mental space.

Switching mentally from transmit to receive involves more than just going directly from one to the other.

You might think of it like an old fashioned telephone switch-board, with lots of cables and plugs and jacks.

After you transmit, you pull the plug out of the "transmit" jack, study the layout of the board, and then plug into a "receive" jack.

If you pull the plug from the "transmit" jack and just sit there without looking at another part of the board, then when you are ready to put the plug into a jack, you will still be focused on the "transmit" jack.

Switching your mind from transmit to receive is similar.

First you transmit your question mentally. Then you must disconnect the transmitter.

You cannot disconnect the transmitter as long as you continue thinking about the original subject.

For instance, if your question is, "Who was the thirteenth President of the United States?" you must stop thinking about the question.

That means that you cannot immediately start thinking about the answer.

You must clear your mind.

How do you clear your mind?

If you attempt to think of nothing, then the original topic will probably remain.

Instead, think of something else.

Here's how:

First, you pose your question:

"Who was the thirteenth President of the United States?" as you turn your eyes slightly upwards and visualize your professor.

After presenting the question, stop thinking about the thirteenth President and start thinking about something else.

Distract yourself.

For instance, you might think about some errands you have to run.

You might think about some items you need to purchase.

You might think of a loved one.

When you change your thoughts to some other topic, you clear your mind of the question about the thirteenth President. This disconnects your mental transmitter, because you are no longer thinking about that topic.

After you do this, then you can start thinking again about the thirteenth President, with the expectation that you will receive an answer.

You can use this procedure, at your level, with the appropriate techniques, to obtain information and make decisions about anything that is important to you. When you do this, you will receive your answers.

Note: You can start learning Silva techniques right now with the Free Lessons in the appendix of this book.

92 Program for the Future In a Past Tense Sense *(1989)*

When you enter your level and seek help from the other side, it is important to complete the project—at the subjective dimension.

What do I mean when I talk about getting help from the other side?

That could mean many things, depending on how you are programming and which technique you are using.

When you use the To Awake Control, you are getting help from human intelligence. You are asking human intelligence to awaken your biological body. That is one way of getting help from the other side.

When you use the Mirror of the Mind or 3-Scenes Technique to program to resolve a conflict, you are getting help from the other side.

You are depending on human intelligence, and possibly Higher Intelligence too, to provide guidance for you and perhaps for the other person as well.

When you work a health case on someone, you are using your subjective faculties to detect and correct a problem. This is another way to get help from the other side.

When you use the MentalVideo technique to seek guidance from Higher Intelligence, this is yet another way to obtain help from the other side.

Regardless of which technique you are using, it is important to remember that the project is completed on the other side before it is completed in the physical dimension.

In a practical sense, that means that you should always program for the future in a past tense sense.

When you program to awaken with the To Awake Control, you mentally picture yourself waking up at the desired time. It has already been done in the subjective dimension, and it will be done in the objective dimension.

You cannot do it halfway on the other side. Either you do it or you don't. So, program yourself to wake up at a specific time, desire it, believe it, and expect it, and you will. Do not question it. Be done with it. Put a period on it.

When you work on the conflict in the relationship, complete it on the other side when you use your visualization/imagination techniques.

When you work the health case, take it for granted that the subject has recovered perfect health—on the other side.

When you seek guidance from Higher Intelligence, take it for granted that the answer is there, and you will become aware of it within three days.

In the physical dimension, you continue to expect the results to manifest objectively.

But never doubt for an instant that the results have already been achieved on the other side.

Of course, just like any other skill, you get better at this with practice. That is why we recommend that you practice working health cases frequently.

This gives you immediate feedback that you are functioning successfully on the other side.

Sometimes people become too active mentally and are no longer functioning on the other side.

You can learn to identify this through experience.

And the quickest way to accumulate a lot of experience is by working health cases.

Learn exactly what it feels like to function on the other side.

Then, on the other side, correct your problems. When you correct a problem, remember to think of it in a past tense sense. It is completed . . . in that dimension.

Put a period on it . . . in the subjective dimension.

Never program halfway. Banish all doubt. Do not program with a vague hope that you might get results.

Pray believing that you have already received. Because on the other side, you have received.

Do it mentally, and keep working and expecting it physically, and you will surely get what you program for.

93 Silva Techniques Expand Learning
(1980)

It is very encouraging to see our graduates get involved in further usage of the methods we have learned through Silva Mind Control.

A case in point is the work being done by Miss Maria Luz Ojeda, a SMC lecturer from Chile.

Miss Ojeda's work is highlighted somewhere else in this newsletter, and I cannot help but comment on it because it demonstrates something which I have contended for a long time.

I firmly believe, and I have done so ever since the Silva Mind Control Method was in its experimental stages, that our method can be a very useful learning tool in the classroom.

In a way, Miss Ojeda's work reflects this belief, and her research in using Silva Mind Control techniques while teaching handicapped children has so far given very positive results.

I believe that the Silva Mind Control Method can be useful in the classroom as an aid in the learning process. And there is already evidence that some other progressive educators are beginning to relate the importance of the multiple roles the brain plays in the learning potential of students.

For one, the brain is our most versatile organ, one that is capable of changing. Yet, I feel that many teachers—perhaps guided by the now discarded theory that the Intelligence Quotient (IQ) of a person is static and is the determinant of the intelligence potential of a person—do not yet realize the flexible wonders of the brain.

We know that by providing the right environment, by feeding the brain positive energies—such as we learn to do in our courses—and by helping to motivate it properly, the brain can achieve a tremendous capacity for learning.

For example, it is generally accepted by educators that learning and emotions cannot be separated, and this is basically true, even accepted by the person who truly believes that his actions and behavior are solely guided by his intellect.

Yet, through the Silva Mind Control techniques, students themselves can make a better distinction between the two areas of intellect and emotions.

By becoming aware of the relationship that exists between the two, the student can better assess the rationality of his actions.

Through Silva Mind Control, the student can make this distinction simply because he has learned how to program his mind to detect the clear implications of both.

One of the techniques that we have learned to master is how to program the mind to accentuate the positive. This technique can be adapted very well to the motivation that is necessary in the classroom in order to enhance learning.

After all, motivation in the classroom is nothing more than expectation of pleasurable experiences, or the wish of students to succeed and thereby to avoid unpleasantries.

Through Silva techniques children can learn how to strengthen their feelings of comfort and security, thus accentuating their learning environment.

Also, visualization can be a tremendous factor in the learning process of students.

For example, students who are having difficulties with linguistics, mathematics, or reading will find it to their benefit to associate their visualizations with the subject at hand.

Children can learn how to visualize their subject matter.

I am certain that the work being done by Miss Ojeda will help to structure these theories into a workable classroom practice.

Doing so will enable students—especially those with learning disabilities—to utilize a system that can be systematically adapted to any educational curricula.

Fortunately, there has been much progress in the implementing of Silva Mind Control techniques in the classroom.

In Central America, government officials are already considering adapting our method as a required course in their educational system.

Preliminary work has already been done, but I am not a liberty to name the country at this time. More definite information, however, will be forthcoming when matters reach concrete terms.

It is personally satisfying to see that the concepts that we researched thirty years ago are now being accepted by many noted educators, and it is my belief that soon we will see a variety of Silva Mind Control techniques being routinely used in the classroom by teachers who have had the benefit of our courses.

If you have not taken a Silva course yet, you can get started right now with the Free Training in the appendix of this book.

94 Wisdom of the Past Can Help Us Build a Better and Better Future *(1989)*

One popular activity of many "truth seekers" is to study the "wisdom of the past."

These studious individuals want to uncover the "secrets" that the ancient people knew.

Of course, there are not really any secrets. All of this information is readily available in many books.

All you have to do is locate the books and allow yourself plenty of time to read them.

But not everything that is written is true.

Separating Fact from Fiction

How can you separate the fact from the fiction? How can you determine what is valid . . . and valuable?

My system for doing this is very simple:

If the information can be used to solve problems, then I consider it to be the truthful truth, and the real reality.

What do I mean by "solve problems"?

To me, if a person is sick and you apply information that helps them get well, you have solved a problem.

If a person has not yet found his or her purpose in life, and therefore is having difficulty earning a satisfactory living, and they apply a technique it helps them determine what they should be doing, and they do it and their life improves as a result, then a problem has been solved.

If you do not have enough information to make a decision, and you apply a technique that helps you gain more information, or insight into the subject, and you then make the correct decision, that's what I call problem solving.

In other words, I want to see tangible results.

Promises Aren't Proof

Writers know how to make things sound attractive, but that does not make their writing true.

Let's apply what they write about, and then the results (or lack of results) will give us the answer as to their truth.

Did the ancient Egyptians have special powers that went into the building of the pyramids?

Were the people of Atlantis so advanced that they literally destroyed themselves by misusing their great power?

Can we somehow learn their secrets? Can we rediscover their techniques, and this time use them more wisely?

Or have these techniques, for some reason, been hidden from us forever?

What I Have Learned

Here is what I have determined, by applying my pragmatic test for truth and reality:

Wisdom and ability accumulate.

Each new generation has the advantage of all of the accumulated wisdom of the past. It is in the genes.

Just look at how our world continues to evolve.

We are constantly building on the successes of the past.

This is true just as much in our genetic structure as it is in our conscious efforts to find new and better ways to do things.

If there were some special secrets in the past, then the people who came later would have built on this wisdom. It would not be "lost."

Oh, it is fun to think that there must be some "secret" that we do not know. Just like it is fun to think that we will win a multi-million dollar lottery. A lot of people seem to want things to be done for them.

But that is not the way of the world. At least, my own research, tested in the fire of actual experience in the real world, indicates that if we want to do any more than just barely survive for a few short years, we must do for ourselves.

Look at how many lottery winners end up miserable. They did not earn the money, they do not know how to handle it, they are not prepared for what happens. When this happens, they often find they have more troubles than before.

How to Have a Better Life

Higher Intelligence rewards us for doing our job.

What is our job?

Again, based on my experience, our job is to help solve problems on the planet.

For three quarters of a century I have been observing that the people who solve the most problems, live the best, most prosperous lives.

But Higher Intelligence must not think that we are doing a very good job.

Perhaps Higher Intelligence notices that we spend more on recreation and fun than we spend on solving problems.

We pay our sports heroes, our movie stars, millions of dollars, while we give only a few thousand dollars to researchers who are trying to find ways to save lives.

We know more today than ever before. We have more wisdom. We have more ability. It is there for us to use.

All we have to do is to apply ourselves to solving more problems and we will be given more of everything, we will become aware of all that we need to help us do our job . . . and more.

Rather than looking for some "secret to success" apply yourself to solving problems, and then you will have all the success that you will ever want.

95 Each One of Us Can Help Bring Peace to Our Planet *(1991)*

1+2=5 Billion

Can one individual make a difference in the world? Can one person actually do anything to help bring peace to our planet?

The answer is definitely Yes.

The formula I have used for years is this:

1 + 2 = 5 billion.

What do I mean by that?

I mean that if each person influences just two other people, and each of those two influences just two people, then soon all 5 billion humans on the planet will get the message.

Spread the Word

What message do people need to hear, in order to bring peace to our planet?

People need to learn that they can get whatever they need to be successful, healthy, prosperous and happy, without taking things away from other people, and without hurting other people.

When people learn to center themselves brain frequency wise, to function at the center of the brain frequency spectrum so they can use both brain hemispheres to think with, then they will be able to get help from the other side, to solve problems on this side—in the physical dimension.

We need to let people know that there is a method for them to do this.

People can learn to actually enter the alpha level with conscious awareness so that they can use the information stored on either the logical left brain hemisphere, or the creative and intuitive right brain hemisphere, to gain more insight, more ideas, and thereby correct more problems.

Reap the Harvest

There is enough of everything in the world for everybody. All we need to do is to learn to correct problems and achieve our goals by using positive, creative and constructive means, rather than negative, destructive means.

I believe that we were put here by the creator to help correct problems and to convert the planet into a paradise.

It makes no sense to see people destroying each other in the name of the creator.

The creator is not a destroyer. The creator does not destroy, but creates.

We can create a paradise on earth if we so desire.

I'm not the first to suggest that. There have been many great religious leaders who have said the same thing, in their own way.

All of these religious leaders were correct in the things that they said. They were all seeking to help people, to lead them in the correct direction.

It is their followers that we need to watch out for.

All too often, the followers misunderstand the message of their leader, and as a result, they get into fights.

Where Misunderstanding Comes From

Why do the followers misunderstand?

Because they are not centered.

They do not know how to center themselves and use both brain hemispheres to think with, and get help from the other side.

Because the followers are not centered, they observe things from a different perspective than their leaders.

The leaders are centered. They have access to information from the other side, from higher intelligence, from God.

The followers, though, are not centered and thus are limited to their own thoughts and feelings and prejudices and misconceptions and false information.

What You Must Do

When you learn to center yourself and see things from a higher perspective, then you function like the leaders of the great religions; you become one who creates rather than destroys; you become a creator—a creator of paradise on this planet.

How can you know when you are centered and connected with higher intelligence?

You can verify this when you are able to obtain information with your mind, information that is not available to your physical senses, and then verify that this information is correct.

Intuition is a faculty of the mind. The better your intuition, the more effective you are in the mental—spiritual—dimension.

When you know that you are able to use your mind to get information and use this information to correct problems, then you will begin to create your own paradise, without hurting anyone else, without taking anything from anyone else.

When you do this, other people will also want to learn how.

Be a Peacemaker

If you will make sure that just two people learn how to center themselves and function in this manner, and each of those people spread the word to just two more people, we can soon bring peace to our planet.

The Silva Courses provide a method that you can use to center yourself. You can easily verify that you can trust your intuition, that you can get information with your mind and then verify that this information is correct.

Then, you can use your mind to help you solve any problem.

It has been said that we are made in the image of the creator.

An image is mental, not physical.

We are not like the creator physically; we all look different from one another.

We are like our creator in what we can do with our mind.

When we use our minds the way the creator intended, we will be at peace.

Let's spread the word to everyone.

Let's get everyone centered, and humanize humanity.

1 + 2 = 5 billion.

Let's make it happen.

96 Here's How to Surpass Even the "Intellectually Superior" People *(1996)*

genius *n.* A person who has extraordinary intelligence surpassing that of most intellectually superior individuals.

Contemplate and meditate on where humanity stands today on this planet. You will readily see that the human race is going in a demoralizing, degenerative, destructive direction. If not corrected, this can only end in disaster.

Indicators indicate that:

- Crime is getting worse all the time, everywhere.
- Drug trafficking is causing great human suffering, and increased violence and killing.
- Water and air pollution are ruining our planet, our home.
- Many individuals are discouraged and no longer even try to lead productive, creative lives.
- Teenage pregnancy, especially to those who are not ready to be parents, is creating a whole underclass that is not functioning creatively and productively.
- Global unrest continues to increase.
- Many nations are going bankrupt.
- Wars are being fought over who gets a piece of land, how a person should worship, and for selfish economic reasons.

This stressful situation is bound to shorten the life span of the human race.

Well, that's the "blue framed" (negative) image. Now that we've identified the problem, the next question is:

"Why do we have all of these problems?"

Who's in charge here?

Studying and contemplating this situation at a deep meditative level, we are led back to one answer:

Human intelligence.

Human beings are the caretakers of the planet. This is our assignment. If we fail to do our job, we will destroy ourselves.

It appears that we have reached a saturation point in our intellectual growth.

Even the "intellectually superior individuals" seem to be unable to find solutions and to correct the problems that plague us today.

If our intellectual capabilities are saturated, then what are we to do?

Is there any solution?

Is there some way that we can surpass the intellectual saturation of the intellectually superior individuals so that we can come up with creative new ways to deal with our problems?

To do this, we cannot depend on just a few individuals. Everybody would have to develop additional mental faculties.

How can people acquire additional mental faculties?

The answer to that lies in the way the human brain and mind function.

Unused Potential Discovered

As you know, we have spent the last fifty years studying the human brain and mind.

Our investigations have revealed that 90 percent of people use only the left brain hemisphere to think with. They do both their thinking and acting with only the left brain hemisphere.

This limits these people to using only logical, intellectual, objective means to correct problems.

Only 10 percent of humanity think with the right brain hemisphere, and then act with the left brain hemisphere.

Is there an advantage in using the right brain hemisphere to think with? It certainly appears so. Those who do:

- Are healthier.
- Make fewer mistakes.
- Have fewer accidents.
- Are luckier.
- Are more successful in life.
- Are happier.

In other words, the 10 percent are classified as geniuses. They have "extraordinary intelligence surpassing that of most intellectually superior individuals."

Think of that for a moment:

Not only do they have more intellectual ability than the average person, they have more intellectual ability than even the intellectually superior people.

They have found a whole new dimension that they can use for problem solving, a dimension that has not been saturated but that has tremendous potential as a means of helping humanity to correct the problems that we are facing on our planet today.

Expanding Your Intellectual Capacity

Once we had identified the problem and had determined what was causing it, then the next question was: What could be done to help the 90 percent of people to become superior geniuses?

We had to find a way to help the 90 percent learn to think with the right brain hemisphere and act with the left, the way the geniuses do.

It appears that the functions of the two brain hemispheres are specialized—they have different tasks to perform. Common sense tells us that there must be a reason for this, and the reason must be to allow one hemisphere to specialize in thinking and the other to be used in taking action.

Since most people are doing their thinking with the hemisphere that was not designed for thinking, but was designed for putting our thoughts into action—the left brain hemisphere—they have saturated the left brain hemisphere and have been stymied.

Biologically, people use both brain hemispheres: The left brain hemisphere controls sensory and motor nerves on the right side of the body while the right hemisphere controls the left side of the body.

But when it comes to intellectual abilities, people are using only half a brain, and they are using the least suitable half. No wonder they have become saturated, and everything is now going in the wrong direction.

How to Get Along Better

Those who think and act with only the left brain hemisphere get sick more often with psychosomatic health problems. They are more accident prone. They make more mistakes. They are less successful in life.

When people think with the right brain hemisphere and act with the left, the results are just the opposite: They are healthier, less accident prone, make fewer mistakes, and are more successful in life.

When the 90 percent think with the left hemisphere, and act with it also, their brain frequency is centered at 20 cycles per second (cps), called the "beta" frequency.

But for the 10 percent who think with the right brain hemisphere, their brain frequency is centered at 10 cps, called "alpha." Then when they act, their brain frequency is centered at 20 cps beta.

It appears that for people to be healthier, happier, and more successful in life, and to make correct decisions more often than not, they need to learn how to think with the right hemisphere, at alpha, and then to act with the left hemisphere, at beta.

When people do this, they will make the correct decisions to help solve problems.

They will come up with creative ideas so that they will gain while helping other people to also gain, rather than gain at other people's loss, as so many are doing now.

When people are centered at 10 cycles alpha, they can find ways to get everything that they need without taking anything away from anyone else, without hurting anybody. Nobody loses; everybody gains.

But that does not happen with left brain thinking, only with right brain thinking.

It has been said that we prey on each other at beta, while we pray for each other at alpha.

A New Field of Science

Our research lead us to develop a method of training the 90 percent who now use only the left brain hemisphere to think with, so that they will be able to use their right brain hemisphere to think with, just as the natural geniuses on the planet do.

This has created a whole new field of science called "psychorientology."

The Silva ESP training is a product of this research, a product of psychorientology.

Over the last thirty years, the Silva Method has helped millions of people learn to think with the right brain hemisphere and act with the left.

Many Benefits

People who practice entering the alpha level, where they can think and make decisions and come up with ideas with the use of the right brain hemisphere, receive many benefits. They are:

- Healthier.
- Luckier.
- Better decision makers.
- More successful.
- Happier.

When you begin to think at the alpha level, with the right brain hemisphere, you gain insight and understanding about many things, such as why we were sent here.

From the alpha dimension, we can understand that the reason we human beings were sent to planet earth is to improve conditions here.

But we have not been doing that. We now know that the reason that our problems are growing faster than our solutions, is that 90 percent of people are thinking at the wrong brain frequency.

The correction for this problem is simple:

Begin using the correct frequency for acting . . . the beta frequency, and the correct frequency for thinking . . . the alpha frequency.

This discovery compares with the discovery made in radio communications many years ago. Broadcast stations had saturated what is called the am (amplitude modulation) band with stations.

This led to the discovery of another dimension, the fm (frequency modulation) band. And as you know from turning on your radio, you get less static and superior high fidelity reception on the new fm band.

Right brain thinking is a superior band for thinking:

It changes the sub-conscious into an inner-conscious level. This allows people to also use the information stored in the subconscious, consciously.

Right brain thinking—through intuition (ESP)—connects us mentally with all information on this planet, so that we can use this information to correct problems.

It also connects us with higher intelligence, so that we can get the guidance and help that we need.

Once people begin using the right brain hemisphere to think with; they will then start to comply with the mission assigned to them, which is to improve living conditions on planet earth.

Everybody Can Be a Winner

This can happen when we gain by helping others to gain, and gain while helping the planet to gain.

In order to do this, all material gains are to be used to help us better carry out our mission here on earth.

Remember, we come here with nothing, and when we leave here, we return to wherever we came from with nothing.

So do not ask for more than what you need; but do ask for no less than what you need.

Besides helping themselves, graduates of the Silva Method are also directly obligated to help improve conditions on the planet by promoting the new science of psychorientology.

When they introduce people to the Silva Method—a product of the science of psychorientology—they are helping many individuals to comply with their mission.

Thus, Silva Method graduates are actually taking part in "The second phase of human evolution on this planet."

This is a highly responsible assignment.

We say congratulations and thank you to all of you who are helping in this movement, and also helping other people to accomplish their mission on planet earth.

You can learn the techniques mentioned in this article with the Free Lessons in the appendix of this book.

97 Reflections On the Purpose of Life During the Holiday Season *(1998)*

As I see it, the story of the coming of Christ represents a birth that must take place in each of us, what is known as being "born again" into the spiritual dimension.

It is appropriate that this symbolism is celebrated at the time of the year when the days are the shortest in the place where Jesus was born, when the future promises longer and warmer and more comfortable days.

It would not seem to matter very much what symbols are used, so long as people realize that there is a spiritual dimension where all things are possible, and that they learn to use that dimension.

Philosophies, religions, belief systems have not prevented wars and suffering on this planet. In fact, often they have caused wars and suffering.

Do religions and belief systems unite people, or do they divide people? We see wars being fought, and society disrupted, because of people's beliefs about what might happen to us in the next world.

Meanwhile, life has become a hell for millions of people on our planet!

It seems to me that all of the avatars tried to teach their followers how to live a better life here on Planet Earth. Buddha taught non-attachment to reduce frustration and fighting; Lao Tsu taught we should flow with the forces of the universe and live in harmony; in the beginning of his ministry, Muhammad brought peace and social reform to his people, only later resorting to force.

Each Avatar Was Unique

Each avatar was unique in what they brought to humanity. Most, from Moses on, have brought rules for better living, and, of course, their own personal example.

But the rules were working for only a few people. Most still suffered.

What made Christ unique, in my opinion, was that He was sent to find out why the rules and practices taught by other avatars worked for so few people. Christ was a trouble shooter, a problem solver.

He found the problem. People had taken the path of least resistance. They were enjoying the pleasures of the world so much that they had gotten out of balance. They were using the physical, but not the spiritual.

In modern scientific terms, they were using the left brain hemisphere, but not the right brain hemisphere, to do their thinking.

When He saw what the problem was, Christ taught a method for people to use so they could once again become balanced and use all of their abilities, use both brain hemispheres.

The Time Is Now

Christ came to bring light and peace and love to the world, just as the new year brings with it longer and warmer days in the land where Christ was born.

My personal journey of awareness, which led to creation of the Silva Method, began during a dark period in the history of the world in 1944.

Again, as this holiday season approaches, we see dark days, with death and destruction.

Let us pledge ourselves to bring light and peace and love in every way we can.

You can help, first by going to level every day and becoming peaceful yourself.

Second, by programming peace in each trouble spot on our planet.

Let us use our spiritual heritage to come together, and help bring all humanity together in peace and partnership on our planet.

You can learn the Silva techniques with the Free Lessons in the appendix of this book.

98 Give Yourself a Special Gift and Humanity Will Benefit Also (1990)

The greatest gift you can give yourself during the busy holiday season is the gift of 15 minutes three times a day—relaxing at alpha.

One of the best things you can do for your loved ones during the holiday season is to spend time at alpha, programming for their health, success and happiness.

One of the best things you can do for humanity during the holiday season is to make your contribution towards world peace by working at alpha to bring peace and harmony to our planet.

The alpha dimension helps everyone.

In the physical dimension, when you give a gift to someone, you receive the satisfaction of having made them happy, but you have less money than before.

In the spiritual dimension, it is just the opposite:

When you program for someone's health, success and happiness, you automatically receive those same things yourself.

In the subjective dimension, everyone benefits, everyone gains.

Let's not wait for New Year's Day to resolve to go to level every day. Let's do it right now. That will make the New Year even better.

For many people, the holiday season is the most stressful time of the year.

We are busy shopping and buying and making decisions and arranging parties and so much more.

The weather is often bad, which adds physical stress along with the psychological stress.

And often we get too little rest, we pay less attention to nutrition, some people drink too much and get too little sleep.

To counteract all of this added stress, make sure that you enter alpha for 15 minutes at least once a day. This 15 minute session will counteract the stress syndrome in your body and will strengthen your immune mechanism.

You can use your level to help you select the perfect gift for each person on your list. There will be less stress in making the decisions, and more joy when they thank you for such thoughtful gifts.

All of your decisions will be easier to make, and better. It will be easier to know when to schedule a party and who to invite.

The time at alpha will help to keep your system in balance. You can program yourself to remember to eat better, dress warmer, and get enough restful, relaxing sleep.

And you can get into the real spirit of the holiday season by programming for others around the world.

Remember that we must program for specific situations.

Imagining light around the world has not proven very effective in bringing about world peace.

Programming specific individuals to desire peace seems to work much better.

That means that it will take some time to achieve world peace.

But the more people who are programming, the sooner we will accomplish that goal.

You can work cases on political hostages and program that they will be treated better and experience less stress.

You can work cases on their captors and program that they will treat the hostages better, and will decide that they want to release them.

And while you are doing this, you will be receiving benefits yourself.

You will be strengthening your immune system so that you will be healthier.

You will be developing your subjective skills and exercising your right brain hemisphere so that you can achieve more of your goals.

Isn't it wonderful that we can receive so much personal benefit while doing so much for someone else.

I can't understand why everyone does not take advantage of this. Take time now to go to level, and to go to level every day.

You will benefit; your loved ones will benefit; humanity will benefit.

Note: You can learn the basic Silva techniques right now with the Free Lessons in the appendix of this book.

99 Life Will Be Like This—One Day
(1986)

One day people will be in such control of their minds that their desire will be sufficient to trigger the manifestation of what they expect.

Methodology will no longer be necessary.

This is pretty difficult for scientists to understand, accept and explain.

Thoughts, feelings and other forms of mental activity are non-measurable in ordinary ways and are therefore not subject to conventional scientific study and explanation.

But, if desire is analyzed and if you go inside the meaning of the word, desire can be seen as a turning on of the computer.

Once the computer is turned on, then belief—based on all the previous solutions obtained by the computer and the infallibility of the programming—proclaims the advent of a solution, and expectation produces the desired end result.

Desire, belief and expectation may permit our mind to function in the way it was designed to function. Lack of desire, lack of belief or lack of expectation are blocks to that normal functioning.

Since you have completed the Silva training, you have been practicing each morning to be able to reach your creative level of mind, quickly and easily. At least I hope you have been practicing, for that is the only way you will develop your proficiency at programming and producing the desired end results.

You practice because you desire to have the benefits of good health, the ability to provide whatever you and your loved ones need to live a healthy, happy and successful life, to accomplish whatever you desire in your personal, family and business life.

You practice because you desire to have the problem solving advantages and mental abilities that this level of mind brings to you.

You practice because you believe you can do more with your mind than you are now doing, and because you expect your desire to be fulfilled.

So your practice could be compared with computer programming.

Your computer is plugged in and turned on (desire). Your computer produced before and it will produce again (belief).

Your computer has the appropriate circuits to handle this job (expectation).

You are succeeding.

Desire that success.

Believe you are attaining it.

Expect it.

It is amazing, isn't it, how some people believe that others can help them, but that they can't help themselves.

How much are you using the Silva techniques to help others and yourself?

The more you use it, the better you will become at succeeding with the techniques.

Note: If you haven't already learned and been practicing the Silva techniques, you can start right now with the free lessons in the appendix of this book.

100 Here Is a Man Who Helped to Make a Better World *(1998)*

(This was used to introduce José Silva for his closing comments at the 1998 Silva International Convention in Laredo, Texas, six months before his passing.)

Here Was a Man

Born to poor parents in the border town of Laredo, Texas, he was orphaned when he was four.

At the age of six he went to work to support his family.

He never had a mentor.

What he learned, he learned on his own.

Until he reached the age of thirty, he never traveled more than 200 miles from the place where he was born.

Yes, here was a man.

As a child, he shined shoes and sold newspapers.

Later, he taught himself electronics, and has worked ever since correcting problems.

As a young father, he studied psychology, to find ways to help his children do better in school.

The techniques he developed over the next twenty-two years helped thousands of people in his home town.

Yet the more successful he was in helping people, the more criticism was heaped upon him.

His friends shunned him.

The government threatened to jail him.

The church cautioned people to avoid him, and even considered excommunicating him.

But here was a man.

Although he conducted careful scientific research, most scientists ignored him because he didn't have any degrees, and would not play their games.

And the President of the United States declined his offer to turn over all his research so that the government could continue the work.

But here was a man.

With no credentials except the genius of his own mind, he took his findings direct to the public.

Over the next three decades, millions of people worldwide benefited from his Method.

He never sought fame.

He never sought fortune.

He continued to live in a modest home in Laredo, with the woman he married in 1940.

He always continued to be what he had been since childhood: A repairman, correcting problems.

Now more than half a century has elapsed since he began his research,

And I think that I am well within the mark when I say that during that time,

No scientist,

No doctor,

No politician or statesman,

No humanitarian,

None of them

Has done more to improve the lot of humanity on Planet Earth as has that:

One extraordinary individual.

Yes! Here is a man.

(This is based on a poem that was very special to José Silva, about the "One Solitary Life" of Christ. A small pamphlet with the "One Solitary Life" poem was given to him as he was being inducted into the army in 1944, the same time that he was first introduced to psychology.)

101 Principles of a Global Ethic
(1997)

(The From the Founder column consisted of the complete "Principles of a Global Ethic" that came from the Parliament of the World's Religions, September 4, 1993, in Chicago, Illinois, which was signed by 143 respected leaders from all of the world's major faiths.)

The Principles

Our world is experiencing a fundamental crisis: A crisis in global economy, global ecology, and global politics. The lack of a grand vision, the tangle of unresolved problems, political paralysis, mediocre political leadership with little insight or foresight, and in general too little sense for the commonweal are seen everywhere: Too many old answers to new challenges.

Hundreds of millions of human beings on our planet increasingly suffer from unemployment, poverty, hunger, and the destruction of their families. Hope for a lasting peace among nations slips away from us. There are tensions between the sexes and generations. Children die, kill, and are killed. More and more countries are shaken by corruption in politics and business. It is increasingly difficult to live together peacefully in our cities because of social, racial, and ethnic conflicts, the abuse of drugs, organized crime, and even anarchy. Even neighbors often live in fear of one another.

Our planet continues to be ruthlessly plundered. A collapse of the ecosystem threatens us.

Time and again we see leaders and members of religions incite aggression, fanaticism, hate, and xenophobia-even inspire and legitimize violent and bloody conflicts. Religion often is misused for purely power-political goals, including war. We are filled with disgust.

We condemn these blights and declare that they need not be. An ethic already exists within the religious teachings of the world which can counter the global distress. Of course this ethic provides no direct solution for all the immense problems of the world, but it does supply the moral foundation for a better individual and global order: A vision which can lead women and men away from despair, and society away from chaos.

We are persons who have committed ourselves to the precepts and practices of the world's religions. We confirm that there is already a consensus among the religions which can be the basis for a global ethic—a minimal fundamental consensus concerning binding values, irrevocable standards, and fundamental moral attitudes.

I. No New Global Order Without a New Global Ethic!

We women and men of various religions and regions of Earth therefore address all people, religious and non-religious. We wish to express the following convictions which we hold in common:

We all have a responsibility for a better global order.

Our involvement for the sake of human rights, freedom, justice, peace, and the preservation of Earth is absolutely necessary.

Our different religious and cultural traditions must not prevent our common involvement in opposing all forms of inhumanity and working for greater humaneness.

The principles expressed in this Global Ethic can be affirmed by all persons with ethical convictions, whether religiously grounded or not.

As religious and spiritual persons we base our lives on an Ultimate Reality, and draw spiritual power and hope therefrom, in trust, in prayer or meditation, in word or silence. We have a special responsibility for the welfare of all humanity and care for the planet Earth. We do not consider ourselves better than other women and men, but we trust that the ancient wisdom of our religions can point the way for the future.

After two world wars and the end of the cold war, the collapse of fascism and nazism, the shaking to the foundations of communism and colonialism, humanity has entered a new phase of its history. Today we possess sufficient economic, cultural, and spiritual resources to introduce a better global order. But old and new ethnic, national, social, economic, and religious tensions threaten the peaceful building of a better world. We have experienced greater technological progress than ever before, yet we see that world-wide poverty, hunger, death of children, unemployment, misery, and the destruction of nature have not diminished but rather have increased. Many peoples are threatened with economic ruin, social disarray, political marginalization, ecological catastrophe, and national collapse.

In such a dramatic global situation humanity needs a vision of peoples living peacefully together, of ethnic and ethical groupings and of religions sharing responsibility for the care of Earth. A vision rests on hopes, goals, ideals, standards. But all over the world these have slipped from our hands. Yet we are convinced that, despite their frequent abuses and failures, it is the communities of faith who bear a responsibility to demonstrate that such hopes, ideals, and standards can be guarded, grounded, and lived. This is especially true in the modern state. Guarantees of freedom of conscience and religion are necessary but they do not substitute for binding values, convictions, and norms which are valid for all humans regardless of their social origin, sex, skin color, language, or religion.

We are convinced of the fundamental unity of the human family on Earth. We recall the 1948 Universal Declaration of Human Rights of the United Nations. What it formally proclaimed on the level of rights we wish to confirm and deepen here from the perspective of an ethic: The full realization of the intrinsic dignity of the human person, the inalienable freedom and equality in principle of all humans, and the necessary solidarity and interdependence of all humans with each other.

On the basis of personal experiences and the burdensome history of our planet we have learned:

that a better global order cannot be created or enforced by laws, prescriptions, and conventions alone;

that the realization of peace, justice, and the protection of Earth depends on the insight and readiness of men and women to act justly;

that action in favor of rights and freedoms presumes a consciousness of responsibility and duty, and that therefore both the minds and hearts of women and men must be addressed;

that rights without morality cannot long endure, and that there will be no better global order without a global ethic.

By a global ethic we do not mean a global ideology or a single unified religion beyond all existing religions, and certainly not the domination of one religion over all others. By a global ethic we mean a fundamental consensus on binding values, irrevocable standards, and personal attitudes. Without such a fundamental consensus on an ethic, sooner or later every community will be threatened by chaos or dictatorship, and individuals will despair.

II. A Fundamental Demand: Every Human Being Must Be Treated Humanely

We all are fallible, imperfect men and women with limitations and defects. We know the reality of evil. Precisely because of this, we feel compelled for the sake of global welfare to express what the fundamental elements of a global ethic should be-for individuals as well as for communities and organizations, for states as well as for the religions themselves. We trust that our often millennia-old religious and ethical traditions provide an ethic which is convincing and practicable for all women and men of good will, religious and non-religious.

At the same time we know that our various religious and ethical traditions often offer very different bases for what is helpful and what is unhelpful for men and women, what is right and what is wrong, what is good and what is evil. We do not wish to gloss over or ignore the serious differences among the individual religions. However, they should not hinder us from proclaiming publicly those things which we already hold in common and which we jointly affirm, each on the basis of our own religious or ethical grounds.

We know that religions cannot solve the environmental, economic, political, and social problems of Earth. However they can provide what obviously cannot be attained by economic plans, political programs, or legal regulations alone: A change in the inner orientation, the whole mentality, the "hearts" of people, and a conversion from a false path to a new orientation for life. Humankind urgently needs social and ecological reforms, but it needs spiritual renewal just as urgently. As religious or spiritual persons we commit ourselves to this task. The spiritual powers of the religions can offer a fundamental sense of trust, a ground of meaning, ultimate standards, and a spiritual home. Of course religions are credible only when they eliminate those conflicts which spring from the religions themselves, dismantling mutual arrogance, mistrust, prejudice, and even hostile images, and thus demonstrate respect for the traditions, holy places, feasts, and rituals of people who believe differently.

Now as before, women and men are treated inhumanely all over the world. They are robbed of their opportunities and their freedom; their human rights are trampled underfoot; their dignity is disregarded. But might does not make right! In the face of all inhumanity our religious and ethical convictions demand that every human being must be treated humanely!

This means that every human being without distinction of age, sex, race, skin color, physical or mental ability, language, religion, political view, or national or social origin possesses an inalienable and untouchable dignity, and everyone, the individual as well as the state, is therefore obliged to honor this dignity and protect it. Humans must always be the subjects of rights, must be ends, never mere means, never objects of commercialization and industrialization in economics, politics and media, in research institutes, and industrial corporations. No one stands "above good and evil"-no human being, no social class, no influential interest group, no cartel, no police apparatus, no army, and no state. On the contrary: Possessed of reason and conscience, every human is obliged to behave in a genuinely human fashion, to do good and avoid evil!

III. Irrevocable Directives
1. COMMITMENT TO A CULTURE OF NON-VIOLENCE AND RESPECT FOR LIFE

Numberless women and men of all regions and religions strive to lead lives not determined by egoism but by commitment to their fellow humans and to the world around them. Nevertheless, all over the world we find endless hatred, envy, jealousy, and violence, not only between individuals but also between social and ethnic groups, between classes, races, nations, and religions. The use of violence, drug trafficking and organized crime, often equipped with new technical possibilities, has reached global proportions. Many places still are ruled by terror "from above;" dictators oppress their own people, and institutional violence is widespread. Even in some countries where laws exist to protect individual freedoms, prisoners are tortured, men and women are mutilated, hostages are killed.

a) In the great ancient religious and ethical traditions of humankind we find the directive: You shall not kill! Or in positive terms: Have respect for life! Let us reflect anew on the consequences of this ancient directive: All people have a right to life, safety, and the free development of personality insofar as they do not injure the rights of others. No one has the right physically or psychically to torture, injure, much less kill, any other human being. And no people, no state, no race, no religion has the right to hate, to discriminate against, to "cleanse," to exile, much less to liquidate a "foreign" minority which is different in behavior or holds different beliefs.

b) Of course, wherever there are humans there will be conflicts. Such conflicts, however, should be resolved without violence within a framework of justice. This is true for states as well as for individuals. Persons who hold political power must work within the framework of a just order and commit themselves to the most non-violent, peaceful solutions possible. And they should work for this within an international order of peace which itself has need of protection and defense against perpetrators of violence. Armament is a mistaken path; disarmament is the commandment of the times. Let no one be deceived: There is no survival for humanity without global peace!

c) Young people must learn at home and in school that violence may not be a means of settling differences with others. Only thus can a culture of non-violence be created.

d) A human person is infinitely precious and must be unconditionally protected. But likewise the lives of animals and plants which inhabit this planet with us deserve protection, preservation, and care. Limitless exploitation of the natural foundations of life, ruthless destruction of the biosphere, and militarization of the cosmos are all outrages. As human beings we have a special responsibility-especially with a view to future generations-for Earth and the cosmos, for the air, water, and soil. We are all intertwined together in this cosmos and we are all dependent on each other. Each one of us depends on the welfare of all. Therefore the dominance of humanity over nature and the cosmos must not be encouraged. Instead we must cultivate living in harmony with nature and the cosmos.

e) To be authentically human in the spirit of our great religious and ethical traditions means that in public as well as in private life we must be concerned for others and ready to help. We must never be ruthless and brutal. Every person, every race, every religion must show tolerance and respect-indeed high appreciation-for every other. Minorities need protection and support, whether they be racial, ethnic, or religious.

2. COMMITMENT TO A CULTURE OF SOLIDARITY AND A JUST ECONOMIC ORDER

Numberless men and women of all regions and religions strive to live their lives in solidarity with one another and to work for authentic fulfillment of their vocations. Nevertheless, all over the world we find endless hunger, deficiency, and need. Not only individuals, but especially unjust institutions and structures are responsible for these tragedies. Millions of people are without work; millions are exploited by poor wages, forced to the edges of society, with their possibilities for the future destroyed. In many lands the gap between the poor and the rich, between the powerful and the powerless is immense. We live in a world in which totalitarian state socialism as well as unbridled capitalism have hollowed out and destroyed many ethical and spiritual values. A materialistic mentality breeds greed for unlimited profit and a grasping for endless plunder. These demands claim more and more of the community's resources without obliging the individual to contribute more. The cancerous social evil of corruption thrives in the developing countries and in the developed countries alike.

a) In the great ancient religious and ethical traditions of humankind we find the directive: You shall not steal! Or in positive terms: Deal honestly and fairly! Let us reflect anew on the consequences of this ancient directive: No one has the right to rob or dispossess in any way whatsoever any other person or the commonweal. Further, no one has the right to use her or his possessions without concern for the needs of society and Earth.

b) Where extreme poverty reigns, helplessness and despair spread, and theft occurs again and again for the sake of survival. Where power and wealth are accumulated ruthlessly, feelings of envy, resentment, and deadly hatred and rebellion inevitably well up in the disadvantaged and marginalized. This leads to a vicious circle of violence and counter-violence. Let no one be deceived: There is no global peace without global justice!

c) Young people must learn at home and in school that property, limited though it may be, carries with it an obligation, and that its uses should at the same time serve the common good. Only thus can a just economic order be built up.

d) If the plight of the poorest billions of humans on this planet, particularly women and children, is to be improved, the world economy must be structured more justly. Individual good deeds, and assistance projects, indispensable though they may be, are insufficient. The participation of all states and the authority of international organizations are needed to build just economic institutions.

A solution which can be supported by all sides must be sought for the debt crisis and the poverty of the dissolving second world, and even more the third world. Of course conflicts of interest are unavoidable. In the developed countries, a distinction must be made between necessary and limitless consumption, between socially beneficial and non-beneficial uses of property, between justified and unjustified uses of natural resources, and between a profit-only and a socially beneficial and ecologically oriented market economy. Even the developing nations must search their national consciences. Wherever those ruling threaten to repress those ruled, wherever institutions threaten persons, and wherever might oppresses right, we are obligated to resist-whenever possible non-violently.

e) To be authentically human in the spirit of our great religious and ethical traditions means the following:

We must utilize economic and political power for service to humanity instead of misusing it in ruthless battles for domination. We must develop a spirit of compassion with those who suffer, with special care for the children, the aged, the poor, the disabled, the refugees, and the lonely.

We must cultivate mutual respect and consideration, so as to reach a reasonable balance of interests, instead of thinking only of unlimited power and unavoidable competitive struggles.

We must value a sense of moderation and modesty instead of an unquenchable greed for money, prestige, and consumption. In greed humans lose their "souls," their freedom, their composure, their inner peace, and thus that which makes them human.

3. COMMITMENT TO A CULTURE OF TOLERANCE AND A LIFE OF TRUTHFULNESS

Numberless women and men of all regions and religions strive to lead lives of honesty and truthfulness. Nevertheless, all over the world we find endless lies and deceit, swindling and hypocrisy, ideology and demagoguery:

Politicians and business people who use lies as a means to success. Mass media which spread ideological propaganda instead of accurate reporting, misinformation instead of information, cynical commercial interest instead of loyalty to the truth;

Scientists and researchers who give themselves over to morally questionable ideological or political programs or to economic interest groups, or who justify research which violates fundamental ethical values;

Representatives of religions who dismiss other religions as of little value and who preach fanaticism and intolerance instead of respect and understanding.

a) In the great ancient religious and ethical traditions of humankind we find the directive: You shall not lie! Or in positive terms: Speak and act truthfully! Let us reflect anew on the consequences of this ancient directive: No woman or man, no institution, no state or church or religious community has the right to speak lies to other humans.

b) This is especially true for those who work in the mass media, to whom we entrust the freedom to report for the sake of truth and to whom we thus grant the office of guardian. They do not stand above morality but have the obligation to respect human dignity, human rights, and fundamental values. They are duty-bound to objectivity, fairness, and the preservation of human dignity. They have no right to intrude into individuals' private spheres, to manipulate public opinion, or to distort reality; for artists, writers, and scientists, to whom we entrust artistic and academic freedom. They are not exempt from general ethical standards and must serve the truth; for the leaders of countries, politicians, and political parties, to whom we entrust our own freedoms. When they lie in the faces of their people, when they manipulate the truth, or when they are guilty of venality or ruthlessness in domestic or foreign affairs, they forsake their credibility and deserve to lose their offices and their voters. Conversely, public opinion should support those politicians who dare to speak the truth to the people at all times; finally, for representatives of religion. When they stir up prejudice, hatred, and enmity towards those of different belief, or even incite or legitimize religious wars, they deserve the condemnation of humankind and the loss of their adherents.

Let no one be deceived: There is no global justice without truthfulness and humaneness!

4. COMMITMENT TO A CULTURE OF EQUAL RIGHTS AND PARTNERSHIP BETWEEN MEN AND WOMEN

Numberless men and women of all regions and religions strive to live their lives in a spirit of partnership and responsible action in the areas of love, sexuality, and family. Nevertheless, all over the world there are condemnable forms of patriarchy, domination of one sex over the other, exploitation of women, sexual misuse of children, and forced prostitution. Too frequently, social inequities force women and even children into prostitution as a means of survival-particularly in less developed countries.

a) In the great ancient religious and ethical traditions of humankind we find the directive: You shall not commit sexual immorality! Or in positive terms: Respect and love one another! Let us reflect anew on the consequences of this ancient directive: No one has the right to degrade others to mere sex objects, to lead them into or hold them in sexual dependency.

b) We condemn sexual exploitation and sexual discrimination as one of the worst forms of human degradation. We have the duty to resist wherever the domination of one sex over the other is preached-even in the name of religious conviction; wherever sexual exploitation is tolerated, wherever prostitution is fostered or children are misused. Let no one be deceived: There is no authentic humaneness without a living together in partnership!

c) Young people must learn at home and in school that sexuality is not a negative, destructive, or exploitative force, but creative and affirmative. Sexuality as a life-affirming shaper of community can only be effective when partners accept the responsibilities of caring for one another's happiness.

d) The relationship between women and men should be characterized not by patronizing behavior or exploitation, but by love, partnership, and trustworthiness. Human fulfillment is not identical to sexual pleasure. Sexuality should express and reinforce a loving relationship lived by equal partners.

Some religious traditions know the ideal of a voluntary renunciation of the full use of sexuality. Voluntary renunciation also can be an expression of identity and meaningful fulfillment.

e) The social institution of marriage, despite all its cultural and religious variety, is characterized by love, loyalty, and permanence. It aims at and should guarantee security and mutual support to husband, wife, and child. It should secure the rights of all family members. All lands and cultures should develop economic and social relationships which will enable marriage and family life worthy of human beings, especially for older people. Children have a right of access to education. Parents should not exploit children, nor children parents. Their relationships should reflect mutual respect, appreciation, and concern.

f) To be authentically human in the spirit of our great religious and ethical traditions means the following:

We need mutual respect, partnership, and understanding, instead of patriarchal domination and degradation, which are expressions of violence and engender counter-violence.

We need mutual concern, tolerance, readiness for reconciliation, and love, instead of any form of possessive lust or sexual misuse.

Only what has already been experienced in personal and familial relationships can be practiced on the level of nations and religions.

IV. A Transformation of Consciousness!

Historical experience demonstrates the following: Earth cannot be changed for the better unless we achieve a transformation in the consciousness of individuals and in public life. The possibilities for transformation have already been glimpsed in areas such as war and peace, economy, and ecology, where in recent decades fundamental changes have taken place. This transformation must also be achieved in the area of ethics and values!

Every individual has intrinsic dignity and inalienable rights, and each also has an inescapable responsibility for what she or he does and does not do. All our decisions and deeds, even our omissions and failures, have consequences.

Keeping this sense of responsibility alive, deepening it and passing it on to future generations, is the special task of religions.

We are realistic about what we have achieved in this consensus, and so we urge that the following be observed:

1. A universal consensus on many disputed ethical questions (from bio- and sexual ethics through mass media and scientific ethics to economic and political ethics) will be difficult to attain. Nevertheless, even for many controversial questions, suitable solutions should be attainable in the spirit of the fundamental principles we have jointly developed here.

2. In many areas of life a new consciousness of ethical responsibility has already arisen. Therefore we would be pleased if as many professions as possible, such as those of physicians, scientists, business people, journalists, and politicians, would develop up-to-date codes of ethics which would provide specific guidelines for the vexing questions of these particular professions.

3. Above all, we urge the various communities of faith to formulate their very specific ethics: What does each faith tradition have to say, for example, about the meaning of life and death, the enduring of suffering and the forgiveness of guilt, about selfless sacrifice and the necessity of renunciation, about compassion and joy. These will deepen, and make more specific, the already discernible global ethic.

Our Appeal to You

In conclusion, we appeal to all the inhabitants of this planet. Earth cannot be changed for the better unless the consciousness of individuals is changed. We pledge to work for such transformation in individual and collective consciousness, for the awakening of our spiritual powers through reflection, meditation, prayer, or positive thinking, for a conversion of the heart. Together we can move mountains! Without a willingness to take risks and a readiness to sacrifice there can be no fundamental change in our situation! Therefore we commit ourselves to a common global ethic, to better mutual understanding, as well as to socially beneficial, peace-fostering, and Earth-friendly ways of life.

We invite all men and women, whether religious or not, to do the same.

Appendix A

About the Silva Centering Exercise

The Silva Centering Exercise helps you discover an inner dimension, a dimension that you can use to become healthier, luckier, and more successful in achieving your goals.

When you learn to function from this inner dimension, you automatically become more spiritual, more human, healthier, safer from accidents, and a more successful problem-solver.

In order for you to use this inner dimension, you need to hear the Silva Centering Exercise a total of ten hours, and to follow the simple directions in the mind exercise.

4 Ways to Learn

There are 4 ways you can proceed to find the alpha brain wave level with the Silva Centering Exercise, so choose the one that is best for you:

1. The Free Lessons at the SilvaNow.com website
2. Record the script below and listen to the recording
3. Have somebody read the script to you
4. Memorize the script—memorize the steps and follow them

How to Read the Silva Centering Exercise

When reading the Silva Centering Exercise, read in a relaxed, natural voice. Be close enough so that the listener can hear you comfortably. Read loud enough to be heard, and read as though you were reading to a seven year old child. Speak each word clearly and distinctly.

Have the listener assume a comfortable position. A sitting position is preferred, but the most important thing is to make sure the listener is comfortable. If uncomfortable, the listener will not relax as much and will not get as much benefit from the exercise.

Avoid distractions, such as loud outside noises. There should be enough light so you can read comfortably, but not extremely bright lights.

If the person shows any signs of nervousness or appears to be uncomfortable, stop reading, tell them to relax and make themselves comfortable. When they are comfortable and ready, then go back to the beginning and start again.

Take your time when you read; there is no need to rush.

Note: Do not read the titles out loud, they are for your benefit.

The Silva Centering Exercise Script
DEEPENING (PHYSICAL RELAXATION AT LEVEL 3)

Find a comfortable position, close your eyes, take a deep breath and while exhaling, mentally repeat and visualize number 3 three times. (pause)

To help you learn to relax physically at level 3, I am going to direct your attention to different parts of your body.

Concentrate your sense of awareness on your scalp, the skin that covers your head; you will detect a fine vibration, a tingling sensation, a feeling of warmth caused by circulation. (pause) Now release and completely relax all tensions and ligament pressures from this part of your head and place it in a deep state of relaxation that will grow deeper as we continue. (pause)

Concentrate your sense of awareness on your forehead, the skin that covers your forehead; you will detect a fine vibration, a tingling sensation, a feeling of warmth caused by circulation. (pause) Now release and completely relax all tensions and ligament pressures from this part of your head and place it in a deep state of relaxation that will grow deeper as we continue. (pause)

Concentrate your sense of awareness on your eyelids and the tissue surrounding your eyes; you will detect a fine vibration, a tingling sensation, a feeling of warmth caused by circulation. (pause) Now release and completely relax all tensions and ligament pressures from this part of your head and place it in a deep state of relaxation that will grow deeper as we continue. (pause)

Concentrate your sense of awareness on your face, the skin covering your cheeks; you will detect a fine vibration, a tingling sensation, a feeling of warmth caused by circulation. (pause) Now release and completely relax all tensions and ligament pressures from this part of your head and place it in a deep state of relaxation that will grow deeper as we continue. (pause)

Concentrate on the outer portion of your throat, the skin covering your throat area; you will detect a fine vibration, a tingling sensation, a feeling of warmth caused by circulation. (pause) Now release and completely relax all tensions and ligament pressures from this part of your body and place it in a deep state of relaxation that will grow deeper as we continue. (pause)

Concentrate within the throat area and relax all tensions and ligament pressures from this part of your body and place it in a deep state of relaxation going deeper and deeper every time. (pause)

Concentrate on your shoulders; feel your clothing in contact with your body. (pause) Feel the skin and the vibration of the skin covering this part of your body. (pause) Relax all tensions and ligament pressures and place your shoulders in a deep state of relaxation going deeper and deeper every time. (pause)

Concentrate on your chest; feel your clothing in contact with this part of your body. (pause) Feel the skin and the vibration of your skin covering your chest. (pause) Relax all tensions and ligament pressures and place your chest in a deep state of relaxation going deeper and deeper every time. (pause)

Concentrate within the chest area; relax all organs; relax all glands; relax all tissues, including the cells themselves and cause them to function in a rhythmic, healthy manner. (pause)

Concentrate on your abdomen; feel the clothing in contact with this part of your body. (pause) Feel the skin and the vibration of your skin covering your abdomen. (pause) Relax all tensions and ligament pressures and place your abdomen in a deep state of relaxation going deeper and deeper every time. (pause)

Concentrate within the abdominal area; relax all organs; relax all glands; relax all tissues, including the cells themselves and cause them to function in a rhythmic, healthy manner. (pause)

Concentrate on your thighs; feel your clothing in contact with this part of your body. (pause) Feel the skin and the vibration of your skin covering your thighs. (pause) Relax all tensions and ligament pressures and place your thighs in a deep state of relaxation going deeper and deeper every time. (pause)

Sense the vibrations at the bones within the thighs; by now these vibrations should be easily detectable. (pause)

Concentrate on your knees; feel the skin and the vibration of your skin covering the knees. (pause) Relax all tensions and ligament pressures and place your knees in a deep state of relaxation going deeper and deeper every time (pause)

Concentrate on your calves; feel the skin and the vibration of the skin covering your calves. (pause) Relax all tensions and ligament pressures and place these parts of your body in a deep state of relaxation, going deeper and deeper every time. (pause)

To enter a deeper, healthier level of mind, concentrate on your toes. (pause) Enter a deeper, healthier level of mind.

To enter a deeper, healthier level of mind, concentrate on the soles of your feet. (pause) Enter a deeper, healthier level of mind. (pause)

To enter a deeper, healthier level of mind, concentrate on the heels of your feet. (pause) Enter a deeper, healthier level of mind. (pause)

Now cause your feet to feel as though they do not belong to your body. (pause)

Feel your feet as though they do not belong to your body. (pause)

Your feet feel as though they do not belong to your body. (pause)

Your feet, ankles, calves, and knees feel as though they do not belong to your body. (pause)

Your feet, ankles, calves, knees, thighs, waist, shoulders, arms, and hands feel as though they do not belong to your body. (pause)

You are now at a deeper, healthier level of mind, deeper than before.

This is your physical relaxation level 3. Whenever you mentally repeat and visualize the number 3, your body will relax as completely as you are now, and more so every time you practice.

DEEPENING (MENTAL RELAXATION AT LEVEL 2)

To enter the mental relaxation level 2, mentally repeat and visualize the number 2 several times, and you are at level 2, a deeper level than 3. (pause) Level 2 is for mental relaxation, where noises will not distract you. Instead, noises will help you to relax mentally more and more.

To help you learn to relax mentally at level 2, I am going to call your attention to different passive scenes. Visualizing any scene that makes you tranquil and passive, will help you relax mentally.

Your being at the beach on a nice summer day may be a tranquil and passive scene for you. (pause)

A day out fishing may be a tranquil and passive scene for you. (pause) A tranquil and passive scene for you may be a walk through the woods on a beautiful summer day, when the breeze is just right, where there are tall shade trees, beautiful flowers, a very blue sky, an occasional white cloud, birds singing in the distance, even squirrels playing on the tree limbs. Hear birds singing in the distance. (pause) This is mental relaxation level 2, where noises will not distract you.

To enhance mental relaxation at level 2, practice visualizing tranquil and passive scenes.

TO ENTER YOUR CENTER

To enter level 1, mentally repeat and visualize the number 1 several times. (pause)

You are now at level 1, the basic level where you can function from your center.

DEEPENING EXERCISES

To enter deeper, healthier levels of mind, practice with the count-down deepening exercises.

To deepen, count downward from 25 to 1, or from 50 to 1, or from 100 to 1. When you reach the count of 1, you will have reached a deeper, healthier level of mind, deeper than before.

You will always have full control and complete dominion over your faculties and senses at all levels of the mind including the outer conscious level.

WHEN TO PRACTICE

The best time to practice the count-down deepening exercises is in the morning when you wake up. Remain in bed at least five minutes practicing the count-down deepening exercises.

The second best time to practice is at night, when you are ready to retire.

The third best time to practice is at noon after lunch.

5 minutes of practice is good; 10 minutes is very good; 15 minutes is excellent.

To practice once a day is good; 2 times a day is very good; and 3 times a day is excellent.

If you have a health problem, practice for 15 minutes 3 times a day.

TO COME OUT OF LEVELS

To come out of any level of the mind, count to yourself mentally from 1 to 5 and tell yourself that at the count of 5 you will open your eyes, be wide awake, feeling fine and in perfect health, feeling better than before.

Then proceed to count slowly from 1 to 2, then to 3, and at the count of 3 mentally remind yourself that at the count of 5 you will open your eyes, be wide awake, feeling fine and in prefect health, feeling better than before.

Proceed to count slowly to 4, then to 5. At the count of 5 and with your eyes open, mentally tell yourself, "I am wide awake, feeling fine, and in perfect health, feeling better than before. And this is so."

DEEPENING (ROUTINE CYCLE)

To help you enter a deeper, healthier level of mind, I am going to count from 10 to 1. On each descending number, you will feel yourself going deeper and you will enter a deeper, healthier level of mind.

10 - 9 - Feel going deeper,

8 - 7 - 6 - deeper and deeper,

5 - 4 - 3 - deeper and deeper,

2 - 1

You are now at a deeper, healthier level of mind, deeper than before.

You may enter a deeper, healthier level of mind by simply relaxing your eyelids. Relax your eyelids. (pause) Feel how relaxed they are. (pause) Allow this feeling of relaxation to flow slowly downward throughout your body, all the way down to your toes. (pause)

It is a wonderful feeling to be deeply relaxed, a very healthy state of being.

To help you enter a deeper, healthier level of mind, I am going to count from 1 to 3. At that moment, you will project yourself mentally to your ideal place of relaxation. I will then stop talking to you, and when you next hear my voice, one hour of time will have elapsed at this level of mind. My voice will not startle you; you will take a deep breath, relax, and go deeper.

1 - (pause) - 2 - (pause) - 3. Project yourself mentally to your ideal place of relaxation until you hear my voice again. Relax. (Reader: remain silent for about 30 seconds.) Relax. (pause) Take a deep breath and as you exhale, relax and go deeper. (pause)

RAPPORT

You will continue to listen to my voice; you will continue to follow the instructions at this level of the mind and any other level, including the outer conscious level. This is for your benefit; you desire it, and it is so.

Whenever you hear me mention the word, "Relax," all unnecessary movements and activities of your body, brain, and mind will cease immediately, and you will become completely passive and relaxed physically and mentally.

I may bring you out of this level or a deeper level than this by counting to you from 1 to 5. At the count of 5, your eyes will open; you will be wide awake, feeling fine and in perfect health.

I may bring you out of this level or a deeper level than this by touching your left shoulder three times. When you feel my hand touch your left shoulder for the third time, your eyes will open; you will be wide awake, feeling fine and in perfect health. And this is so.

GENIUS STATEMENTS

The difference between genius mentality and lay mentality is that geniuses use more of their minds and use them in a special manner.

You are now learning to use more of your mind and to use it in a special manner.

BENEFICIAL STATEMENTS

The following are beneficial statements that you may occasionally repeat while at these levels of the mind. Repeat mentally after me. (Reader: Read slowly.)

My increasing mental faculties are for serving humanity better.

Every day, in every way, I am getting better, better, and better.

Positive thoughts bring me benefits and advantages I desire.

I have full control and complete dominion over my sensing faculties at this level of the mind and any other level, including the outer conscious level. And this is so.

I will always maintain a perfectly healthy body and mind.

EFFECTIVE SENSORY PROJECTION STATEMENTS

Effective Sensory Projection statements for success.

I am now learning to attune my intelligence by developing my sensing faculties and to project them to any problem area so as to be aware of any actions taking place, if this is necessary and beneficial for humanity.

I an now learning to correct any problems I detect.

Negative thoughts and negative suggestions have no influence over me at any level of the mind.

POST EFFECTS—PREVIEW OF NEXT SESSION

You have practiced entering deep, healthy levels of mind. In your next session, you will enter a deeper, healthier level of mind, faster and easier than this time.

POST EFFECTS—STANDARD

Every time you function at these levels of the mind, you will receive beneficial effects physically and mentally.

You may use these levels of the mind to help yourself physically and mentally.

You may use these levels of the mind to help your loved ones, physically and mentally.

You may use these levels of the mind to help any human being who needs help, physically and mentally.

You will never use these levels of the mind to harm any human being; if this be your intention, you will not be able to function within these levels of the mind.

You will always use these levels of the mind in a constructive, creative manner for all that is good, honest, pure, clean, and positive. And this is so.

You will continue to strive to take part in constructive and creative activities to make this a better world to live in, so that when we move on, we shall have left behind a better world for those who follow. You will consider the whole of humanity, depending on their ages, as fathers or mothers, brothers or sisters, sons or daughters. You are a superior human being; you have greater understanding, compassion, and patience with others.

BRING OUT

In a moment, I am going to count from 1 to 5. At that moment, you will open your eyes, be wide awake, feeling fine and in perfect health, feeling better than before. You will have no ill effects whatsoever in your head, no headache; no ill effects whatsoever in your hearing, no buzzing in your ears; no ill effects whatsoever in your vision and eyesight; vision, eyesight, and hearing improve every time you function at these levels of mind.

1 - 2 - coming out slowly now.

3 - at the count of 5, you will open your eyes, be wide awake, feeling fine and in perfect health, feeling better than before, feeling the way you feel when you have slept the right amount of revitalizing, refreshing, relaxing, healthy sleep.

4—5 - eyes open, wide awake, feeling fine and in perfect health, feeling better than before.

Reader: Be sure to observe whether or not the person is wide awake. If in doubt, touch the person's left shoulder three times and while doing so say: "Wide awake, feeling fine and in perfect health. And this is so."

It is recommended that you practice staying at your Center for fifteen minutes a day to normalize all abnormal conditions of the body and mind.

Appendix B
40-Day Countdown System for Finding the Alpha Level

If you do not have someone to read the Silva Centering Exercise to you, or you don't want to record it yourself or memorize the steps and do it on your own, here is an alternative. It is not necessary to do this if you are using the Silva Centering Exercise.

This alternative method gives you a simple way to relax, and you will do better and better at this as you practice.

I will also give you a beneficial statement to help you.

This is how you train your mind:

You relax, lower your brain frequency to the alpha level, and practice using imagination and visualization.

Because you cannot read this book and relax simultaneously, it is necessary that you read the instructions first, so that you can put the book down, close your eyes, and follow them.

HERE ARE YOUR INSTRUCTIONS
1. Sit comfortably in a chair and close your eyes. Any position that is comfortable is a good position.
2. Take a deep breath, and as you exhale, relax your body.

3. Count backward slowly from 50 to 1.
4. Daydream about some peaceful place you know.
5. Say to yourself mentally, "Every day, in every way, I am getting better, better, and better."
6. Remind yourself mentally that when you open your eyes at the count of five, you will feel wide awake, better than before. When you reach the count of three, repeat this, and when you open your eyes, repeat it ("I am wide awake, feeling better than before").

You already know steps one and two. You do them daily when you get home in the evening. Add a countdown, a peaceful scene, and a beneficial statement to help you become better and better, and you are ready for a final count-out.

Read the instructions once more. Then put the book down and do it.

Learning to Function Consciously at the Alpha Level

As stated previously, you learn to enter the alpha level and function there with just one day of training when you attend the Silva UltraMind ESP Systems live training programs. You can use the audio recordings to learn to enter the alpha level within a few days with either a Silva home-study program or the free lessons at the SilvaNow.com web site. You can also record the Silva Centering Exercise in appendix A and listen to it, or have someone read it to you.

If you have already learned to enter the alpha level by one of those methods, you can skip the following instructions for practicing countdown-deepening exercises for the next forty days.

If not, then follow these instructions from José Silva:

When you enter sleep, you enter alpha. But you quickly go right through alpha to the deeper levels of theta and delta.

Throughout the night, your brain moves back and forth through alpha, theta, and delta, like the ebb and flow of the tide. These cycles last about ninety minutes.

In the morning, as you exit sleep, you come out through alpha, back into the faster beta frequencies that are associated with the outer-conscious levels.

Some authors advise that as you go to sleep at night, you think about your goals. That way, you get a little bit of alpha time for programming. The only trouble is, you have a tendency to fall asleep.

For now, I just want you to practice a simple exercise that will help you learn to enter and stay at the alpha level. Then, in 40 days, you will be ready to begin your programming.

In the meantime, I will give you some additional tasks that you can perform at the beta level that will help you prepare yourself so that you will be able to program more effectively at the alpha level when you are ready at the completion of the 40 days.

YOUR FIRST ASSIGNMENT

If you are using the Silva Centering Exercise (also known as the Long Relaxation Exercise) on the SilvaNow.com web site to enter the alpha level, then you can skip the information that follows.

If you do not want to use the recording of the Silva Centering Exercise, and you have not attended a Silva seminar or used one of our home-study courses to learn to enter the alpha level, then you will need to follow the instructions here to learn to enter the alpha level on your own.

Here Is Your Alpha Exercise:

Practice this exercise in the morning when you first wake up. Since your brain is starting to shift from alpha to beta when you first wake up, you will not have a tendency to fall asleep when you enter alpha.

Here are the steps to take:

1. When you awake tomorrow morning, go to the bathroom if you have to, then go back to bed. Set your alarm clock to ring in fifteen minutes, just in case you do fall asleep again.
2. Close your eyes and turn them slightly upward toward your eyebrows (about 20 degrees). Research shows that this produces more alpha brainwave activity.

3. Count backward slowly from 100 to one. Do this silently; that is, do it mentally to yourself. Wait about one second between numbers.

4. When you reach the count of one, hold a mental picture of yourself as a success. An easy way to do this is to recall the most recent time when you were 100 percent successful. Recall the setting, where you were and what the scene looked like; recall what you did; and recall what you felt like.

5. Repeat mentally, "Every day in every way I am getting better, better, and better."

6. Then say to yourself, "I am going to count from one to five; when I reach the count of five, I will open my eyes, feeling fine and in perfect health, feeling better than before."

7. Begin to count. When you reach three, repeat, "When I reach the count of five, I will open my eyes, feeling fine and in perfect health, feeling better than before."

8. Continue your count to four and five. At the count of five, open your eyes and tell yourself mentally, "I am wide awake, feeling fine and in perfect health, feeling better than before. And this is so."

These Eight Steps are Really Only Three

Go over each of these eight steps so that you understand the purpose while at the same time become more familiar with the sequence.

1. The mind cannot relax deeply if the body is not relaxed. It is better to go to the bathroom and permit your body to enjoy full comfort. Also, when you first awake, you may not be fully awake. Going to the bathroom ensures your being fully awake. But, in case you are still not awake enough to stay awake, set your alarm clock to ring in 15 minutes so you do not risk being late on your daily schedule. Sit in a comfortable position.

2. Research has shown that when a person turns the eyes up about 20 degrees, it triggers more alpha rhythm in the brain and also causes more right-brain activity. Later,

when we do our mental picturing, it will be with your eyes turned upward at this angle. Meanwhile, it is a simple way to encourage alpha brainwave activity. You might want to think of the way you look up at the screen in a movie theater, a comfortable upward angle.

3. Counting backward is relaxing. Counting forward is activating. 1-2-3 is like "get ready, get set, go!" 3-2-1 is pacifying. You are going nowhere except deeper within yourself.

4. Imagining yourself the way you want to be—while relaxed—creates the picture. Failures who relax and imagine themselves making mistakes and losing, frequently create a mental picture that brings about failure. You will do the opposite. Your mental picture is one of success, and it will create what you desire: success.

5. Words repeated mentally—while relaxed—create the concepts they stand for. Pictures and words program the mind to make it so.

6–8. These last three steps are simply counting to five to end your session. Counting upward activates you, but it's still good to give yourself "orders" to become activated at the count of five. Do this before you begin to count; do it again along the way; and again as you open your eyes.

Once you wake up tomorrow morning and prepare yourself for this exercise, it all works down to three steps:

Count backward from 100 to 1.

Imagine yourself successful.

Count yourself out 1 to 5, reminding yourself that you are wide awake, feeling fine, and in perfect health.

40 Days That Can Change Your Life for the Better

You know what to do tomorrow morning, but what about after that? Here is your training program:

Count backward from 100 to 1 for 10 mornings.

Count backward from 50 to 1 for 10 mornings.

Count backward from 25 to 1 for 10 mornings.

Count backward from 10 to 1 for 10 mornings.

After these 40 mornings of countdown relaxation practice, count backward only from 5 to 1 and begin to use your alpha level.

People have a tendency to be impatient, to want to move faster. Please resist this temptation and follow the instructions as written.

You must develop and acquire the ability to function consciously at alpha before the mental techniques will work properly for you. You must master the fundamentals first. We've been researching this field since 1944, longer than anyone else, and the techniques we have developed have helped millions of people worldwide to enjoy greater success and happiness, so please follow these simple instructions.

Appendix C
Conditioning Cycle to Use When Impressing Formulas

Reader: Read this Entry to the Alpha Level first, then move ahead to the formula or formulas you want to impress. After reading the formulas move ahead to the Preview, Post Effects, and Bringout.

Remember: Do not read the headings out loud.

Entry to the Alpha Level
We will start this exercise with the 3 to 1 method.

Find a comfortable position, close your eyes, take a deep breath and while exhaling, mentally repeat and visualize the number 3 three times. (pause)

Take another deep breath and while exhaling, mentally repeat and visualize the number 2 three times. (pause)

Take another deep breath and while exhaling, mentally repeat and visualize the number 1 three times. (pause)

You are now at level 1, the basic plane level that you are learning to use for a purpose, any purpose you desire.

Deepening (routine cycle)

To help you enter a deeper, healthier level of mind, I am going to count from 10 to 1. On each descending number, you will feel yourself going deeper and you will enter a deeper, healthier level of mind.

10 - 9 - Feel going deeper,

8 - 7 -

6 - deeper and deeper,

5—4 -

3 - deeper and deeper,

2 - 1

You are now at a deeper, healthier level of mind, deeper than before.

You may enter a deeper, healthier level of mind by simply relaxing your eyelids. Relax your eyelids. (pause) Feel how relaxed they are. (pause) Allow this feeling of relaxation to flow slowly downward throughout your body, all the way down to your toes. (pause)

It is a wonderful feeling to be deeply relaxed, a very healthy state of being.

To help you enter a deeper, healthier level of mind, I am going to count from 1 to 3. At that moment, you will project yourself mentally to your ideal place of relaxation. I will then stop talking to you, and when you next hear my voice, one hour of time will have elapsed at this level of mind. My voice will not startle you; you will take a deep breath, relax, and go deeper.

1 - (pause) - 2 - (pause) - 3. Project yourself mentally to your ideal place of relaxation until you hear my voice again. Relax. (Reader: remain silent for about 30 seconds.)

Relax. (pause) Take a deep breath and as you exhale, relax and go deeper. (pause)

Rapport

You will continue to listen to my voice; you will continue to follow the instructions at this level of the mind and any other level, including the outer conscious level. This is for your benefit; you desire it, and it is so.

Whenever you mentally or verbally mention the word, "Relax," all unnecessary movements and activities of your body, brain, and mind will cease immediately, and you will become completely passive and relaxed physically and mentally.

I may bring you out of this level or a deeper level than this by counting to you from 1 to 5. At the count of 5, your eyes will open; you will be wide awake, feeling fine and in perfect health.

Genius Statements

The difference between genius mentality and lay mentality is that geniuses use more of their minds and use them in a special manner.

You are now learning to use more of your mind and to use it in a special manner.

Beneficial Statements

The following are beneficial statements that you may occasionally repeat while at these levels of the mind. Repeat mentally after me. (Reader: Read slowly.)

My increasing mental faculties are for serving humanity better.

Every day, in every way, I am getting better, better, and better.

Positive thoughts bring me benefits and advantages I desire.

I have full control and complete dominion over my sensing faculties at this level of the mind and any other level, including the outer conscious level. And this is so.

Protective Statements

The following statements are for your protection.

This is **MIND CONTROL**, your own self-**MIND CONTROL**. You are always in control. You may accept or reject anything I say, any time, at any level of the mind. You are always in control.

Preventive Statements

The following preventive statements are for your better health. Keep in mind that from now on, I will occasionally be speaking in your place. (Read slowly.)

I will never learn to develop physically or mentally, mental disorders nor psychosomatic or functional ailments or diseases.

I will never learn to develop physically or mentally, a dependence on drugs or alcohol.

Negative thoughts and negative suggestions have no influence over me at any level of the mind.

I will always maintain a perfectly healthy body and mind.

Mental Projection Statements

Mental projection statements for success.

I am now learning to attune my intelligence by developing my sensing faculties, and to project them to any problem area, so as to become aware of any abnormalities, if this is necessary and beneficial for humanity.

I am now learning to apply corrective measures and to correct any abnormality I detect.

Negative thoughts and negative suggestions have no influence over me at any level of the mind.

Reader: At this time move ahead to the formula/s you want to impress and after reading the formula/s move ahead to the Preview/ Post Effects/Bringout.

Formula-Type Techniques

(Scroll down the page to the Technique/s you want to program)

TO AWAKE CONTROL

Impression of information for your benefit, programming a formula-type technique.

To Awake Control, a formula-type technique that you can use to practice awakening without an alarm clock. This helps in your development of MIND CONTROL. To use To Awake Control, practice awakening without an alarm clock.

You can also learn to use Awake Control to remain awake longer when necessary.

Enter level 1 with the 3 to 1 method just before going to sleep.

At level 1 visualize a clock. Mentally move the hands of the clock to indicate the time that you want to awaken and tell yourself mentally, "This is the time I want to awaken and this is the time I am going to awaken."

Stay at level 1 and go to sleep from Level 1. You will awaken at your desired time and be wide awake, feeling fine and in perfect health.

AWAKE CONTROL

To use Awake Control for learning to remain awake longer.

Whenever you feel drowsy and sleepy, and don't want to feel drowsy and sleepy, especially when you are driving, pull to the side of the road, stop your motor, and enter level 1 with the 3 to 1 method.

At level 1 mentally tell yourself, "I am drowsy and sleepy; I don't want to be drowsy and sleepy; I want to be wide awake, feeling fine and in perfect health."

Then tell yourself mentally, "I am going to count from 1 to 5. At the count of 5 I will open my eyes, be wide awake, feeling fine and in perfect health. I will not be drowsy and sleepy; I will be wide awake.

Count mentally, slowly: 1, 2, 3; at the count of 3 mentally remind yourself that, at the count of 5, "I will open my eyes, be wide awake, feeling fine and in perfect health."

Then mentally count slowly to 4, then 5; at the count of 5 and with your eyes open, tell yourself mentally, "I am wide awake, feeling fine and in perfect health, feeling better than before."

DREAM CONTROL

Impression of information for your benefit, programming a formula-type technique.

Dream Control, a formula-type technique that you can use to practice remembering dreams. This helps in your development of Mind Control.

Dream Control step 1. To practice remembering a dream, you will enter level 1 with the 3 to 1 method. Once at level 1, you will mentally tell yourself, "I want to remember a dream, and I am going to remember a dream." You will then go to sleep from level 1.

You will awaken during the night or in the morning with a vivid recollection of a dream. Have paper and pencil ready to write it down. When you are satisfied that Dream Control step 1 is responding, then start with Dream Control step 2.

Dream Control step 2. To practice remembering dreams, you will enter level 1 with the 3 to 1 method. Once at level 1, mentally tell yourself, "I want to remember my dreams, and I am going to remember my dreams." You will then go to sleep from level 1.

You will awaken several times during the night and in the morning with vivid recollections of dreams. Have paper and pencil ready to write them down. When you are satisfied that Dream Control step 2 is responding, then start with Dream Control step 3.

Dream Control step 3. To practice generating a dream that you can remember, understand, and use for problem solving. You will enter level 1 with the 3 to 1 method. Once at level 1, mentally tell yourself, "I want to have a dream that will contain information to solve the problem I have in mind." State the problem and add, "I will have such a dream, remember it, and understand it." You will then go to sleep from level 1.

You may awaken during the night with a vivid recollection of the desired dream, or you may awaken in the morning with a vivid recollection of such a dream. You will have this dream, remember it, and understand it.

HEADACHE CONTROL

Impression of information for your benefit, programming a formula-type technique.

Headache Control, a formula-type technique that you can use to practice stopping headaches. Tension type headaches, 1 application; migraine type headaches, 3 applications, 5 minutes apart.

Headache Control, a formula-type technique that you can use to practice stopping tension type headaches. If you have a tension type headache, enter level 1 with the 3 to 1 method. Once at level 1 mentally tell yourself, "I have a headache; I feel a headache; I don't want to have a headache; I don't want to feel a headache.

"I am going to count from 1 to 5 and at the count of 5, I will open my eyes, be wide awake, feeling fine and in perfect health. I will then have no headache. I will then feel no headache."

You will then count slowly from 1 to 2, then to 3, and at the count of 3 you will remind yourself mentally that, "At the count of 5, I will open my eyes, be wide awake, feeling fine and in perfect health; I will then have no discomfort in my head; I will then feel no discomfort in my head."

Notice that we have made a change at level 3, from ache to discomfort. We left the ache behind. You will then proceed to mentally count slowly to 4, then to 5, and at the count of 5, and with your eyes open, you will say to yourself mentally, "I am wide awake, feeling fine and in perfect health. I have no discomfort in my head. I feel no discomfort in my head. And this is so."

Headache Control, a formula-type technique that you can use to practice stopping the migraine type headache. If you have a migraine headache, enter level 1 with the 3 to 1 method. Once at level 1 go through the same procedure as in the tension type headache application, but use 3 applications, 5 minutes apart.

You will note that the first application will have reduced the discomfort by a certain amount. Wait five minutes, then apply the second application. The second application will take care of a greater amount of the discomfort. Wait five more minutes and apply the third application. With the third application all of the discomfort will have disappeared.

From then on, when symptoms appear, one application will take care of the migraine problem. As you continue to take care of this problem in this manner, the symptoms will appear less frequently, until the body forgets how to cause them, bringing to an end the migraine problem without the use of drugs. And this is so.

To correct health problems, controls are applied under a doctor's supervision.

MENTAL SCREEN

We will now impress new information for your benefit, programming the Mental Screen.

To locate your Mental Screen, begin with your eyes closed, turned slightly upward from the horizontal plane of sight, at an angle of approximately 20 degrees.

The area that you perceive with your mind is your mental screen.

Without using your eyelids as screens, sense your Mental Screen to be out, away from your body.

To improve the use of your Mental Screen, project images or mental pictures onto the screen, especially images having color. Concentrate on mentally sensing and visualizing true color.

3-FINGERS TECHNIQUE

We will now impress information for your benefit, programming a formula-type technique, the Three Fingers Technique. At this time, bring together the tips of the first two fingers and thumb of either hand. (pause)

By bringing together the tips of the first two fingers and thumb of either hand, your mind adjusts to a deeper level of awareness for stronger programming.

Stronger programming of information results in easier recall, producing a better memory.

To read a lesson, enter level 1 with the use of the 3 to 1 method. Tell yourself mentally that you are going to count from 1 to 3 and at the count of 3 you will open your eyes and read the lesson. Mention the lesson title, and subject.

Add: "Noises will not distract me, but will help me to concentrate. I will have superior concentration and understanding." Count from 1 to 3, open your eyes and read the lesson.

When you have read the lesson, once again enter level 1 with the 3 to 1 method. Tell yourself mentally, "I will recall the lesson I have just read (mention title and subject) anytime in the future with the use of the Three Fingers Technique."

To hear a lecturer, enter level 1 with the 3 to 1 method, and tell yourself mentally that you are going to hear a lecture and mention the title, subject, and lecturer's name.

Tell yourself that you are going to use the Three Fingers Technique. Keep your eyes open during the lecture.

Tell yourself that noises will not distract you, but will help you to concentrate; that you will have superior concentration and understanding; and that you will recall the lecture (mention title, subject, and lecturer's name) anytime in the future with the use of the Three Fingers Technique.

For test taking with the Three Fingers Technique, follow the 3-cycle method.

First: Read your test questions the way you always do, but do not stay too long on any of them. If you have a ready answer put it down; if not, skip that question and move to the next one.

Second: Use the Three Fingers Technique, and do as in the first cycle, but stay a little longer on the unanswered question. When an answer comes, put it down; if not, skip that question and move to the next one.

Third: Use the Three Fingers Technique, read the unanswered question, and if still no answer comes, close your eyes, turn them slightly upward, visualize or imagine your professor on your mental screen and ask for the answer. Then clear your mind, and start thinking again to figure out the answer. The answer that comes, is your professor's. Write it down. Do not turn in a blank paper.

3-SCENES TECHNIQUE

We will now impress and program the 3-Scenes Technique, a technique that you can use to help you implement your decisions and the guidance that you receive.

When you desire to use the 3 Scenes Technique, go to your center with the 3 to 1 method. Create and project onto your mental screen, directly in front of you, using visualization, an image of the existing situation.

Recall details of what the situation looks like in this first scene. Make a good study of the existing situation so you are completely aware of all aspects of it.

If you have programmed for this project previously, then take into account any changes that have taken place since your most recent programming session.

After making a good study of the existing situation, then shift your awareness to your left, approximately 15 degrees. In a second scene, to the left of the first scene, use imagination to mentally picture yourself taking action and doing something to implement your decisions, and to follow the guidance you have received, and imagine the desired changes beginning to take place.

Now in a third scene, another 15 degrees farther to your left, use your imagination to create and project an image of the situation the way you desire for it to end up. Imagine many people benefiting. The more people who benefit, the better.

Anytime in the future when you think of this project, visualize (recall) the image that you created of the desired end result in the third scene.

DECISION MAKING

Here is how to proceed when you need to analyze a project, and make decisions about it, at the optimal time to obtain the best results:

At night before you go to sleep, enter your level using the 3 to 1 Method. Once at your level, program yourself to awaken automatically at the best time, when all conditions are optimal to obtain the best results on the project you have in mind. Stay at your level and go to sleep from Level 1.

When you awaken automatically, take it for granted that all conditions are optimal. Assume a sitting position, head lowered approximately 20 degrees, and eyes turned upward approximately 20 degrees relative to your face, re-enter your level, and work on your project.

When there are two options and you desire to know which is better, you bring both to mind: Option Number 1 and Option Number 2.

Then clear your mind from thinking about the project, and think of something else that is not relevant to the project at all, such as: I need to buy a new pair of shoes tomorrow.

Then immediately start thinking again about the two options. The one that enters your mind first is usually the right one, and the one you should go for.

When there are more than two options, work two at a time using the same procedure. The one that comes to mind first can be compared to a third option.

Always retain the option that enters your mind first, until you have dismissed all except one option.

That option is the best one.

WEIGHT AND HABIT CONTROL

We will now impress and program Habit Control, formula-type techniques you can use to control the eating and smoking habits.

Formula type techniques for Habit Control, Weight. When you desire to reduce weight, enter level 1 by the use of the 3 to 1 method and analyze your weight problem. At level 1, mentally mark a big red "No" over every item of food considered to be causing the problem.

Program yourself that hunger between meals will vanish by eating a piece of carrot, celery, or apple, or some such helpful foods, or by taking three deep breaths.

Program yourself to leave something on your plate, realizing that you do not need all the food you have taken. Program yourself not to eat dessert.

Visualize yourself in the Mirror of the Mind or the 3-Scenes Technique the way you are now. Then in the solution scene, stamp what you want to weigh on one corner and the size of suit or dress you want to wear on the other corner, and imagine yourself at your ideal weight and size.

Thereafter, when you think of your weight, always visualize the image you have created of yourself the way you want to be in the solution scene.

Whenever you are eating, visualize the image you have created of yourself the way you want to look and visualize your desired weight stamped on one corner and your desired size of clothing stamped on the other corner of the solution screen.

If you desire to gain weight, eat those foods that you sense at level 1 will help you gain; eat slowly, savoring every bite. Learn to improve your taste and smell by concentrating on your food as you eat.

Visualize yourself the way you want to be; do this every time you think of your weight.

Formula-type techniques for Habit Control, Smoking. Whenever you wish to reduce or discontinue cigarette smoking, enter level 1 by the 3 to 1 method, and at level 1 analyze the problem.

Determine when you smoke the first cigarette of the day, then program yourself at level 1 to smoke it one hour later. When that becomes effective, program yourself to smoke the first cigarette still one hour later, and continue to make these changes by programming at level 1, until you smoke only a few cigarettes a day; it will then be a simple matter to stop smoking altogether.

You can also program yourself to smoke only 1 cigarette per hour on the hour; when this has become effective, then program yourself to smoke only on the even hours. After this has taken effect it will be a simple matter to stop smoking completely.

You can also program yourself at level 1 to stop smoking altogether 30 days from the date of your initial programming.

You can mark a date on a calendar, thirty days from the present and tell yourself mentally that on this date you will stop smoking, and never smoke again in your life. Reinforce this programming for this purpose at level 1 daily, and this will be so.

Tips that help in your programming at level 1 to stop smoking:

Change brands frequently.

Do not inhale the cigarette smoke.

Program that 3 deep breaths will stop the immediate desire to smoke.

Stop smoking for the sake of your loved ones.

JOSÉ SILVA'S MENTALVIDEO TECHNIQUE

Whenever you need to solve a problem, make a decision, or obtain guidance with the MentalVideo Technique, proceed in the following manner:

At beta, with your eyes open, mentally create, with visualization, a MentalVideo of a problem, or the existing situation. Include everything that belongs to the animate matter kingdom. Animate matter means everything that contains life.

After you have completed the MentalVideo of the problem, use visualization to review it at beta, with your eyes closed.

Later, when you are in bed and ready to go to sleep, go to your center with the 3 to 1 method. Once you are at your center, review the MentalVideo that you created of the problem, or the existing situation, when you were at the beta level.

After you have reviewed the problem, mentally convert the problem into a project. Then create, with imagination, a MentalVideo of the solution.

The MentalVideo of the solution should contain a step-by-step procedure of how you desire the project to be resolved.

After both of the MentalVideos have been completed, go to sleep with the intention of delivering the MentalVideos to your tutor while you sleep. Take for granted that the delivery will be made.

During the next three days, look for indications that point to the solution. Every time you think of the project, think of the solution that you created in the MentalVideo, in a past tense sense.

Appendix D

How to Develop Your
Natural God-Given ESP

ESP is beyond the scope of this book. You can learn and start using your EPS in just a few days time with expert guidance from a Silva ESP Instructor, either in a live seminar or webinar, or in one of our Online Learning,Courses. Courses are also available to download.

Visit the SilvaESP.com website for more information. If you want to get started immediately with our recorded courses, when you check out enter the coupon code MM15 for a special discount.

Meanwhile you can use the MentalVideo. It works best if you analyze your problem at the alpha level, but will work even if you don't know how to function at the alpha level.

Appendix E

Resources and Contact Information

FREE INTRODUCTORY LESSONS AND VIDEOS
Visit the SilvaNow.com website.

SPECIAL OFFER
As an owner of this book, you qualify for a special discount on genuine authentic José Silva home study courses and workshops. Visit SilvaESP.com and submit the coupon code MM15 when you check out.

INFORMATION ABOUT SILVA COURSES AND PRODUCTS
Visit the SilvaESP.com website.

HELP FOR HEALTH PROBLEMS
If you have a health problem and want Silva ESP graduates to program for you, or if you are a Silva ESP graduate and want health cases to work, please visit the SilvaHealthCases.com website.